SILVER THROUGH THE AGES

THE BELLE SAUVAGE LIBRARY

SILVER

Through the Ages

GERALD TAYLOR

CASSELL · LONDON

CASSEL & COMPANY LTD

35 Red Lion Square · London WCI
and at
MELBOURNE · SYDNEY · TORONTO · CAPE TOWN
JOHANNESBURG · AUCKLAND

———

© Gerald Taylor 1956, 1963
Originally published by Penguin Books
in 1956

This edition first published 1964

Printed in Yugoslavia

Contents

List of Plates

H = Height   D = Diameter   L = Length

1 King John's Cup. 14th century (H 15 ins). *King's Lynn.* Earliest known English standing cup. *See* N. M. Penzer, *Connoisseur,* CXVIII (1946), pp. 12–16, 79–84, 120, illustrated (fig. 15 and pp. 75–6)

2 a Head of Pastoral Staff. About 1370 (D of crook 7⅜ ins). *New College, Oxford.* Elaborated from a shepherd's crook; figures in volute represent a bishop (? William of Wykeham, the testator) kneeling in adoration before Our Lord, with attendant angel; ten panels on each side, each containing the figure of an angel musician, enamelled in colour; architectural motifs of the Decorated period (p. 74)

 b Head of Pastoral Staff. About 1487–1501 (D of crook 5 ins). *Corpus Christi College, Oxford.* At head of staff a six-sided knop (as on a chalice of 14th–15th century) with medallions of pelicans reserved on blue enamelled ground; two tiers of six Transitional niches, containing figures of the twelve Apostles (Bartholomew and James the Less are prominent); below the volute, figures of an angel (cf. plate 2a) and a pelican vulning herself (pp. 74, 106)

3 a Detail of volute from plate 2b. In volute, seated figure of St Peter beneath open canopy; round the sides engraved running patterns of roses and pelicans (which occur in the College arms) reserved on a blue enamelled ground

 b Detail of niches from plate 2a. Three figures of Apostles (Simon, Paul, John) in Decorated curvilinear niches. Cf. crockets with cresting in plates 1 and 38, the machicolation with fig. 13a (pp. 74, 106)

4 a Mazer. Later 15th century (D 8 ins). *Oriel College, Oxford.* Thin maplewood body with rather broad lip-band; Latin couplet, advising temperance, engraved in Gothic black-letters reserved on hatched ground (cf. plate 4b, fig. 14, and p. 75): *Vir racione bibas non quod petit atra voluptas sic caro casta datur lis lingue suppeditatur.* Cf. the regularity of ornament on modern foot with that on original lip-band (p. 78)

 b Studley Bowl. 14th century (H 5¼ ins). *Victoria and Albert Museum.* Black-letter alphabet (less W) and other symbols and contractions used in Latin MSS. engraved on bowl and cover reserved on hatched ground (p. 77). Repetitive stamped strip

7

of five dots; foot raised on band of openwork rings, with cable-moulding

5 Election Cup. About 1554 (H 17½ ins). *Winchester College.* Bell-shaped bowl, finial, mouldings and cresting of 15th-century type. But scrolling of cresting recalls ionic volute, and hints at date well after the introduction of neo-classical motifs; cf. ornamental straps round bowl in plate 8. Jewels applied to the rim of cover and foot (p. 77)

6 Font Cup. 1515 (H 7¾ ins). *Corpus Christi College, Oxford.* Large, collared finial (print engraved with Tudor rose) lobular motifs, cable-moulding, etc., characteristic of late medieval plate (cf. plates 5 and 38) (p. 77)

7 Two-handled Cup. 1533 (H 7¼ ins). *Corpus Christi College, Oxford.* Classical motifs used, viz., three cast dolphins to support baluster finial; chased triple volutes of foliage reserved on pounced ground. Cast handles (cf. plate 12a). Stamped pattern of foliated scrolls. Marks visible; *maker's mark* (illegible), *leopard's head* and *date letter* (pp. 96, 97)

8 Bowes Cup. 1554 (H 19¼ ins). *Goldsmiths' Company.* About same date as plate 5. Crystal bowl and knop. Full Classical influence visible; five sculpted figures, gadrooning below rim, grotesques in relief, and stamped egg-and-dart moulding round foot (pp. 93, 94)

9 Cup and Cover. 1569. Bunch of Grapes (H 21 ins). *Corpus Christi College, Cambridge.* Directly comparable with plate 8 in general shape and details. Sculpted finial; embossed fruit and foliage round foot: medallion heads, strapwork, and moresques engraved in relief show rather Germanic influence (p. 94)

10 Steeple Cup. 1613 (H 23 ins). *Wallace Collection.* Tripod open-work 'steeple' finial (pp. 115–16) on low platform (cf. plate 9), repetitive stylized flower pattern in low relief, reserved on pounced ground; acanthus leaves on tall foot; stamped mouldings (cf. plates 17c, 20, 21, 33b, etc.). Cast scrolled brackets (cf. plates 8 and 64)

11 Pepys Cup. About 1677 (H 23 ins). *Clothworkers' Company.* Pierced and repoussé foliage, birds, etc., on sleeve containing bowl, and on cover; acanthus leaves, embossed and in full relief at base of stem (cf. plate 10). Engraved Latin inscription on plain panel, date visible, Anno MDCLXXVII (p. 140)

12 a Two-handled Cup and Cover. 1657. A.M. (H 6 ins). *Castle Museum, Norwich.* Punched and chased stylized floral orna-ment with pouncing. Ring-handle and foot-ring of cable moulding; cast handles. Engraved arms in heater shield. Marks visible: *date letter, leopard's head* (p. 118)

b Two-handled Cup and Cover. 1664. I.W. (H 6½ ins). *Ashmolean Museum.* So-called 'caudle cup'. Netherlandish repoussé orna-

8

ment of fruit and flowers, cast grotesque handles, with human heads for thumbpieces (cf. plate 12a)

13 a Two-handled Cup and Cover. 1675. T.M. (H 5½ ins). *Ashmolean Museum*. So-called 'porringer', with solid cast scrolled handles; three cast handle-feet on cover-salver. Cut-card work and casting. Unidentified engraved arms, in heater shield with feather ornament (p. 141)

b Two-handled Cup. 1699. Joseph Ward (H 7¼ ins). *Ashmolean Museum*. Surbase embossed with swirled flutes and gadroons alternately (foot treated in reverse), pounced strip surmounted by punched ornament of alternate designs. Graduated beading on hollow cast handles. Marks visible: *maker's mark, Britannia, leopard's head erased, date letter*

14 a Two-handled Cup and Cover. 1730. Paul de Lamerie (H 7 ins). *Ashmolean Museum*. Small specimen; cast broken scroll handles with leaf thumb-piece; calyx of applied tapering strips of alternate designs (repeated on domed cover) and medial band. Flat-chased bands of reticulation, stars, etc. Engraved arms (of Chardin) in elaborate, so-called 'Hogarth', ornament (p. 193)

b Two-handled Cup and Cover. 1737. Paul de Lamerie (H 15 ins). *Fishmongers' Company*. So-called 'dropped bottom' elevation to the bowl, with rocaille calyx; alternate flutes chased with guilloche and chevrons. Handles modelled naturalistically as snakes (p. 193)

15 a Two-handled Cup and Cover. 1785. Daniel Smith and Robert Sharp (H 18 ins). *Hoare's Bank*. Four bands each of beading and acanthus leaves, embossed and chased; reeded loop handles, issuing from a sheath of foliage. Oval panel with arms of the bank (two-headed eagle) in low relief: 'made out of old plate'

b Brighton Cup. 1805. John Emes (H 17¾ ins). *Brighton Museum*. Combination of Classical, medieval and contemporary motifs; frets, *paterae*, palm leaves, bas-relief, wreathed masks, etc.; engraved inscription in black letters (cf. plate 4); coronet and Prince of Wales's feathers

16 a Wine Cup. 1587. I.N. (H 5½ ins). *Goldsmiths' Company*. Engraved ornament with egg-and-dart pattern punched on foot rim (cf. plate 15b). Marks visible: *date letter, lion passant, leopard's head, maker's mark*

b Wine Cup. 1603. Three Bells (H 5 ins). *British Museum*. Punched ornament, perhaps imitating *reticelli* glass; chased lobes with strapwork (cf. same motif in relief plate 8, and stamped, plate 17c; cf. also plate 24b)

c Wine Cup. 1616. H.S. (H 7½ ins). *Armourers' and Brasiers' Company*. Octagonal bowl and baluster stem, with three cast scrolls; calyx of acanthus leaves; flat chased panels of stylized flowers in low relief on pounced ground

d Wine Cup. 1637. W.C. (H 6½ ins). *Victoria and Albert Museum.*
Marks visible: *maker's mark, leopard's head, lion passant,
date letter*

17 a Tumbler Cup. York 1680. George Gibson (H 2¼ ins). *Ashmolean
Museum.* Repoussé acanthus calyx (cf. plate 16c)

b Mug. 1692. I.C. (H 4¾ ins). *Ashmolean Museum.* Engraved
ornament of flowers, etc., with boys, birds, etc.; lines softened
by ? rolling with a knurler, producing effect like wriggle-work
on pewter. Reeded scroll handle

c Beaker. Norwich, about 1595. Orb and Cross (H 7 ins). *Ashmolean Museum.* Engraved panels of scrolled foliage with three
groups of three dependent flowers (cf. fig. 22). Inscription
RYCHARD BROWNE OF HEIGHAM. Stamped egg-and-dart (cf.
plates 8, 9, 16, etc.) and lobed ornament (cf. plates 8, 10, etc.)

d Beaker. 1664. S.R. (H 5 ins). *Ashmolean Museum.* Repoussé
floral ornament in Dutch manner: reverse of ornament visible
in interior (p. 143)

18 a Tankard. 1571. Dove. (H 6½ ins). *Corpus Christi College, Cambridge.* Scrolled handle with imbricated ornament. Scrolled
thumb-piece (cf. fig. 26); rayed pedestal on cover; cf. ornament
in plate 9 (cf. p. 99)

b Tankard. 1653. A.F. (H 6½ ins). *Abingdon Corporation.* Twin
cusp thumb-piece (cf. plate 18c); broad pounced band on
drum; skirted base

c Tankard. 1679. T.C. (H 7¼ ins). *Magdalen College, Oxford.*
Engraved arms on cover with feather ornament (cf. plate 13a)
and on drum with crest and mantling; contemporary Latin
inscription recording the gift

d Tankard. 1683. Anthony Nelme (H 6½ ins). *Goldsmiths' Company.* Engraved *chinoiseries.* Marks visible: *maker's mark,
leopard's head, lion passant* (upside down), *date letter* (on its
side)

19 a Tankard. Hull, about 1689. Thomas Hebden (H 8 ins). *Hedon
Corporation.* Scandinavian type, with cast 'pomegranate' feet,
double ball thumb-piece

b Tankard. 1703. Samuel Wastell (H 8 ins). *St Edmund Hall,
Oxford.* 'William and Mary' ornament, including elaborate
applied cut-card work, graduated beading (cf. plate 19a), separated bands of fluting and gadrooning. Contemporary inscription in capitals and minuscules, Roman and Italic (cf. plate
18c)

c Tankard. 1717. Humphrey Payne (H 9½ ins). *Ashmolean
Museum.* Domed and moulded cover (cf. plate 19b); double
corkscrew thumb-piece. Moulded foot and medial band

d Tankard. 1772. Louisa Courtauld & George Cowles (H 8 ins).
Private Collection. Hoop (applied) and stave (engraved) in

imitation of a cask with hooped thumb-piece. Flat cover with feather edging

20 Flagon. 1616. E.L. (H 12¾ ins). *The Queen's College, Oxford.* Swags of fruit (cf. plates 8, 9, etc.), stylized flowers, sea monsters in strapwork (cf. plate 15a) chased in low relief reserved on pounced ground. Marks visible: *date letter, lion passant, leopard's head, maker's mark.* Immediately above, pricked inscription, *Deo O.M. et Collegio Reginae in usum Sacrae Mensae*

21 Flagon. 1598. I.D. (H 13½ ins). *Wadham College, Oxford.* Engraved strapwork enclosing pounced panels with stylized flowers and foliage reserved. Marks visible: *maker's mark, leopard's head, lion passant, date letter*

22 a Monteith. 1700. Francis Garthorne (D 12½ ins). *Tallow Chandlers' Company.* Repoussé scrolls, etc., with embossed beading, drop handles suspended from lions' masks. Contemporary engraved arms of donor, James Wood, Master

   b Punch Bowl. 1735. John White (D 12 ins). *Oriel College, Oxford.* Elaborate applied castings round calyx, flat-chased ornament of rococo panels (urns of flowers and masks alternately separated by reticulation). Two engraved arms (City of Bristol and Edmunds) in rococo ornament. Inscription (? later) round foot-rim: COLL ORIEL OXON

23 a Punch Bowl (George Boothby) and Ladle (William Fordham). 1727 (D 15 ins). *Hastings Corporation.* Finely engraved seated figure of George II; italic inscription. Ladle, with cartridge-shaped handle

   b Punch Bowl and Ladle. 1814. Paul Storr (D 12¼ ins). *Dover Corporation.* Combination of rococo (dropped-bottom outline, chased rim, and shell ladle) with classical motifs (oval medallions, guilloche ornament, and ovolos). Cf. handle of ladle with handles in plate 52b

24 a Wine Cistern. 1694. George Garthorne (H 13 ins). *Bank of England.* Drop-handles suspended from lions' masks (cf. plate 22a); lobed bowl with dependent husks between; lion's claw and bun feet; gadrooned rim, by leading English maker

   b Wine Cistern. 1697. Pierre Harache (H 7 ins). *Barber Surgeons' Company.* Handles cast as female terms springing from foliage, gadrooned mouldings, by leading Huguenot maker. Both a and b are largely based on classical motifs (p. 169)

25 a Wine Cooler. 1775. Frederick Kandler (H 7½ ins). *Victoria and Albert Museum.* Form based on Classical altar, drop-handles suspended from rams' heads; reeding with ribbon binding, wave pattern (cf. fig. 26)

   b Wine Cooler. 1810. Paul Storr (after John Flaxman) (H 9½ ins). *Victoria and Albert Museum.* Form based on calyx krater;

lions' masks, gadrooning, shells; full blazon of Royal Arms in low relief

26 a Tea Pot. About 1685. Benjamin Pyne (H 5¼ ins). *Ashmolean Museum*. Form based on Chinese wine-pot: panels of matted ornament (cf. plate 18b); spout stopper on chain (cf. hinged flap, plate 28) (p. 147)

b Tea Pot. 1718. James Seabrook (H 6 ins). *Ashmolean Museum*. Oblong octagonal plan, pear-shaped elevation with mouldings. Spout chased in form of bird's head. Wooden handle. Later engraved crest

27 a Tea Pot. 1735. Paul de Lamerie (H 5½ ins). *Ashmolean Museum*. Flat-chased band round flush lid; cast sockets for spout and handle; wooden handle and knop in finial, as in plate below

b Tea Pot. 1785. Daniel Smith & Robert Sharp (H 5 ins). *Barber Institute of Fine Arts*. Oval plan, with vertical sides, and beaded ornament; wooden knop and handle. On small stand to match

28 Coffee Pot. 1702. William Lukin (H 10 ins). *Burrell Collection*. Hinged flap on spout; fluting on domed lid which is removable (chained pin in hinge); elaborate cut-card work to mask joints of handle and spout; volute thumb-piece. Wooden handle, with pierced silver band, at right angles to spout

29 Coffee Pot. About 1735. Charles Kandler (H 8½ ins). *Ashmolean Museum*. Pear-shaped body with vertical moulding, flat-chased scrolls with panels of reticulation, etc. Cf. leaf on spout with those on handles in plate 14a, and base of spout with that in plate 27a

30 a Jug. 1718. Thomas Parr (H 3½ ins). *Ashmolean Museum*. Plain, pear-shaped, with separate lid; lip at right-angles to wooden handle

b Jug. 1740. William Gwillim (H 3½ ins). *Ashmolean Museum*. Plain, pear-shaped, with spout opposite handle

c Jug. 1750. John Pollock (H 3¾ ins). *Private Collection*. Repoussé flowers, etc. (cf. plate 31c); broken scroll handle, three cast feet

d Jug. 1785. Robert Hennell (H 7⅛ ins). *Victoria and Albert Museum*. Cf. shape of bowl and handles in plate 15a; shallow fluting and beading

31 a Tea Canister. 1759. Wiliam Shaw & William Priest (H 5 ins). *Victoria and Albert Museum*. Repoussé *chinoiseries* and foliage

b Tea Canister. 1761. A.S. (H 5 ins). *Ashmolean Museum*. Rectangular bombé form, with repoussé foliage, etc.

c Set of Tea Canisters. 1752. Samuel Taylor (H 5¾ ins and 5¼ ins). *Ashmolean Museum*. Set of two tea canisters (cf. (a) above), flanking a covered sugar bowl to match (fitted in shagreen-covered box with silver mounts and lock)

32 Tea Kettle and Stand. 1727–37. Charles Kandler (H 13¼ ins). *Victoria and Albert Museum.* Combination of classical and rococo ornament in the rococo period. For antithesis see plate 23b (p. 202). Salver not made to match

33 a Basin. 1556. M. (D 17½ ins). *Goldsmiths' Company.* Combination of engraved moresque ornament (cf. fig. 18) with repoussé masks and swags of fruit, both with strapwork; the outer band of ornament is repeated four times, the inner thrice. Enamelled arms on print of Legh of Lyme

b Basin. 1605. W.I. (D 18¼ ins). *Merton College, Oxford.* Similar size and proportions to 33a, but with flat-chased scrolls and formal flowers, in conjunction with sea-monsters and swags of fruit in low relief (cf. plates 20, 21). Pattern of outer and inner bands repeated thrice, of that between four times

34 Parker Ewer. 1545. Maiden's Head (H 8½ ins). *Corpus Christi College, Cambridge.* Alternate facets engraved with moresque ornament; concave swirled lobes on cover, and stamped moulding point back to late Middle Ages. Marks visible: *date letter, maker's mark, leopard's head, lion passant* (p. 102)

35 Henslowe Ewer. 1562. (H 8½ ins). *Winchester College.* Engraved moresque ornament and medallions in strapwork; cf. handles and thumb-pieces in plates 20, 21, and bosses in preceding three plates. Cf. also general form of bowl and cover in plate 9 (p. 102)

36 Ewer. 1617. I.V. (H 13¾ ins). *Norwich Corporation.* Elaborate cast grotesque handle; composition of mermaids and tritons in low relief; bands of stamped ornament and acanthus calyx. Perhaps work of immigrant from France or Netherlands (pp. 103, 123)

37 Ewer. 1724. Paul de Lamerie (H 8½ ins). *Ashmolean Museum.* Applied cast and chased ornament. Contemporary engraved arms of Treby, from same toilet service as salver in plate 48b (p. 211)

38 Warden Hill's Salt. About 1490 (H 19½ ins). *New College, Oxford.* Cresting and crockets in Decorated style (cf. plate 2); embossed swirled lobes. Legend round foot in black and Lombardic letters on cross-hatched ground: super+WA+montes+ TER+stabunt+HIL + aque+M = the waters stood above the hills, a punning reference from Psalm 104 in the Vulgate to the name of the donor, Walter Hill, Warden (p. 81)

39 Gibbon Salt. 1576. Three trefoils (H 12 ins). *Goldsmiths' Company.* Classically inspired architectural composition, with four Ionic columns, repeated use of stamped egg-and-dart ornament; crystal column in centre (cf. plate 8) (pp. 103–4)

40 Bell Salt. 1613. I.M. (H 10 ins). *Holburne of Menstrie Museum, Bath.* Flat-chased pattern of stylized flowers and foliage in

in simplicity, with beading. Contrast plates 44b and 45b. Contemporary shield of arms with outline of four curves (p. 229)

b Sauce Tureen. 1819. Paul Storr (H 7⅜ ins). *Victoria and Albert Museum.* Massive metal, cast and chased with foliate ornament, including oak-leaves (p. 245)

46 a Sauce Boat. 1730. (H 3 ins). *Castle Museum, Norwich.* Boat-shaped, with two handles and two spouts. Contemporary engraved arms of Buxton impaling Gooch (p. 198)

b Sauce Boat. 1764. John Vere and William Lutwycke. (L 7¾ ins). *Holburne of Menstrie Museum, Bath.* Similar in form to the above, but in the late rococo style (p. 198)

47 Centre Piece. 1811. Paul Storr (for Rundells) (H 21¾ ins). *Wellington Museum.* Surmounted by a circular tureen, with band of chased bay leaf in low relief, handle chased as a wreath, others as tendrils. Three winged figures of Victory in Classical dress, with wreaths; anthemion ornament below. Three naturalistic lions on circular plinth alternate with full Royal arms in low relief on a three-sided pedestal (p. 247)

48 a Salver. 1686. W.I. (D 9 ins). *Ashmolean Museum.* Cast and chased composition in low relief of four Classical gods within a border of oval depressions, and bead and reel ornament (p. 149)

b Salver. 1724. Paul de Lamerie (W 5 ins). *Ashmolean Museum.* Square, with incurved corners; moulded rim; border flat-chased with narrow strips of reticulation, interlacing straps, and foliage on brick-work. Four scrolled feet (cf. plate 62a). Engraved arms of Treby in contemporary ornament, with the crest, a demi-lion rampant, in a panel in each corner. From same toilet service as plate 37 (p. 211)

49 a Salver. 1750. Paul de Lamerie (D 9¾ ins). *Ashmolean Museum.* Flat-chased composition of flowers and scrolls; three scrolled foliate feet. Contemporary engraved arms of Hyde (p. 207–8)

b Salver. 1753. William Peaston (D 12½ ins). *Victoria and Albert Museum.* Piecrust and shell border of six repeated sections. Contemporary engraved arms and crest of Stacye (p. 208)

50 a Fruit Dish. 1649. E.S. (D 10¼ ins). *Victoria and Albert Museum.* Stylized plants reserved in eight pounced panels, round boss engraved with arms in feather ornament; border of twenty-two circular panels of punched and flat-chased ornament (p. 122)

b Tray. 1799. (?) Thomas Robins (L 23¼ ins). *Messrs Tessiers Ltd.* Oval, with gadrooned edge; loop handles springing from leaves (cf. plate 45a); bright-cut border of twenty oval panels with acanthus swags between (p. 228)

51 a Fruit Dish. 1734. Paul de Lamerie (L 8¼ ins). *Ashmolean Museum.* Oval; moulded border with shells and leaves; flat-

chased ornament; ribbed depression (cf. plates 49a, b). Set completed by a matching dish, a larger, and four smaller (p. 199)

b Tray. Dublin 1705. Joseph Walker (D 17 ins). *Ashmolean Museum*. Octagonal, plain, except for contemporary engraved arms of ten quarterings, supporters, motto and crest, of Tichborne (p. 183)

52 a Sugar Bowl. 1728. Samuel Laundry (D 5¼ ins). *Ashmolean Museum*. Shape derived from Chinese porcelain (cf. plate 26a); hammer marks visible inside. Contemporary engraved arms of ? Hereford in oval shield; crest on cover. Cf. plate 31c, centre (p. 206)

b Sugar Vase. 1805. Digby Scott & Benjamin Smith (H 6¾ ins). *Victoria and Albert Museum*. Gadrooned surbase; elaborated fret between beading; egg-and-dart moulding. Cf. handles in plates 36, 37. Contemporary engraved crest. Marks visible: *maker's mark, lion passant, leopard's head, date letter, Sovereign's head* (p. 250)

53 Sugar Vase. 1810. Benjamin & James Smith (H 8 ins). *Wellington Museum*. Gadrooned surbase, etc., loop handles (cf. plate 45b); band of acanthus husk and leaf in low relief. Cf. scrolling foliage in plate 7 (p. 250)

54 a Basket. 1731. Paul de Lamerie (L 14¾ ins). *Ashmolean Museum*. Looped rope handles; pierced sides of reeded strapwork; flat-chased panels of reticulation enclosed by straps. Contemporary engraved arms of Paulet (p. 207)

b Basket. 1744. Paul de Lamerie (L 15 ins). *Ashmolean Museum*. Flat-chased swing handle with chased scrolls; sides pierced with scrolls; cast and chased openwork feet and skirt; flat-chased bottom (p. 207)

55 a Basket. 1747. Paul de Lamerie (L 14 ins). *Ashmolean Museum*. Scallop-shaped, with pierced scrolls and diaper-work; gadrooned border; three feet, cast and chased as dolphins; handle cast and chased as female term above dolphins (p. 207)

b Basket. 1783. Charles Aldridge & Henry Green (L 17¼ ins.) *Ashmolean Museum*. Boat-shaped, with pierced *paterae* and criss-cross bands; applied beading (p. 227)

56 a Candlestick. 1673. I.B. (H 10¾ ins). *Ashmolean Museum*. Fluted Doric column with moulded base, constructed of thinnish metal. Unidentified contemporary engraved crest. *Maker's mark* visible (one mark on each side) (p. 155)

b Candlestick. 1673(?) T.D. (H 10 ins). *Ashmolean Museum*. Constructed, in rather thin metal, of repoussé scallop shells, scrolled brackets and lobed knop; short clustered column round socket; detachable nozzle (p. 155)

c Candlestick. 1715. John Broake (H 6¾ ins). *Ashmolean Museum*.

Cast with facets. Cf. plate 57a, a later treatment of the same outline (p. 180)

d Candlestick. 1700–2. Joseph Bird (H F$\frac{1}{4}$ ins). *Ashmolean Museum.* Tripod, with shell feet; acanthus husks, swags, and gadrooning in low relief. Engraved contemporary cypher (p. 180)

57 a Candlestick. 1729. James Gould (H 6$\frac{1}{4}$ ins). *Ashmolean Museum.* Cast, chased, and flat-chased; leaf calyx to reel-shaped socket (p. 209)

b Candlestick. 1741. John Jacob (H 9$\frac{1}{2}$ ins). *Ashmolean Museum.* Cast and chased with rocaille, masks, dolphins, shells, etc., in high relief (p. 209)

c Candlestick. 1770. William Abdy (H 13 ins). *Merton College, Oxford.* Ionic column of architectural proportions, on square pedestal (p. 228)

d Candlestick. Sheffield 1791. Maker's mark overpunched with that of William Robertson of Edinburgh (H 12 ins). *Ashmolean Museum.* Shallow fluting; foliate calyx to bell-shaped socket; ˙ detachable nozzle; circular pedestal (p. 228)

58 Candelabrum. 1816. Benjamin Smith (H 57 ins). *Wellington Museum.* Massive sculptural work, cast and chased in full relief with combination of Classical imagery (figure of Victory, bas-reliefs) with contemporary realism (cannon, arms, soldiers, etc.) (p. 243)

59 Candelabrum. 1823. Paul Storr (H 29 ins). *Keble College, Oxford.* Heavy cast and chased foliate ornament, with acanthus leaves, shells and scrolls; tripod base. Cf. plate 45b (p. 244)

60 a Apostle Spoon (St John). 1504. A plant (L 7$\frac{1}{4}$ ins). *Ashmolean Museum* (p. 83)

b Apostle Spoon (St Simon). 1555. I.F. (L 7$\frac{1}{4}$ ins). *Ashmolean Museum* (p. 105)

c Apostle Spoon (St Jude). 1601. C enclosing W (L 7 ins). *Ashmolean Museum*

d Seal Top Spoon. 1635. E.H. (L 7 ins). *Ashmolean Museum*

e Puritan Spoon. 1669. Lawrence Coles (L 7$\frac{1}{2}$ ins). *Ashmolean Museum* (p. 126)

f Engraved Trifid Spoon. 1695. Indistinct mark (L 6$\frac{1}{4}$ ins). *Ashmolean Museum*

g Trifid Spoon with Lace ornament. 1691. T.Z. (L 7$\frac{1}{4}$ ins). *Ashmolean Museum.* Marks visible, from top to bottom: *date letter, lion passant, leopard's head, maker's mark.* Fluted rat's tail visible (p. 154)

h Pointed end with Lace pattern. Provincial, about 1695. R.S. (L 8$\frac{1}{4}$ ins). *Ashmolean Museum*

61 a Waved end. 1706. Joseph Barbitt (L 7 ins). *Ashmolean Museum.* Contemporary engraved crest (p. 181)

b Hanoverian. About 1725. No marks (L 6¾ ins). *Ashmolean Museum*. Cast and chased ornament in low relief; cf. plates 44a, etc. (p. 181)

c Old English spoon, with reeded edge. 1806. Stephen Adams (L 8¾ ins). *Private Collection*. Contemporary engraved initials in monogram (p. 201)

d Three-pronged Trifid Fork. 1689. I.C. (L 5¼ ins). *Ashmolean Museum*. Late engraved crest (p. 154)

e Four-pronged Reeded Fiddle pattern Fork. 1810. Eley, Fearn & Chawner (L 6½ ins). *Private Collection*. Contemporary engraved crest and later initials (p. 231)

f Four-pronged King's pattern Fork. 1837. John & Henry Lias (L 8 ins). *Private Collection*

g Ladle. 1769. T. Evans (L 13¼ ins). *Private Collection*. Feather-edging, Onslow finial, scalloped bowl (p. 201)

62 a Inkstand. 1735. Paul de Lamerie (L 12½ ins). *Ashmolean Museum*. Cf. salver in plate 48b. Pots for ink and sand; bell between (p. 210)

b Inkstand. 1773. AF (L 10 ins). *Holburne of Menstrie Museum, Bath*. Combination of rococo motifs (cast openwork feet, piercing in lid of jar on left) with Classical (gadrooning, beading, regular curves and straight lines). Depressions along each side for pens, etc. Glass jars for sand, ink, and ? wafers (p. 228 f.)

63 a Dish Ring. Dublin, about 1770 (D 8 ins). *City Museum, Leeds*. Pierced and repoussé pastoral capriccio, with scrolls, birds, architecture, human and animal figures, etc. (p. 230)

b Wine Coaster. 1814. Paul Storr (H 5¾ ins). *Wellington Museum*. Appropriate Classical motif of children amid vines, repoussé and partly pierced, with ribboned reeding and chased foliage. Inscription visible: RUNDELL BRIDGE ET RUNDELL AURIFICES REGIS FECERUNT (p. 249 f.)

64 Queen's Cup. 1953. R. Y. Goodden (H 15 ins). *Goldsmiths' Company*. Combination of raised steeple (cf. plate 10), spherical finial (cf. plate 38), acanthus calyx (cf. plate 11) with fluting and gadrooning, and scrolled brackets. Marks visible: *maker's mark, lion passant, leopard's head, date letter*, and *Coronation mark* (p. 257)

List of Figures

LIST OF FIGURES

Acknowledgements

THANKS are due to the following for permission to reproduce articles in their possession: the Trustees and the Director of the British Museum; of the Victoria and Albert Museum; and of the Wallace Collection; the Brighton Museum; the Norwich Museums Committee; the Holburne of Menstrie Museum, Bath; the Barber Institute of Fine Arts, Birmingham; the Glasgow Art Gallery; the Museum of Art, Boston, Mass.; and the City Museum, Leeds; the Corporations of Abingdon, Dover, Hastings, Hedon, King's Lynn, and Norwich; the Company and Governor of the Bank of England; the following Worshipful Companies: the Fishmongers' Company, the Goldsmiths' Company, the Clothworkers' Company, the Barbers' Company, the Tallow Chandlers' Company, and the Armourers' and Brasiers' Company; the Benchers of the Middle Temple; and to the following colleges, at Cambridge, Corpus Christi, and at Oxford, Corpus Christi, Keble, Magdalen, Merton, New College, Oriel, the Queen's College, St Edmund Hall, Wadham; the Warden and Fellows of Winchester College; His Grace the Duke of Bedford; Messrs Hoare and Co., Bankers; Messrs Sotheby and Co.; Messrs Tessiers Ltd; and finally to the Visitors of the Ashmolean Museum who allowed no less than fifty objects to be reproduced.

The photographs of the objects in the Victoria and Albert Museum and the Wellington Museum are Crown Copyright; those for plates 8, 14b, 15a, 16a, 16c, 18d, 19a, 22a, 23a, 23b, 24a, 24b, 33a, 36, 39, 44b, and 64 have been kindly supplied by the Worshipful Company of Goldsmiths; and for plate 50b by Messrs Christie, Manson, and Woods.

The author is especially grateful to Mr A. G. Grimwade for his help in reading the proofs and for much advice.

NOTE

We are indebted to Frederick Bradbury Publications Ltd, for permission to reproduce the Assay Office Mark, the Sterling Mark, the Duty Mark, and the first Date Letter of each cycle from the late Frederick Bradbury's pocket book *Guide to Marks of Origin on British and Irish Silver Plate, from Mid 16th Century to the Year 1959, and Old Sheffield Plate Makers' Marks 1743–1860*, published by J. W. Northend Ltd, West Street, Sheffield, England.

Introduction

MANY of the books written about domestic silverware made in the British Isles are either historical and rather narrow in their scope, or detailed records of public and private collections. Almost as numerous are the comprehensive inventories of church plate, which are interspersed with descriptions of domestic plate that has become ecclesiastical property. Other works are concerned principally with hall-marks or the goldsmiths themselves, individually or corporately as the Worshipful Company of Goldsmiths. Such works are of the greatest interest to the collector and antiquary.

So large and, in some aspects, controversial a subject cannot be comprehensively expounded in a short book. The present volume is therefore intended to present to a wider public no more than a general introduction to the history of British plate which draws, more or less, on all such works and on many other published sources. It is an attempt to describe concisely many of the factors which from time to time have affected the manufacture of plate in the British Isles, and to describe and illustrate the development and variety of its design and ornament, and the many forms of vessels and utensils which have been made in succeeding centuries for display and daily use. The first chapter is devoted to the general properties, discovery, processing and working of gold and silver, the two precious metals first known to man. The remaining chapters deal with successive convenient periods, and are all divided into three parts. Each begins with a general introduction dealing with external forces, political, economic, and social, which affected the art of the plate-worker, and with some of the principal goldsmiths; little is known of their personalities, and their work seldom shows any personal idiosyncrasies beyond the characteristics common to their period. Next follows a section explaining how current artistic styles may be reflected in the ornament and to a lesser extent in the shapes of the objects made. The third section describes the principal types of plate made and their uses. The epilogue touches on Victorian and modern plate and some of the problems that silversmiths now face.

Silver and gold are rare and costly metals; from early times their possession has been associated with prestige, power, and wealth. Their attraction lies not only in their rarity, but also in their fine appearance, weight, and solidity. They were from the beginning the obvious metals for ceremonial objects of great importance. In Christian times they have been used to make vessels and ornaments in the worship of God. Under the feudal system the principal owners of secular plate were kings and nobles; they were later imitated by the rich merchants, and by the professional classes, until today there are few people who have not some article of silver or gold – be it but a spoon or a ring. The fact that the two metals share certain physical characteristics naturally led to the working of both for similar purposes by the same craftsmen – the goldsmiths, silversmiths, or plate-workers – who composed the most highly respected group among the metal-workers, and figured among the most prosperous and important tradesmen of their times.

Gold and silver are almost indestructible, though both are wasted by wear, and the latter by corrosion also; broken or damaged articles or discontinued coins can be melted down and turned into something else; fresh supplies are constantly being added and the total quantity in use continues to accumulate.

The two metals are suitable for a great variety of uses, from massive castings, such as those reproduced on plates 24, 58, 59, etc., to the most delicate chains, and a fine clean finish can always be achieved. They can therefore be put to more varied uses than most other metals, earthenware, porcelain, or glass. Vessels made in solid metal are more expensive, yet cannot be easily broken. They can be imitated, though seldom satisfactorily, in base metals gilded or silvered, or in base metal alloys such as pinchbeck, or stainless steel, or in aluminium. All these base metals and base metal alloys have certain disadvantages; the covering wears off exposed parts to reveal the metal beneath, and they are either too soft to wear well or too hard to manipulate with the fluency needed to emulate goldsmiths' work. Above all, the weight and the intrinsic value of the solid gold or silver are unmistakable in the vessels made of them. It is a curious coincidence that the small amount of gold and silver, by comparison with the base metals whose production may be measured in millions of tons per year instead of millions of ounces, makes them even more valuable than their unique qualities for ornamental working would in any case ensure.

Silver suffers from particular disadvantages; the normal alloys used for plate can tarnish rapidly in impure air or in contact with salt or egg-yolk. Silver utensils were originally acquired by those who employed enough servants to keep their plate clean and polished. In recent conditions the domestic situation has altered so that many who were accustomed to use lavish ornamental plate now tend to restrict themselves to simpler items which can be easily kept clean in the course of normal daily use. Were the experiments successful that are now being made to introduce some element into silver alloys which would retard, if it cannot entirely prevent, discoloration, more ornamental plate would be wanted for use today.

Plate produced at the present time may be divided into three categories; the first and largest comprises products of contemporary and traditional designs which are made by machinery in large quantities for retailing widely, in Britain and abroad; the second, the specially designed articles of high quality, hand wrought with machine aids in limited quantities; and the third the small number of pieces specially commissioned and made by the hands of designer-craftsmen.

Happily there is evidence of a great effort in certain parts of the industry to mass-produce attractive modern plate designed by the best artists, and to combine in such products cheapness, functionalism, and variety. The middle years of the twentieth century may come to be remembered for a nucleus of impressive master-pieces which are matched in style and quality by much excellent plate for daily use. Thus once again we may see restored in the silversmiths' craft the homogeneity which in former times has characterized the products of an age.

Some aspects of style must be touched on at this point; not those which are relevant to personal pleasure or distaste but those which help in the correct assessment of a piece of plate. The weight or size of a piece or set, the amount and quality of its ornament, may, being dependent largely on the wealth of the client, be considered as irrelevant. Plate is essentially functional and its form depends much on social usages. But those forms most obviously suitable for certain purposes may be modified by fashionable ideas of proportion, elegance, or ornament. The types of tools in use, the availability of craftsmen with certain skills, and the shortage or abundance of bullion may likewise modify the appearance of the finished product.

Far more often and reliably than in any other branch of British art, whether fine or applied, can the maker of a piece of plate, no less than the year and place of manufacture, be found out by reference to the marks stamped on it. Study of plate thus authenticated will gradually result in the acquisition of a sense of style, an understanding of the characteristics of sequent styles and the recognition with increasing assurance of discrepancies between form, ornament, workmanship, and marks. In short, a piece of plate should be self-consistent from every aspect. Some characteristics may be typical of a few years earlier, some of a few years later, just as some workers concerned in a piece of plate may be young and imbued with a newly fashionable style, while others may be old and unable entirely to forget the styles and habits of their earlier days. But if the characteristics of a piece of plate disagree irreconcilably, then, one may be sure, the piece is 'wrong'. 'Wrongness' is a matter of degree, for some inconsistencies may be explicable and have occurred in one of several proper and lawful ways, as in the instances of repairs and alterations, while others are due to fraudulent deceptions, old and new.

Techniques and tools used in the manufacture of plate have gradually improved, and the difference between rolled sheet and hammered sheet, or between hand and machine piercing are only two of the features that are generally distinguishable. There should be, for instance, no difficulty in recognizing at sight a nineteenth-century replica of a sixteenth-century vessel. The change in the traditions of manufacturing techniques and the craftsman's unfamiliarity with the old styles will generally give both imitations and replicas a meticulous but wooden finish lacking the vigour and spontaneity that only a craftsman working in his own idiom can give (see note to plate 4a). When an object falls into one of the more common patterns that are illustrated in this book, it should not be difficult to assign it to its correct period, even though it has been mended, transformed, or subsequently ornamented. Even an unmarked piece of strange design can often be placed by an experienced judge near to its date; if it was made after the fifteenth century, within a bracket of ten or twenty years: the more ornament it carries the easier this will be, because the sum of its characteristics, rather than any salient characteristic, reflects those other vessels known to have been made during a given period.

The sequence of ornamental styles on British plate always reflects those in current use in British architecture and in the other decorative arts. The goldsmiths of each successive generation have introduced new elements of design and pattern, either borrowed from the Continent or of their own devising. Some motifs, particularly those of classical origin, have often recurred, others have been confined to a certain period – one might almost say that in a country where Latin was for long a familiar language, and where Greek was taught in the universities from the later Middle Ages, and in the schools from the sixteenth century, classical ideas and imagery were familiar. Nor has the Orient been neglected.

The two medieval pastoral staves (plates 2, 3) seem to show that in the later Middle Ages a repertory of patterns had been built up which mainly incorporated motifs from gothic architecture, such as crockets, pointed arches, and quatrefoil piercings.

The Renaissance inspired the first break with the Middle Ages, at first under Italian and South German influences, and in the later Tudor period by way of Netherlandish and Rhenish art.

For a short time before and after the Civil War, a naïve style confined to Britain seems to have excluded more monumental continental baroque designs. The cartilaginous style diffused for a short time from the Netherlands, and the more effusive and longer-lived style employing embossed flowers came in shortly before the Restoration, only to be vanquished by the magnificent classicism of the 'Louis XIV' style fostered by the Huguenots, and by the 'William and Mary' style, characterized by contiguous fluting and gadrooning with baroque motifs. During the early years of the eighteenth century the 'Queen Anne' style prevailed with sober but graceful designs with little ornament and was gradually elaborated with low relief ornament in 'Régence', a Franco-German, style (see p. 187). The middle years of the eighteenth century were characterized by the florid asymmetrical rococo style, which often included fantastic, naturalistic, classical, and oriental elements. In reaction a rather pure and neo-Greek, or 'Adam', style became popular about 1770, with some motifs in common with Tudor and 'William and

Mary' ornament. At the turn of the century this was elaborated into the Regency style, more reminiscent of Imperial Rome, with which rococo, Gothic, Romantic, and naturalistic motifs were associated. Since the middle years of the nineteenth century, from the confusion of imitation and mixture of all that had gone before, two or three subsidiary but well-defined characteristics can be discerned. At the end of the century the Art Nouveau style shows the impact of fresh Japanese influences to be seen in the flowing plant-like shapes and ornament. In the present century simple forms, mechanically and geometrically inspired, with an emphasis on straight lines and curves, have predominated.

The practice, customary in the trade, of classifying plate under the name of the monarch at the time of its manufacture is useful, but it may be misleading, especially when one style overlaps two or three short reigns, or when two or three styles obtained during a single reign. The description 'Georgian' is very unsatisfactory because it applies equally to four successive reigns and to a span of more than a century.

Although progress is never regular, it may be seen that increases in the manufacture of plate, in the number of manufacturers, and in the number of purchasers will result in a more than corresponding increase in the variety of objects made and in their shape and ornament. As a corollary the proportion of objects surviving from each period increases from medieval times until the present day. Therefore the number of extant objects which fall to be examined in connexion with each successive period increases rapidly till, by the middle of the eighteenth century, it is fruitless to attempt a systematic list of the multitudinous types of every category of object known to have been made, or to do more than generalize about combinations of their shapes or ornament. On the other hand this increase allows a wide general view of the periods of the eighteenth and nineteenth centuries, whereas of the medieval and Tudor periods a general picture must be built up from many isolated examples. While the field of medieval plate has been almost exhaustively examined, no comparable studies have been made of plate from the more recent centuries, and very little has been written about domestic plate of the nineteenth and twentieth centuries. With few exceptions, plate of the last hundred years has not yet been selectively collected in the way that earlier plate has been. Moreover, it is difficult to study because its period is seldom described more fully than as 'Victorian' or 'modern'.

The principal owners of ecclesiastical plate continue to be parishes or cathedrals of the Church of England, as well as churches of other sects; some plate has passed out of their possession, and some very important or rare vessels have been lent to public museums or temporary exhibitions.

As the results of changes in municipal government and in the relative prosperity and importance of towns and industries, some municipal and corporate plate, too, has passed into private or public ownership.

Domestic plate is for the most part where it should be, in the hands of private families, or in the ownership of municipal corporations, livery companies, colleges – especially those of Oxford and Cambridge – or in parish churches, for use or as memorial gifts.

The last two major wars have been so expensive that rich families have been expected to contribute to the cost great parts of their accumulated wealth, in land, money, and goods, and have therefore been forced to part with many of their treasures by sale or, instead of paying heavy duties, by presentation to a public museum. Plate of all kinds constitutes a large part of such treasure, having been habitually used in former times for entertaining and display as befitted its owners' positions, rank, and wealth.

Only during the last hundred years have works of art, or

of applied art, been on permanent public exhibition in so many cities and towns. The idea of improving the taste and encouraging the inventiveness of young designers of manufactured articles by showing them works of art and facilitating the study of the best work at the public expense was begun by the Royal Society of Arts (founded in 1754) and more widely canvassed and practised in the early nineteenth century; the results were not always so satisfactory as the organizers had hoped. More recently large sums of money have been spent in approaching the same end by providing temporary and permanent displays of such works to afford pleasure to the public generally, and through such enjoyment to create a demand for higher standards of manufactured goods, and the rejection of ill-designed and badly made articles. Many people, neither antiquarians nor collectors, have in this way become interested in various art-forms yet lack the facilities to study them comprehensively or the money to collect examples of them.

Some important and many representative pieces are now in museums where they help to illustrate the ways of life in earlier centuries, the development of the goldsmiths' craft, and the highest achievements of which they were capable.

The principal British national collection of plate is in the Victoria and Albert Museum, where a long and varied sequence of English plate, both domestic and ecclesiastical, from the thirteenth to the nineteenth century, is shown, as well as a wide selection of continental plate. In the British Museum is some English and continental plate, as well as work in precious metals from many epochs and civilizations. The Wellington Museum (Apsley House) and the London Museum have some fine specimens of plate, principally of the eighteenth and early nineteenth centuries, and other specimens of royal provenance are in the Tower of London.

In the provinces, the principal displays are in the Ashmolean Museum, Oxford (Carter and Farrer Collections;

about 1660–1750); the National Museum of Wales, Cardiff (Collection formed by the late Sir Charles J. Jackson); the Royal Scottish Museum, Edinburgh (Scottish plate); the Castle Museum, Norwich; the McLellan Galleries, Glasgow (Burrell Collection); the Holburne of Menstrie Museum, Bath; the City Museum and Art Gallery, Birmingham; and Museums at Brighton, Leeds, Manchester, Newcastle, Plymouth, Sheffield, York, and elsewhere.

Public exhibitions of ancient or contemporary plate have been organized from time to time since the middle of the nineteenth century so that examples of the finest craftsmanship still in private hands may be more generally appreciated.

There was a show of some important Cambridge plate in the Fitzwilliam Museum in 1895, followed by others there in 1931 and 1951. Two important exhibitions of plate were organized in London by the now dissolved Burlington Fine Arts Club at the beginning of the century, in 1901 and 1903 respectively. In 1928 much Oxford plate was shown in the Ashmolean Museum, and in 1929 two comprehensive exhibitions of privately owned plate were held in London, at Seaford House and 25 Park Lane respectively. Some plate was included in an exhibition at the Victoria and Albert Museum of works of art belonging to the Livery Companies of the City of London, staged in 1926, and in that of Medieval Art in 1930. A large selection of royal plate from Buckingham Palace and Windsor Castle was shown in that museum in 1954.

The Worshipful Company of Goldsmiths has recently organized a series of summer exhibitions, of Modern Silver and of Historic Plate of the City of London in 1951, of Municipal Plate in 1952, of Oxford Treasures in 1953, and of Cambridge Treasures in 1959. Many provincial museums have held smaller exhibitions devoted to, or inclusive of, plate.

The information set out in this book has depended primarily on general histories of plate and other more specialized works, on official publications, on exhibition and sale catalogues, on numerous articles, some of which are of prime importance, in periodicals, both English and foreign, and on the many thousands of photographs and drawings reproduced in trade advertisements.

Present knowledge of the history of plate is based on the assiduous research and study of many learned men. The first to work seriously on its history was the antiquarian, Charles Octavius Swinnerton Morgan (1803–88). L. Jewitt and W. St John Hope published their work on *Corporation Plate* in 1895, two years after the exhibition of municipal plate in the Mansion House.

William Chaffers (1811–92) was responsible for a book on hall-marks that has been republished in several editions, and for a *History of English Goldsmiths* (1883). The then Clerk of the Worshipful Company of Goldsmiths, Sir Walter S. Prideaux, published abstracts from its records in two volumes in 1896, wherein he set out chronologically much material that is interesting for the history at once of the Company and of the manufacture of plate. It was Sir Charles James Jackson (1849–1923) who set out to produce a comprehensive illustrated record of British hall-marks: his first edition, published in 1905, was succeeded by the larger and revised second edition in 1921; now in its third (photographically copied) edition of 1949, it remains the standard work of reference. Its index and layout may be criticized and inevitably mistakes and omissions will be found, but it is, in most matters, reliable; each chapter is introduced by a history of the assay office in question. In part, this work has been superseded by that of the late Commander G. E. P. How, whose third volume in great detail and with photographic accuracy records London and provincial hall-marks up to the death of Edward VI.

Sir Charles Jackson also published, in 1911, his *History of English Plate* in two volumes, which, with more than fifteen hundred photographic reproductions and drawings, is the most important historical treatise yet written.

E. Alfred Jones (1872–1943) devoted more than forty

years to the study of English and American silver, and produced nearly thirty volumes with comprehensive descriptions and excellent photographs of objects in many important private collections, and several hundred illustrated contributions to periodical literature. W. W. Watts (1862–1948), besides his illustrated single-volume survey (*Old English Silver*, 1924), wrote many articles and catalogues. His successor as Keeper of the Department of Metalwork in the Victoria and Albert Museum, Mr C. C. Oman, has introduced a more analytical historical method into the study of the subject, notably in his *English Church Plate, 597–1830*, published in 1958, in which he has also consolidated the work of others.

The Church plate of Scotland and of many counties has been surveyed and recorded in detail (Berkshire, Brecon, Cardiganshire, Carmarthenshire, Devonshire, Dorset, Essex, Gloucestershire, Hampshire, Kent, Hereford, Isle of Man, Lancashire, Leicestershire, London, Middlesex, Norfolk, Northampton, Oxfordshire, Pembrokeshire, Radnorshire, Rutland, Somerset, Surrey, Sussex, Wiltshire, and Yorkshire. and the dioceses of Bangor and Carlisle). The most constant worker in this field was the Rev. J. T. Evans.

The reproductions in this book have been chosen for a variety of reasons: some choices were inevitable for the early chapters, such as the King's Lynn Cup (plate 1), or the Gibbon Salt (plate 39), because of their unique importance. Other objects have been selected because they illustrate at once a combination of several features. In some few cases the objects, especially smaller articles in public collections, have not been published before. The great majority of them will be familiar to those who have studied the history of plate in any detail, and in any case no satisfactory history could be written without the inclusion of some of the best-known specimens (which after all are best known because they are of exceptional interest). Considerations of format and clarity limited the number of objects reproduced photographically to an average of two on each of sixty-four plates; additional illustration has been afforded in the text by fifty line-drawings specially executed by Mrs F. M. Russell, of which some are schematic patterns to illustrate the more common ornamental motifs and others are outlines of items that are excluded from the plates.

CHAPTER ONE

The Sources and Working of Gold and Silver

THROUGHOUT historic time only the two metals gold and silver had been classified as precious, until by the discovery in 1803 of palladium, and the later isolation of the related metals platinum and rhodium, another group was added to this category; but the rarity of these last confines their use to jewellery and so excludes their further consideration in this book.

Gold and silver are distinguished from all other metals by their combination of four valuable qualities, their lustre, their permanence, their responsiveness to manipulation under easily produced conditions, and, above all, their scarcity. That the annual production of silver is about ten times that of gold, is reflected in its fluctuating current price of over six shillings (95c.) per fine ounce as compared with over two hundred and fifty shillings (about $35) per fine ounce of gold. The search for gold is thus more intense and its discovery more rewarding. In certain circumstances easier to find and in others much more laborious, it always occurs in its metallic form, while silver is seldom found except compounded with another substance. Some gold is occasionally found in association with silver; some silver is nearly always found mixed with gold. The techniques used in their production may be very different even when both are found together in a metallic alloy such as electrum; on the other hand the details of the techniques used in transforming them into objects for use and decoration are so nearly the same that emphasis will be given to silver as the more common of the two.

Although most formations of rock contain some gold, few bear a proportion sufficient to justify the cost of its extraction. The metal occurred below the earth's crust in the molten masses which were thrust up from time to time and solidified into rocks. It is therefore chiefly found embedded in igneous rocks, in greater or less concentrations where it appears in a crystalline wiry branch-like form. This phenomenon understandably encouraged the widespread belief that gold grew as a plant in the rocks, a misconception which, persisting as late as the sixteenth century, the Swiss metallurgist Agricola found it necessary to contradict.

The richest gold-bearing rocks are the bankets of Witwatersrand, in which vein-gold and alluvial deposits are mixed. The three other important sources of gold are veins containing sulphides and pyrites, quartz-reefs in which the gold is embedded in minute flakes, and the siliceous rocks of Mount Morgan in Queensland. Many of these gold-bearing veins were exposed as outcrops to erosion by ice, rain, or heat for perhaps as long as thirty million years. The resulting stones and grit were washed down along the valleys and even out into the oceans, often settling very far from their original sources. The great density of the metal (specific gravity about 19·4) caused the particles of gold to sink down into the accompanying matter so that they became more concentrated near the bedrock than at the surface of the alluvial sands and gravels. Two other characteristics of gold, its permanence in water and air, and its softness, have caused its preservation in particles that vary in size from dust invisible to the eye, and small flakes, to pellets and nuggets of worn and rounded shapes. The largest nugget yet recovered weighed no less than one hundred and ninety pounds.

The second precious metal, silver, is just as widely distributed in many different rocks, as an alloy or a compound. It occurs as a native metal in the extraordinary deposits at Kongsberg in Norway, and exceptionally in Peru, Spain, and elsewhere. Electrum, a native gold which is alloyed more or less heavily with silver, was an ancient source of the latter metal and from it is derived in modern times about fifteen per cent of the world's production of silver. The principal silver ores, of which galena is the most widespread, are associated with and overlie lead ores. The absence of alluvial deposits of silver is explained by its decomposition in contact with chlorides which occur in rain water.

Copper in its metallic form and, more rarely, meteoric iron are also widespread, and the distribution of these metals on the surface of the ground largely determined the order in which they were found on the various continents. There is evidence that gold was the first metal known in South Africa and Mexico, but among the Kaffirs it was preceded by iron, and in other parts of Africa, and among the North American Indians, by copper. Archaeologists have shown that gold was known early in the fourth millennium B.C., and used by widely scattered peoples who probably could not have communicated the knowledge to each other. The discovery of silver came relatively later.

During the Late Stone Age, implements were made from non-metallic substances and man-made fires were not hot enough to melt the metals then known; a wood-fire generates temperatures up to about 700°C., at which gold and silver redden, but they do not melt until the temperature reaches about 1065°C. and 1000°C. respectively. It may therefore be assumed that under such conditions no metal can have been of any practical value in its unworked forms as grains or small lumps, though there is evidence that gold, by virtue of its untarnishing yellow lustre, had acquired some magical significance and was already symbolic of the sun. If metals were worked at all during this early period they were probably carved or beaten into simple shapes. It may also have been found that the metals responded to hammering more satisfactorily when they were heated, but it was not until they were actually melted that true metallurgy began. This was the critical point in the development of the use of metals and some accident in a potter's furnace may well have furnished the clue to further progress. Early pottery was fired at temperatures ranging from 900°C. to 1200°C., which were achieved by supplying oxygen more rapidly to the area of combustion by blow-pipes or primitive bellows.

During the First Metal Age (3000–2200 B.C.) the advantages of these metals over stone for certain purposes had become apparent, and especially attractive were their colours, malleability, permanence, and, in the case of copper and iron, their property of taking and retaining a more regular and sharper cutting edge than that of any stone.

The occasions when metals can be picked up on the surface of the ground are so rare that the demand for them only began to be satisfied very gradually. Gold was commonly obtained from alluvial deposits (placers) until the Second Metal Age (2200–1200 B.C.), when it became possible to supplement these sources by working auriferous veins (see Glossary, p. 273); it was not until about one hundred years ago that the quantity of gold extracted from mines rivalled that from placers. Because gold always occurs in its metallic form, the methods of extracting it from both veins and placers are comparatively simple in principle, and the methods employed today are, for the most part, merely mechanical improvements on those used in earliest historical times.

The simplest way to gather the gold from a placer is to pick out the bigger particles by hand from the earth or gravel with which they are mixed. But even when the material is sifted or winnowed to concentrate the metal, the wastage is very great because the smaller grains escape notice. Where water is near, washing is a convenient, and was in early times the common, process of extraction; washing by hand, though to a limited extent improved on by the Romans, was ousted only by the application of mechanical power during the last century and it is now probably used only by prospectors. A shallow pan is filled with pay-dirt, that is, earth which is expected to contain gold, and shaken in the water until the bulk of the lighter earth has been floated away and only the heavier particles remain at the bottom of the pan. Whenever enough of this enriched earth has been collected, the gold is recovered by a more careful repetition of the process in a smaller pan.

A third method, also used in ancient times, is sluicing. The pay-dirt is thrown into the head of a sluice, a continuous artificial sloping channel of running water, which may extend for several hundred feet. Along its entire length the gold is collected by transverse bars (riffles), notches, or other obstructions while the waste material and much of the flake-gold is washed on. The amount of gold arrested may be increased by placing fat or the skins of certain animals on the riffles to hold or enmesh the particles more securely; it is to the latter practice round the Black Sea that the legend of Jason and the Golden Fleece probably alludes. In more modern times, the riffles are lined with mercury which, readily amalgamating with the gold (as the Romans knew it did), serves the double purpose of catching the metal more effectively and of making its recovery easier.

A more advanced method, not known before Roman times, is hydraulic mining (hushing), where the whole operation is carried out by water-power. The water is directed from a reservoir, in more recent times under great pressure, on to that part of the bank being worked, and carries away the gravel into and along a sluice in the manner already described. Yet even under the most favourable conditions as much as twenty per cent of the gold escapes with the impoverished gravel.

This principle has been further extended for the exploitation of auriferous river-beds, particularly in New Zealand and America, where sluice systems are mounted on dredgers and fed from the river itself, into which the waste gravel is afterwards discharged.

The extraction of both gold and silver ores from below the surface began early in the First Metal Age. Quartz-veins and galena, a lead-silver ore, were worked during the third and second millennia B.C. The quarrying of outcrops must soon have been followed by the driving of more or less horizontal adits in pursuit of veins into the sides of a valley.

The exploration of later systems in Egypt and the Eastern Mediterranean area has shown that, although often complicated by primitive methods of underground surveying, they sometimes reach a depth of 250 feet, with horizontal galleries frequently extending for half a mile or more. Drainage presented an almost insuperable obstacle and only at great risk could shafts be sunk below the natural water-level of the site. The use of buckets was the most obvious remedy, though during the later classical period water-wheels, Archimedean screws, and primitive pumps were among the contrivances used to overcome the dangers of seepage and flooding. Ventilation, especially needed in the Spanish silver mines on account of the sulphur dioxide gases, presented formidable problems which were partially solved by additional vertical shafts, or by artificial draughts either created by flapping cloths or induced by fires in parallel galleries.

Until iron was in general use, it seems that mining was not developed on any considerable scale. The rock-face was attacked with iron-tipped tools and cracked by alternately heating it with fires and then dousing it with cold water, at least until the Middle Ages, when gunpowder was applied to this purpose. The rocks were then prised out, broken down into lumps, and carried in buckets or dragged on sledges to the surface: wheeled haulage below ground is a comparatively recent development, partly because the galleries of early mines were of small diameter and had uneven floors.

In ancient times the cost of developing mines in terms both of capital and of equipment was beyond the means of the landowners and even of the wealthiest merchants, so that mines were generally controlled and operated by the State, notably in the Hellenistic states and in the Roman Empire. On the other hand, because the work was mainly carried out by slaves and criminals, the actual labour costs were low in comparison with those obtaining under present conditions, when wages account for as much as two-thirds of the total cost of production.

After the gold ore has been brought to the surface, it must always be ground to a very fine powder before the metal can be extracted. In early times the ore was pounded in mortars and finally ground in mills worked by hand or other means. The powder was spread over sloping boards and the gold was then separated from the waste matter with the aid of water in a manner similar to that already described. By far the greatest proportion of the quartz now mined in California, Australia, and Africa is treated on the same principle, but by greatly improved, power-operated machines. The ore is crushed in rock-breakers into lumps about two inches in diameter and then fed into stamp-mills, batteries of large, mechanically propelled pestles and mortars. The pestle may weigh as much as half a ton and be dropped, sometimes at the rate of one hundred times a minute, from a height of up to eighteen inches, while the mortar is constantly supplied with water and mercury, At each blow some matter is discharged through small perforations near the bottom of the mortar and carried forward by the flowing water over a sloping table covered with copper plates filled with mercury. A subsequent sluicing operation increases the yield. The amalgam is collected and pressed in wetted canvas or buckskin to remove the surplus mercury; the solid lumps are then distilled to yield the gold, which is melted and cast into ingots.

Gold can also be extracted from auriferous powders by many processes, both wet and dry, all of which may include electrolysis (see pp. 44, 49, and 56). Of the former the MacArthur-Forrest process, used in South Africa, is the most important: the ore is dissolved in a solution of potassium cyanide, from which the gold is precipitated. The chief dry process, called after its inventor, Plattner, requires the reduction by calcination to oxides of all metals except gold and silver; this product is filtered in solvents which dissolve the gold and silver; the gold-silver alloy is precipitated and finally cast into ingots more than ninety per cent pure.

Gold has the property of imparting many of its attributes to alloys of which the gold itself forms as little as half; this property is to a less degree shared by silver. These phenomena in valuable metals have always been such a temptation to fraud that it has been widely found convenient to introduce standards affording purchasers a guarantee of quality. The metalworkers themselves, moreover, evolved empirically and independently various alloys less expensive, harder, and more durable which retain most of the qualities, and lack some of the defects, of the pure metals.

The gold produced by all the methods described is not pure enough for coinage or modern commercial use, because it is almost always still alloyed with a proportion of silver, as well as with base metals; conversely, silver is generally alloyed with some gold. The separation of the two precious metals is a process of some antiquity, and several superseded methods are mentioned in the Bible and by classical authors. The alloy may be immersed in nitric acid or boiling sulphuric acid, both of which dissolve the silver and base metals but do not affect the gold. The most economical method, however, free from such disadvantages as poisonous fumes, is electrolysis, whereby the silver from the alloy on the positive pole is carried by an electric current through a diluted solution of silver nitrate and deposited on the negative pole. The base metals alloyed with the gold remaining on the positive pole are removed by boiling in nitric acid and the gold is left almost one hundred per cent fine.

Until early in the nineteenth century most English goldsmiths made up their own alloys of 22 or 18 carats

Figure 1 – Wire-drawing. Detail from an engraving by
A. and I. Kirk (1743)

(see Glossary) from fine grain gold, and copper or silver.
The addition of copper results in an alloy redder than
pure gold, while silver imparts a paler, greenish colour;
a combination with both silver and copper results in a
tone rather yellower than that of the pure metal. White
gold containing twenty-five per cent of platinum is
marked as 18 carat gold. Thus the variations in both
colour and quality are often considerable, and two or
more of these alloys were often contrasted in a single
piece of work, especially during the eighteenth century,
in order to emphasize the range of colours which can be
obtained, from pale yellow to rich red, or from white to
green. Silver, on the other hand, is seldom alloyed with
any metal except copper, the presence of which is not
betrayed by a dulling of the silver's whiteness until the
proportion of copper reaches about a quarter. But the
recent introduction of mechanical methods of manufacture, with all their attendant advantages and disadvantages, has made it easy for the majority of goldsmiths to
buy sheets or wires of metal of the required gauge, colour,
and fineness, already cut to shape.

   Although gold is almost as soft as lead, so ductile that
a single grain may be drawn into a wire five hundred feet
in length, and so malleable that it may be beaten into a
leaf four millionths of an inch thick, much hammering of
the metal causes a brittleness which must be remedied by
annealing, a fundamental process in metal-work. The

45

metal is heated to a temperature of about 600°C.; only after the work has been cooled from about 400°C. by quenching in cold water do the molecules regain their natural shape and the metal its former properties. If the cooling is too rapid, stresses may be set up, and if from too high a temperature, the plunge into water may cause a fracture; on the other hand, if the cooling is too slow, the metal may remain hard and unworkable.

Silver has many of the characteristics of gold; it is less dense (average specific gravity 10·5) and almost as malleable and ductile, but its most noticeable feature, and that which led the Romans to use it on their military standards, is its very brilliant and lasting lustre. In its pure state it does not oxidize and remains bright indefinitely in unpolluted air, although it quickly tarnishes if exposed to some sulphides or chlorides. The former cause the blackness on silver spoons which have come into contact with egg yolks; and objects which have been long buried are often so badly affected that they may be almost unrecognizable not only for what they were but even for metal. Like gold, silver amalgamates with mercury.

The lead ores proper, of which galena is the most important, also contain silver in quantities varying from 20 to 200 ounces per ton of lead. Technical and archaeological evidence shows that the extraction of silver, and indeed all metallurgy, was closely linked with the production of lead from the galena deposits which stretch across the northern part of Asia Minor. The complicated processes involved would have required many generations of accumulated experience, and satisfactory results were not obtained until the third millennium B.C., when they spread gradually through the Near East. Development may have been retarded because neither lead nor silver was of great practical value at this period, although the latter was soon used as a medium of currency and acquired a magical significance; it was used for amulets and magic missiles and, just as gold was associated with the sun, so silver became associated with the moon, a connexion common throughout the ancient Near East and one which survived among the medieval alchemists and persists to this day in the term lunar caustic (silver nitrate).

The European silver mines of Spain and Hungary do not seem to have been worked till after the division of the Roman Empire, and in the tenth century mines were opened in Germany. By the sixteenth century mines in Austria and Hungary together were producing about half of the European output. Indeed, both gold and silver have been found in various parts of the British Isles, though never in large enough quantities to make their exploitation industrially successful. German miners were brought over to work gold at Crawford Muir in 1566, and silver was produced in Wales, Devon, and Somerset in the seventeenth century. Evidence of mining in the latter county may be seen in the shape of the Mendip Cup, now in the City Art Gallery, Bristol. The annexation of territory in the New World was closely followed by the discovery of rich mines in Mexico and the north-west coast of South America during the first decades of the sixteenth century, and the famous Potosi mines of Peru were opened in 1545. From these colonies a plentiful flow of silver and gold was directed principally towards Spain and Portugal and thence into the larger commercial centres of Europe. The production of European mines fell sharply; and for the next three centuries silver from Spanish America formed the most important supply, until revolutions early in the nineteenth century both diminished the export to Europe and caused the European mines to be reopened and expanded with great vigour. In Spain, Germany, and Austria-Hungary production rose more or less steadily, until in 1900 these three countries accounted for almost the whole European production of more than 18m. ounces per annum.

But this represented no more than a tenth of the world's annual output in that year. During the middle decades of the nineteenth century, huge deposits of silver ore were found and put into production all over the world, among them the famous Comstock lode and the Eureka mines in Nevada, the Leadville mines of Colorado, others in the United States, Mexico, and Canada, as well as the Broken Hill mines of Australia, and more in Japan, India, Burma, China, and Siberia. The world's annual output, about 25 m. ounces in 1850, rose rapidly and steadily, doubled itself by 1870, again by 1890, and yet again by 1908, until a peak of 230 m. ounces was reached in 1912. The coincidence of the First World War with the exhaustion of many lodes caused an appreciable but temporary drop, and in 1929 the total output reached a new level of about 260 m. ounces, from which it has since fluctuated considerably.

Of all these countries, Mexico has during the last half-century been the world's largest supplier of silver, producing no less than one-third of the total, and, with the United States in the second place, the American continents between them are responsible for eighty per cent of the world's supply. Of this almost half is derived from lead and other associated ores, about one-fifth from straight silver ores, fifteen per cent from gold bullion, and the remainder from copper, tin, and other base metal ores.

In the pre-Roman and Roman periods the only method of producing large quantities of silver required the treatment of galena, after it had been mined and powdered, by a mixed process. This may be explained more clearly by a comparison with modern methods, in which each step is now understood to be part of a logical sequence of chemical changes, whereas the ancient workers had to rely entirely on a limited accumulation of experience. If a lump of galena is dropped into a fire, the lead will burn away and a small particle of silver will be left, a simple phenomenon which probably furnished the starting-point for further progress. Production on a larger scale began with the smelting of the powdered ore; the resulting crude lead is purified either by liquation, when the low melting-point of lead allows it to be poured off before other components have melted, or by oxidation, when the dross is skimmed off the molten lead. The next stage is to desilver the lead, at first by a process, known in Roman times, whereby advantage is taken of a peculiar property of lead-silver alloys; when melted and cooled again, the first crystals are formed of pure lead, so that the silver content of the remainder becomes, on repetition, progressively and proportionately greater and, from the resulting concentration, silver can be extracted by cupellation.

By the modern Parkes process, silver is extracted from lead by allowing it to amalgamate with zinc filings, and the zinc-silver alloy is purified by distillation to yield pure silver. In addition to these two methods, which depend on smelting, the silver may be extracted by milling, in a manner similar to that described in connexion with the production of gold. However, the increased yield from smelting in heavily industrialized countries more than repays the greater outlay.

Some silver ores are not amenable to amalgamation with mercury, but must, after being converted into a chloride, be amalgamated under heat. The amalgam is then leached by dissolving the silver, which is precipitated and cast into ingots.

For commercial use silver must be refined and, although many improvements have since been devised, the Moebius process, patented in 1884, will serve to illustrate the principles of electrolysis. A crude silver anode and a silver cathode are suspended, about two inches apart, in a tank containing a half per cent solution of silver nitrate and a weak current is passed between them; the powder deposited on the cathode is easily scraped off, and after it has been washed, melted, and cast into ingots, is almost one hundred per cent pure silver.

Although absolutely pure silver can be obtained by producing a pure silver chloride and then reducing this to metal, in general commercial use the best fine silver contains one or two parts of impure matter in each thousand parts, when it is referred to as 999 or 998 parts fine.

The spread of silver and gold technology in the second

millennium A.D. provided a stimulus to the development of methods for testing the purity of the metals, knowledge of which was essential to trade and to the maintenance of a guaranteed coinage. Cupellation was used, and later the tests of specific gravity and colour were found adequate to provide a rough check of their quality.

The process of assay by cupellation was, until 1925, carried out at Goldsmiths' Hall, and other assay offices, in precisely the same manner as it had been for the last five hundred years. A portion (diet) of metal is scraped from different parts of the article and carefully weighed; this is wrapped in lead and the whole melted in a shallow porous bowl of bone ash, known as a cupel, until the lead and other base metals have been oxidized and the oxides absorbed into the bone ash, leaving only a small button of pure silver. The difference between the weight of this button and the weight of the original diet is therefore the weight of alloy. The process for testing gold is a little more complicated; the diet of gold is weighed, and to it added three times its weight of silver; these are wrapped together in lead and heated in a cupel; the silver and gold combine and the oxides are absorbed, leaving a button of pure gold and silver, which is flattened and coiled into a 'cornet'; this is placed in hot diluted nitric acid, which dissolves the silver but not the gold; after the improved gold has been treated in stronger nitric acid, washed, and made red-hot, it is cooled and weighed again; the difference between the two weights will once more be the weight of the adulterant.

An earlier method of trying gold and silver by the touch required sets of touch-needles each of which was alloyed with a different known proportion of base metal. A streak made on the touchstone by the piece of plate under examination was compared with streaks made by the needles, and although in the testing of silver little difference in colour can be seen, the experienced assayer could derive much information from the sensations of greasiness or dryness, roughness or smoothness imparted by the stroke, or the relative pressure required by the hardness of the metals. The use of sulphuric acid on silver or of aqua regia, a mixture of nitric and hydrochloric acids, on gold furnishes additional evidence.

Fine silver like fine gold is too soft for everyday use in plate or coinage; it is therefore alloyed, generally with copper, to make it harder and to improve its working qualities. In England the alloy is made up of 11 ounces 2 dwt of silver and 18 dwt of copper in each Troy pound; that is 925 parts fine and is known as the Sterling standard. (See table on p. 281.) Although Troy weight has been statutorily abolished since 1879 (except for the Troy ounce, its decimal parts and multiples) the pennyweight continues to be widely used. The alloyed metal was formerly hammered from the ingot into a sheet; it is now rolled. As it is gradually reduced in thickness, or goes through the many other forms of treatment at the hands of the silversmith, the individual crystals are distorted and broken down into small fragments. The stresses thus formed in the metal reveal themselves by an increasing resistance to further work. In order to soften the metal again, it must be annealed, that is, heated to a temperature of about 700°C. (when it glows a cherry red) and cooled. To gauge the correct temperature for each occasion requires considerable skill and experience, because overheating will cause the metal to become 'burnt' and liable to fracture under further manipulation. In the heat the crushed distorted grains begin to recrystallize into their natural form, the stresses are released, and the metal regains its former softness and malleability. Any slight variations in hardness or temper can be compensated for by the craftsman, but where mechanical devices of manufacture are employed, the most careful control in each stage of production after the mixing of the alloy is imperative to ensure complete uniformity of structure and reaction throughout the piece of metal.

While being melted silver absorbs more than twenty times its own volume of atmospheric oxygen, which, however, is not retained but expelled on rapid cooling with great violence, a phenomenon known as 'spitting'. Likewise the copper in the alloy dissolves oxygen very freely when molten, and the cuprous oxide spreads on solidification, causing weaknesses and a surface discoloration known as 'firestain', the penetration of which is increased by each successive heating operation. This stain, visible on much plate (cf. plates 28 and 34), can only be removed with difficulty by hard polishing or even stripping, operations which waste both time and metal; or it may be concealed by silver-plating. It has recently been discovered that firestain can be prevented either by the use of special furnaces or by the addition of a hundredth part of aluminium to the alloy.

A very strong way to join two pieces of silver is by soldering them with silver solders, which melt at temperatures several hundred degrees below the normal silver alloys. Powdered borax is the traditional flux which is applied to dissolve the existing oxides and prevent their further formation and thus to make the solder adhere more effectively. The areas to which the solder will be applied are scraped clean and bright and gradually heated to a temperature at which the solder will melt on contact with them; the work is then reheated so that the solder runs along the joint and fills it well to allow for shrinkage on solidification. The excess of flux is removed by immersion in a weak hot solution of sulphuric acid and brushed off, and the joint is filed flush.

The principal methods of fashioning plate merit a brief description, so that the objects to be described may be better appreciated for the skill of their creators. For example, the body of a tea pot of the late eighteenth century (plate 27b) is constructed by soldering together a number of sheets of silver which have been cut and bent into the required shapes; the carved wooden handle is fixed into its sockets by silver pins and the knob on the lid is attached by a threaded bolt and wing-nut. A plain bowl (plate 52a) or a tumbler cup (plate 17a) is raised from a circular sheet by hammering it on a stake (fig. 2) in a series of concentric rings from the centre to the outer edge, first strongly and then more and more carefully, while from time to time the work requires annealing. To remove the hammer-marks from all over the surface a broad smooth-faced planishing hammer is used; these marks can nevertheless be often seen on the surface (plates 13b and 52a). When the bowl or cup has at last, after much work and continual testing of its measurements with calipers and gauges, assumed its final form, it is ready for what used to be the tedious process of polishing. First it may be pumiced; afterwards the modern craftsman is aided by electrically powered buffing wheels which are used with tripoli paste to produce a satin finish; and finally all the minute rough-nesses on the surface are flattened with jewellers' rouge

Figure 2 – Raising plate. Detail from an engraving by
A. and I. Kirk (1743)

to produce that brilliant lustre which only comes from a completely smooth and unscratched surface.

More solid objects or parts of complex shape, such as the spout of a tea pot (plate 26b), the handle of a ewer (plate 36), or a candlestick (plate 57b) are cast in one or more moulds and, if necessary, the parts are soldered together. The imperfections of the cast are removed, and a crisp modelling is achieved by filing, chasing, and polishing.

Decoration may be added to the plain flat surfaces in a variety of ways. With a scorper, or graver (fig. 3), decorative lines may be cut out of the metal to produce the inscriptions (plates 4, 17c, 18c, 19b, 15b, etc.), armorial bearings (plates 51b, 52a, 48b, 49, etc.), figures (plates 18d and 23a), and patterns (plates 33a and 17c and b) which are often found. The excised grooves may be filled with a black alloy, called *niello* (see p. 276), to present a strong contrast like that of a woodcut, though this practice was generally confined to the decoration of smaller articles and watch cases. Both opaque and translucent enamels can be employed, either *champlevé* (plate 1) or *cloisonné*; the former term indicates that the fields to be filled with enamel are cut out of the solid metal with a scorper, and the latter that the fields are bounded by wire soldered to the ground to form a series of troughs. *Bassetaille* is a rather more sophisticated form of enamelling in which the ground is decorated with engraving, often engine-turned as in the snuff boxes of the later eighteenth century, or in relief, so that the pattern or modelling appears through the translucent enamel to be darker or lighter according to its thickness. A further effect was obtained, especially in the last quarter of the eighteenth century, by placing a blue glass container, which incidentally helps to protect the metal from corrosion, in the decoratively pierced frame of a salt cellar (plates 42d and e) or mustard pot, where its colour formed an attractive foil to the whiteness of the silver.

An effect superficially like that of engraving may be produced by flat-chasing (fig. 3), whereby punches are hammered along the surface, without removing any of the metal, to indent it with a broader and less clearly defined line (plate 49a); on thinnish plate the pattern will be more or less distinctly visible on the reverse side. Decoration may also be executed in relief on thinnish plate by punching, embossing, or chasing. The first term indicates that each indentation of the surface is made by the single stroke with a plain or shaped punch (plates 16b and 50a);

the second means that the relief is raised from the back by strokes from one or more rounded punches to produce the required surface modelling, while the rather indefinite term 'chasing' indicates that a similar technique is used from the front, either alone or in conjunction with embossing. The more complicated figure scenes in embossed

Figure 3 – Chasing (above) and engraving (below). Detail from an engraving by A. and I. Kirk (1743)

and chased relief are generally described by the French word *'repoussé'* (plate 63b).

Ornament may take the form of decorative wires, sheets of metal cut into patterns, stampings or castings, all of which are applied by solder; such work is illustrated by cut-card (plates 13a, 19b, and 28), applied strapwork (plates 14a and 22b), cast reliefs (plates 18a, 15b, 44b, or 25b), or by the many varieties of moulding (plate 23a), rope-moulding (plate 13a), or reeding (plate 17b), which were intermittently used on plate made during the last four hundred years.

Silver was often given the colour of gold by one of several methods of gilding. Mercury, it will be recalled, amalgamates with both silver and gold and can be evaporated by distillation; the common technique of mercury- or fire-gilding takes advantage of this phenomenon. The gold is melted and mixed with mercury in a crucible; the excess of mercury is extracted and the creamy amalgam is then spread with a brush onto the surface of the silver; when the remainder of the mercury has been evaporated by heat, a thin film of gold has fused to the silver and the surface can be safely polished. By another method, which avoids the poisonous mercury vapour, a linen rag is soaked in a solution of chloride of gold, dried, and burnt; the ashes are rubbed onto the surface of the silver, to which the gold adheres securely. Gilding has been more efficiently and easily applied during the last century by electrolysis but it is inferior in appearance.

While the tools and facilities available to contemporary silversmiths are unquestionably superior to those of their predecessors from the earliest times until the Renaissance, and while the advantages of advanced metallurgical knowledge and the experience of centuries are now at their disposal, it must be emphasized that their practical and technical ability, as demonstrated by the finished products, cannot be expected to show a corresponding advance, for the variety of techniques and the quality of surviving works from ancient Egypt and from the classical period reveal a complete mastery of the art of working in precious metals.

CHAPTER TWO

The Middle Ages

WHILE the barbarians from the north were breaking up the Western Roman Empire from the fourth century onwards, Christianity continued to gain increasing support. Its influence extended north and west until Rome again became the centre of Europe when the Frankish king Charlemagne was crowned there by Pope Leo III in 800. This alliance allowed the freer spread of ecclesiastical power throughout Western Europe and, temporarily, more stable and unified government.

During these dark and confused centuries the servants of the Church contrived to preserve some fragments of the culture of Greece and Rome. Nor had all the traditions of art and craftsmanship died. Churches and abbeys were built and decorated, sacred and secular manuscripts were copied and re-copied with much elaborate ornament and illustration, and gold and silver were wrought into a variety of sacred vessels and images and domestic plate. Eloi, for example, who began his distinguished career as a goldsmith-monk at Limoges, was later canonized and adopted as patron saint of the French goldsmiths. Indeed, his reputation extended so far that he was likewise honoured by the Guild of Hammermen of Scotland.

The conversion of the mixed peoples of Britain to Christianity was due not only to the dynamic St Augustine (d. 604) sent directly from the Pope, but also to a succession of Irish missionaries. The latter brought to Northern Britain many elements of the vigorous Christian art, derived from the Continent, that was flourishing in Ireland; its characteristic interlacing ornament combined with

Figure 4 – Interlacing ornament with animal forms (6th century).
Based on the rim of the Taplow Horn

animal forms can be seen on stone crosses and other objects that were made in the north. Rather more bizarre is the interlacing ornament found in mid-Britain dating from the sixth and seventh centuries such as that on the rim mount of the Taplow Horn (fig. 4). But the silver and copper-gilt Ormside Bowl (Yorkshire Museum), of the early eighth century, is the only vessel remaining to represent the art of Northern England during this epoch (fig. 5). So few examples of Anglo-Saxon plate, as opposed to jewellery, remain that their origins are still disputed. An example of the geometrical ornament found on jewellery of *cloisonné* gold and enamel in South-East England, best represented by objects from the Sutton Hoo Burial in the British Museum, is shown in the Faversham Brooch (fig. 6). It is clear that there were a number of distinct regional styles but their development and interrelationship are still largely conjectural. Moreover, the invasions from Scandinavia and Jutland and the movement of populations during the whole of this period make it very difficult to decide where and when any particular piece may have been wrought. For example, a bowl found at Fejø in Den-

Figure 5 – Interlacing ornament (8th–9th century). Based on the Ormside Bowl

Figure 6 – Stepped ornament in *cloisonné* enamel (6th–7th century). Based on the Faversham Brooch

58

mark is thought to have been made in Southern England towards the end of the eighth century, while the Halton Moor Bowl (fig. 7) and a similar bowl and cover, both in the British Museum, have been variously assigned an English or a continental origin during the last two centuries before the Norman Conquest. But wherever they were made, they show strong Sassanian and other Eastern influences. The bowl from the Trewhiddle find has been accepted as Southern English work of about 875 in a style that spread gradually northwards after the unification of England. Its chief ornamental motifs are scrolls, ivy leaves, and palmettes of classical origin, loose interlacings of thin

Figure 7 – Animal and foliate ornament (9th–11th century).
Based on the Halton Moor Bowl

lines of Celtic origin, and the curiously distorted beasts that are associated with Sassanian work.

The existence of considerable quantities of plate, both secular and ecclesiastical, besides the names of many goldsmiths, is recorded in contemporary documents, but not one of these pieces survives. In 801 the King of Mercia presented a fine large silver dish to Worcester Cathedral. In the following century Athelstan included two silver cups amongst his gift of plate to the shrine of St Cuthbert, Durham. King Egbert and King Ethelwulf took presents of plate to Rome and the reputation of Anglo-Saxon goldsmiths was so well established throughout Western Europe that during the eighth and ninth centuries a succession of papal orders for English plate is recorded in the *Liber Pontificalis*.

The esteem in which English plate was held was perhaps directly due to the influence of two historic personalities. Alfred the Great (849–901) not only secured peace for his subjects but determined to improve the standards of British craftsmanship by bringing from abroad artificers skilled in many trades. An example of his success is the Alfred Jewel (Ashmolean Museum), perhaps a representation of Christ, in *cloisonné* enamels elaborately mounted in crystal and gold. Its form and decoration reflect Coptic and other Eastern motifs typical of the Carolingian style that was centred on Charlemagne's capital at Aachen; but its workmanship is Anglo-Saxon. This style, common throughout the Holy Roman Empire, incorporates a mixture of motifs which may be traced back to Sassanian work of the New Persian Kingdom, to Byzantine work of the Eastern Roman Empire (which was itself based on Hellenistic and Near Eastern art), as well as more directly to Greek and Roman motifs that during the centuries of the extensive domination of the Roman Empire had been widely carried through Europe and the Mediterranean world.

Alfred's policy was carried on by the mystic and ascetic (Dunstan (924–88) who acquired much influence as Archbishop of Canterbury. In accordance with the custom by which monks combined craftsmanship with their devotional routines (though they employed skilled laymen as well), Dunstan became a goldsmith, working at a forge in his small cell on plate such as crosses, censers, and chalices for his own abbey, and also on secular plate. One day, it is related, a strange man came in with a large order for plate; Dunstan at once recognized him as the Devil disguised and as the story goes

> He seized the Devil by the nose;
> With red-hot tongs to make him roar,
> Till he could be heard ten miles or more.

Dunstan, like St Eloi, was canonized and later chosen as 'blessed patron, protector, and founder' of the goldsmiths of London and all England. His effigy, of silver gilt set with gems, stood for many years in the hall of the London goldsmiths, and much of their corporate plate was engraved with his image. St Dunstan's Light was kept burning in St John Zachary's Church and on every St Dunstan's Eve (18 May) it was ordered that 'all the holle companye of the lyverye shall assemble at the hall in their second lyverye and shall have iiij chapeleynes to wayte and goo before them' to their chapel in St Paul's Cathedral. Though none of his work is known today, a royal inventory of 1280 listed 'a gold ring with a sapphire of the workmanship of St Dunstan'. An improbable tradition tells that he advised King Edgar to order pegs to be placed at vertical intervals inside all drinking vessels so that a man might be warned against excess by their measure.

During the ninth and tenth centuries Scandinavian influence was strong in the north-east as the invaders gradually extended their hold, small objects being mostly characterized by asymmetrical ribbon patterns and animal forms. During the tenth and eleventh centuries this was to a certain extent ousted by a strong German influence – the Ottonian style which succeeded the Carolingian – characterized by heavy bejewelling with precious stones, or pastes, set in clasps, or cloisons. At the same time the influence of Byzantium continued undiminished, and was often combined with Ottonian motifs, especially in church vessels.

While there is no evidence on which to assess the effect of the Norman Conquest on the goldsmiths in this country, the subsequent freedom from any further effective invasions allowed the population to settle down and develop both agriculture and trade in security, a trend encouraged during the following centuries by the feudal system. Just as Saxon architecture gave place to Norman (the English version of the continental Romanesque style), so a predominantly French influence was felt in this country which rendered its products almost indistinguishable from those of North-Western Europe. Until Gothic architecture superseded Romanesque at the end of the twelfth century, architectural forms with much application of jewellery, filigree and enamelling, and the introduction of human figures predominated.

Much plate made during the Dark Ages, especially that belonging to the abbeys and churches, was handed over to the Norman conquerors, either against their demands for gold or in the hope of obtaining their good will. To the latter end the monks of Ely, which stood in the centre of an area not yet occupied, presented to William I a large gift of silver and gold melted from the possessions of their cathedral.

Little more than a century after the Norman Conquest a further large quantity of melted plate was subscribed by churches and laity alike towards the ransom of Richard I. In 1338 Edward III borrowed another huge sum from various abbeys and cathedrals, promising to replace the vessels melted down, or at least to repay their value. The culmination of these political depredations of ecclesiastical property came with the Reformation when all church plate was called in for replacement.

But if much plate was destroyed, its very destruction must have provided work for the goldsmiths by its replacement. Moreover, additional encouragement was afforded to secular craftsmen by the fact that the clerics who came from France seem to have been imbued with a less strong tradition of monastic craftsmanship than had been fostered in England by Dunstan, or earlier in their own land by Eloi. Indeed, with the exception of writing and illuminating, they were inclined to employ laymen for the production of all kinds of artefacts.

THE EARLY HISTORY OF THE
GOLDSMITHS' COMPANY

There had been a form of guild among the Roman goldsmiths during the Republic and this kind of trade organization survived the division of the Empire: in the Eastern

Empire it achieved such efficiency that marks were punched on plate made there during the fifth and sixth centuries to denote the makers and the cities where they worked. It is not to be expected that any such organization could have existed in England until well after the Conquest, although some loose forms of association of local goldsmiths may well have existed, because the members of such a highly esteemed craft would naturally be jealous of their techniques and some form of joint action would have been necessary to protect their interests.

Such a body is first noticed historically when, in 1180, the goldsmiths, together with members of other trades, were fined for having established organizations without the consent of the king. Nothing seems to have been done officially, however, to control the quality of gold and silver made up into plate until the ordinance *De auro fabricando civitate Londiniarum* of 1238. This decree empowered the mayor and aldermen to choose six of the most discreet goldsmiths in the city to superintend the craft, and to be responsible that all work was done in the public street and not in secret; that the silver used should not be worse in fineness than that used for coinage at the Mint; that the gold so used should not be worth less than one hundred shillings for a mark of Tower weight (see table, p. 281); that gold should be of no colour but its own; and that latten (see Glossary) and copper should not be gilded. The inclusion of provisions about the use of counterfeit and precious stones reminds us that the goldsmith was not then so narrow a specialist as he later became and that he was equally prepared to work on jewellery and on base metals which had similar properties to gold or silver.

After this vague order, the responsibilities of the goldsmiths were gradually defined and suitable sanctions were imposed for frauds by a series of statutes, grants of incorporation, and measures agreed by the goldsmiths among themselves, until, by the beginning of Henry VII's reign, an effective system had been built up under the immediate control of the members of the craft themselves and backed by the law, that had no equal in the world.

Because the 'gardiens' are again mentioned in an Act of 1300, it may be assumed that their appointment continued for the benefit of the goldsmiths and the public alike. But that their disciplinary powers and personal authority were limited is shown by the number of riots in which members of the company took part, notably the affray between them and the tailors in 1267, when about one thousand persons were engaged; many were killed or injured before the bailiffs were able to disperse them and to arrest the ringleaders.

This Act is very important historically because it contains the first mention of the assay and the punch of the Leopard's Head (fig. 8). It ordained that 'no goldsmith of England, nor none otherwhere within the King's dominion ... shall from henceforth make or cause to be made any manner of vessel, jewel or any other thing of gold or silver, except it be of good and true allay, that is to say, gold of a certain touch, and silver of the esterling allay or of better, at the pleasure of him to whom the work belongeth; ... and that no manner of vessel of silver depart out of the hands of the workers until it be assayed by the gardiens of the Craft, and further that it be marked with a leopard's head; and that they work no worse gold than of the touch of Paris; and that the wardens of the Craft shall go from shop to shop among the goldsmiths to essay if their gold be of [that] touch ... And that all the good towns of England, where any goldsmith be dwelling, shall be ordered according to this statute as they of London be; and that one shall come from every good town for all the residue that be dwelling in the same unto London for to be ascertained of their touch'. All plate made in England between 1300 and 1363 ought therefore to bear a single punch, the Leopard's Head.

In spite of this Act the goldsmiths petitioned the king

Figure 8
Leopard's head
mark

with complaints that they had the trouble of melting down the inferior plate that was being imported in order to find its true value, and that public confidence was lowered because many goldsmiths were working secretly and fraudulently with base alloys and plated tin. As a result Edward III granted the incorporation by letters patent of 'The Wardens and Commonalty of the Mystery of Goldsmiths of the City of London' in 1327. The word 'mystery' has no implication of secrecy but is the anglicization of the Latin '*ministerium*' which means trade or craft. The charter recited some of the provisions of the Act and further required 'that those of the trade may by virtue of these presents elect honest sufficient men, best skilled in the trade, to enquire of the matters aforesaid and that they who are chosen reform what defects they shall find, and inflict punishment on the offenders, and that by help of the mayor and sheriffs if need be'.

The first preserved entry in the records of the company was made in 1334. These extensive and informative documents (see Bibliography) deal almost exclusively with the day-to-day affairs of the officials and are most important sources of evidence about the development of the goldsmiths' craft in England.

While it is clear that the goldsmiths as a body were already quite influential, it is difficult to estimate how many of them were working at this time in London. Between 1336 and 1344 twenty apprentices on the average were notified each year and paid their fine of admission of two shillings. But the list of goldsmiths who were sworn in to obey the ordinances of the mystery in 1368 contains only 135 names, rather less than a quarter of the number which might be expected. This figure, however, takes no account of the Black Death and the two other plagues that intervened.

In 1335 a second *Statutum de Moneta* refers to the importation of counterfeit money and makes stringent regulations against the exportation of sterling. Export licences were needed and embarkation for abroad was allowed only at Dover. Innkeepers in every port were sworn to search their guests 'so that no man, of whatsoever state or condition he be, shall carry out of our realm sterling money, silver or plate, neither in vessel of gold nor of silver, without our leave'.

The next important Statute (1363) repeated many earlier regulations and introduced the *maker's mark* (fig. 9). Every master goldsmith 'should have a mark by himself, which mark shall be known by them assigned by the King to survey their work and allay; ... and that after the assay made the surveyor should set the King's mark (*Leopard's Head*) upon it, and then the goldsmith his mark for which he should answer'. Plate made between 1364 and 1458 should thus bear two punched marks. The Act also restricted the price of silver.

Figure 9
A maker's mark
(16th century)

Yet these enactments were frequently evaded; 'gold and silver, which is wrought by the goldsmiths in England, is oftentimes less fine than it ought to be, because the goldsmiths are their own judges'. This complaint led to the re-enactment in 1378 of many clauses from earlier legislation.

The London company was given jurisdiction by its charter over all goldsmiths in the realm, a power which they seldom seem to have exercised in the remoter parts. The growing importance of London as the mercantile and political capital of the country did not prevent a considerable production of plate in the provinces. Many names of provincial goldsmiths in the early Middle Ages have been preserved, but cannot be connected with any of the very few existing works; some achieved a national reputation, as Nicholas 'the great goldsmith' who is mentioned at Chester in 1271. In 1285 John Aurifaber and a dozen other goldsmiths were working there. At Exeter Johannes Wewlingworth was a flourishing goldsmith in the early fourteenth century and the names of several hundred more are recorded from other cities and towns. But after the Act of 1300 and the charter, they must have worked under considerable restraint, being required to bring their wares to London to be marked. Unreasonable as these provisions may seem, no other interpretation of them is possible, and perhaps the London goldsmiths estimated that it would be easier for purchasers to order plate directly from the capital, with the assurance of quality, than to have it made by craftsmen, probably less skilled, in their nearest city and then sent to London and back again. Indeed their policy seems to have been directed towards the elimination of their provincial rivals and the creation of a form of national monopoly entirely under their own control.

Another Act of 1378 defined the penalties for having sold plate without the maker's mark or below the sterling standard. The offender would have to pay damages to the complainant of double the value of the vessel, be put in prison, or pay a fine according to the extent of the trespass. It was in force for a limited period 'to try whether within that time it be useful or no'; it was not repeated after its expiry, but similar provisions appear in later statutes.

Within three years Parliament complained again 'of the great mischief which the realm suffereth and long hath done for that gold and silver ... is carried out of the realm so that in effect there is none left, which thing, if it should be longer suffered, would shortly be the destruction of the same realm, which God forbid'. This anxiety can be well understood because the country depended for its coinage, and hence on its internal and external trade, on supplies of imported silver. So once again, in 1381, the export of all forms of gold and silver was forbidden.

In 1392 Richard II renewed the London goldsmiths' charter and in 1414 Henry IV did likewise, extending their jurisdiction to the gold and silver work of the cutlers.

The fourteenth century was thus remarkable for continual efforts by the legislature and the goldsmiths themselves to keep gold and silver within the kingdom, to standardize the quality of plate throughout the country so that the public might be protected from fraud and the trade from lack of public confidence, and to allocate the responsibility for such frauds directly to the guilty maker or to the conniving or inefficient official. England, however, was not alone, nor even the leader, in such reforms, which were based on the regulations evolved in France, particularly in Paris and at Montpellier.

The preamble to the Statute *What things may be plated with gold or silver and what not* (1403) presents another aspect of the closer definition of fraudulent practices and at the same time shows the range of smaller items that were being commonly made in precious metals. 'Fraudulent artificers, imagining to deceive the common people, do daily make locks, rings, beads, candlesticks, harness for girdles [i.e. buckles and studs], hilts, chalices and sword pommels, powder boxes, and covers for cups, of copper and of latten, and the same overgild and silver, like to gold or silver, and the same sell and put to gage to many men not having full knowledge thereof for whole gold and whole silver, to the great deceit, loss, and hindrance of the common people, and the wasting of gold and silver.' This act forbade the gilding of base metals except for church ornaments and only then if some part were left bare. In 1420 the exception was extended to 'knights' spurs and all the apparel that pertaineth to a baron or above that estate'.

Silver-gilt wares were commonly sold for double the value of ungilt wares 'which seemeth to the King very outrageous and too excessive a price'. It was therefore laid down that no plate except of sterling standard should be gilt and the price was fixed at 46s. 8d. for the Troy pound gilt: the penalty was a fine of the value of the thing sold.

The consumption of silver seems to have been very heavy at this time, for in 1423 the Master of the Mint was required to pay full value, fixed at 22s. per pound, for all silver brought to him for sale; the King's Assayer and the Controller of the Mint ('credible, substantial and expert men, having perfect knowledge of the mystery of goldsmiths and of the Mint') being present at such dealings to fix the true value in case of difference, and to convert into coin all gold and silver, wrought or unwrought, coined or uncoined, that was offered to them.

Another statute was passed in the same year to re-enact earlier provisions about the standard and hall-marks, and to direct that an allowance be made for necessary solder. A penalty of double the value of the article was imposed on the 'keeper of the touch for every harness of silver which he shall touch that is worse than sterling'. 'Divers touches' were allotted to York, Newcastle upon Tyne, Lincoln, Norwich, Bristol, Salisbury, and Coventry, the first time that provincial assay towns are mentioned by name. However, Chester, Exeter, and other lesser places where goldsmiths worked are not mentioned.

In 1462 the London Company was, by its fourth charter, constituted a body corporate and politic with power to use a common seal and to hold lands in perpetuity, powers of search, inspection, assay, and punishment, and the regulation of all gold and silver manufactures in the City of London and its suburbs, in all fairs and markets, and in all cities, towns, and boroughs, and all places whatsover throughout England, thereby confirming more emphatically its existing jurisdiction.

The introduction of a third compulsory stamp, the annual *date letter* (fig. 10) seems to have resulted from an act of 1477, though it is not mentioned until more than a century later, when a minute of the London company refers to the 'letter of the year'. In the indictment of two goldsmiths in 1597 'for making divers parcels of counterfeit plate de-based' it is described as the 'alphabetical mark approved by ordinance among the goldsmiths'. Indeed, this last reference provides the only clue to its origin, but its purpose was, and still is, to indicate the year within which any piece of plate was made so that the assayer and the keeper of the touch in office in that year could be subsequently brought to account. It was not

Figure 10
Date Letter
(1544)

until recently that a convincing theory was put forward to account for a cycle of letters incorporated in the *Leopard's Head* itself. From the beginning, alphabetical cycles of twenty letters were employed, omitting J, V, W, X, Y, and Z; the letter was changed annually on St Dunstan's Day to the next in sequence, and at the end of each cycle the alphabet was begun again with a different outline to the punch, and with different characters (see Appendix, p. 263). Sir Charles Jackson's comprehensive tables of the separated London alphabets begin with the letter A for 1478.

Thus after nearly three hundred years of parliamentary legislation and regulations devised by officers of the Goldsmiths' Company, there was established an enforceable system of controls whereby the purchaser of plate could with confidence buy gold and silver wares of guaranteed quality, or, if he had cause for complaint, seek redress at law against the officers of the Goldsmiths' Company or the goldsmith, or both. The statutes were generally designed to protect public interests in the widest sense, giving the individual purchaser the protection he needed against easily practised frauds through the common law, ensuring that the economic position of the country was not upset through lack of currency, preventing the provincial goldsmiths from being ruined by their more powerfully organized London rivals and ensuring that the elected officers of the London and provincial companies did their duties honestly and impartially. The London goldsmiths themselves devised an effective administrative machinery to execute the will of Parliament without placing unduly heavy burdens on any member of their mystery. Thereafter, the system was only adjusted in detail and not in principle.

STYLE AND ORNAMENT*

Less than four hundred articles of plate, including spoons, remain from the medieval period, of which the propor-

* See plates 1, 2a, 2b, 3a, 3b, 4a, 4b, 5, 6, 38, 60a.

tion increases in successive centuries until 1525, the arbitrary date which has been chosen to mark the decline of the Gothic style and the beginnings of the first neo-classical or Renaissance style in English plate. About two-thirds of this amount is made up of ecclesiastical plate and the remaining third of domestic plate. But enough is available for an assessment of the general developments in ornament (if not in shape) of the various vessels that were used domestically. Further complementary evidence has been obtained from the illustrations to manuscripts as well as from the many descriptions, sometimes detailed, but more often brief and even incomprehensible, contained in inventories and wills.

The influx of Norman knights and clerics and the rule by English kings of dwindling areas in North and West France until at last the port of Calais was lost in Mary's reign, resulted in close cultural ties between England, Normandy, and Picardy. Merchants, architects, and craftsmen of all kinds moved from one country to another as opportunity offered or patrons bade. It is not surprising, therefore, to find records of goldsmiths with French, Netherlandish, or German names in York, East Anglia, and London, or with English names in France and elsewhere on the Continent. Nor is it uncommon to find plate of the 'touches' of Paris, Bruges, or Nuremberg specifically mentioned in medieval inventories – though relatively little English plate seems to have been sent overseas at this time. For example, the Founder's Cup at Trinity Hall, Cambridge, was shown to be Avignon work of about 1350; the Royal Gold Cup in the British Museum was made in France in the fourteenth century, and the Founder's Cup at Oriel College, Oxford, bears a French hall-mark of the late fifteenth century. In addition to these three existing cups, documents show that John of Gaunt (1340–99) bought a gold chalice made at Bordeaux and a gold retable made at Amiens. The inventories of royal plate of Edward III (1338), Henry IV (1399), Henry VI (1439 and 1450), Edward IV (1451), are impressive.

Most items were probably English: a mirror in a gold frame set with jewelled and enamelled roses, of which the back was enamelled with the figure of a queen; a ewer engraved and enamelled with birds, on whose knop sat a lady within a paling; a pair of silver-gilt basins embossed

Figure 11 – Cast openwork ornament (12th century). Based on the Trivulzio Candelabrum

and enamelled with roses, and engraved with the sun and the royal arms, within a vine leaf border.

While some idea of the magnificence of the royal treasure has been given, it must not be overlooked that huge collections of plate belonged also to the nobles. An inventory of Sir John Fastolf (d. 1459) records domestic plate weighing 1,175 pounds with a further 110 pounds in his private chapel; and the will of the 13th Earl of Oxford, about 1509, mentions comparable amounts which together probably exceed by far all English plate that remains today from the Middle Ages.

While unmarked medieval plate can seldom be certainly assigned to any European town or any specific year, and while many hall-marks still remain unassigned, the collation of punched marks, as well as the growing literature on goldsmiths' work, in this country and abroad, have recently helped to make attributions, at least as between France and England, more certain. Moreover, comparison with objects made from other materials may in cases of doubt help to fix not only the country of origin but also, approximately at least, the date.

The elaborate openwork of interlaced foliage interspersed with human or grotesque animal figures on the Gloucester Candlestick (Victoria and Albert Museum) and the Trivulzio candelabrum (Milan; fig. 11), both of bronze, may be considered typical of the elaborate goldsmiths' work of the twelfth century. The limited knowledge of thirteenth- and fourteenth-century work is un-

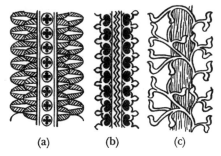

(a)　　　　(b)　　　　(c)

Figure 12 – Vertical stamped, pierced, and openwork ornament (15th century)

likely to be much increased, but from the later fifteenth century enough remains to form a reasonable estimate.

Many ornamental motifs employed in the fifteenth century were derived directly from contemporary ecclesiastical architecture (plates 2 and 3). The horizontal edges and bases of the larger vessels are decorated with cabling (plate 4b), simple mouldings, stamped ornamental mould-ing of beading (plate 4a), foliage, or crosses, mouldings pierced with quatrefoils (figs. 12a and 13a and b) or tre-foils, and other repetitive and often complicated devices of geometrical or stylized foliate forms (figs. 12c and 13b). These are often surmounted by parapets, plain, battle-mented (fig. 13a), or elaborately crested with foliage, sometimes in-verted (fig. 13b). Vertical straps to secure eggs, coconuts, and other materials in metal mounts show similar characteristics. The denticu-late feather edge in fig. 12a is bent on to the contours of the cup, as is the horizontal vandyke edge from a mazer bowl shown in fig. 13c. The bases of vessels are often supported on three or four small feet which take the form of little turrets, of human or animal figures. The finials on their covers recall those on the stonework of the wooden pew-ends of Decorated or Perpendicular churches. Some elaborate examples of church plate, such as the Oxford pastoral staffs (plates 2 and 3) or the Ramsey Abbey Censer (Victoria and Albert Museum) are almost entirely architectural, emulating as they do such magnificent tracery as may be seen on the Bishop's throne in Exeter Cathedral or on the stalls of York and Westminster.

(a)

(b)

(c)

Figure 13
Horizontal cast,
pierced, and
engraved ornament
(15th century)

Many vessels are embossed with bold lobular motifs, often imbricated (plates 38 and 6). Others are plain or have applied relief patterns or pierced panels backed with glass or enamel.

The common use of ornamental lettering is exemplified by the late fourteenth-century Studley Bowl (Victoria and

Albert Museum; plate 4b) whose exterior is engraved all over with the alphabet in a Gothic script reserved on a hatched ground. Inscriptions in Gothic or Lombardic lettering in Latin, English, or French are frequently found on the mounts of mazers and on cups, chalices, and patens, the words often being separated by little devices as in the engraved inscriptions *Soli Deo Honor et Gloria* round the bowl of the Campion Cup dated 1500 (Victoria and Albert Museum; fig. 14) and the Oriel Mazer from a century later (plate 4a). One mazer is inscribed typically with a short prayer *Benedictus Dominus in donis suis*, and another *In the name of the Trinite fille the kup and drinke to me.* Cups were often given names that were engraved on them

Figure 14 – Engraved inscription (1500). From the Campion Cup

such as *Christmas* or *Crumpeldud.* Coats of arms were engraved, but more often enamelled, especially on the prints or bosses of mazers and on the finials of covered cups.

Human and other figures have almost always provided a fruitful source of ideas for ornament. Silver figures of men and women in contemporary costumes reserved against translucent enamel grounds are the principal ornament of the King's Lynn cup of the early fourteenth century (fig. 15 and plate 1). Sacred groups and emblems are engraved on surviving chalices and patens; and on the Swinburne Pyx, of about 1310, some of the compositions have been shown to depend on manuscript illustrations. The Head of Christ (fig. 16) from this small box, once enamelled, indicates an approach more dependent upon architecture. Both this and the preceding figure show the characteristic use in triangular spaces of formal trefoils such as occur in spandrels. The Giant Salt (All Souls' College, Oxford) has several little figures of huntsmen and hounds at the feet of the large bearded figure in a

Figure 15
Champlevé enamel
ornament (about 1320).
Detail from King John's
Cup (see plate 1)

jerkin. The base of the Monkey Salt (New College, Oxford) is supported by wodewoses (wild men). The receptacle for the salt in both these vessels is made of rock crystal. Ostrich eggs, coconuts, mazers, and oriental ceramics were also mounted in this way to hold the vessel firm. The edges of the mounts are notched and bent and engraved with feathers or hatching (plate 4a and figs. 12a and 13c).

PRINCIPAL ARTICLES OF DOMESTIC PLATE

Standing Cups. Most of the twenty or so extant vessels belong to two main groups of well-defined shapes, i.e. with bell-shaped bowls on tall stems or rather smaller cups with font-shaped bowls. Of the former group, the earliest by a century is King John's Cup, a gilt and enamelled cup and cover (plate 1) (Corporation of King's Lynn) which is now generally accepted as English work. Standing on an Early English pillar of five attached columns that continue the pentagonal form of the base, the cover, bowl, and foot are divided by foliate straps with raised ornament into shaped fields, each containing a male and a female figure reserved in a field of blue enamel, relieved with scrolling stems of leaves and flowers in other colours (fig.

Figure 16
Engraved Head of Christ
(about 1310). Based
on the Swinburne Pyx

76

15). From about 1480 are the rather plain Anathema Cup
(Pembroke College, Cambridge) and the embossed Warden's Grace Cup (New College, Oxford), whose trumpet
stem is separated from the bowl by a collar of eight balls.
It is embossed all over with imbricated lobes, the foot and
cover surrounded by open Gothic cresting, and the large
openwork finial of foliage, surmounted by a chestnut fruit,
raised oñ a pinnacle above the openwork cover. Still more
elaborate is the gilt cup of about 1499 which Sir Thomas
Leigh gave to the Mercers' Company in the following century, redecorated with their emblems, pilgrims' bottles
and maidens' heads. John Richmond's Cup (Armourers'
and Brasiers' Company) of more or less the same period
resembles the New College cup, in its over-all embossed
lobes, and comes closer to the slender 'columbine cups'
which are mentioned in the early sixteenth century in
England and which were one of the three patterns· required of German goldsmiths for their master-pieces. The
latest example (Winchester College; plate 5) is known as
the Election Cup presented by the then Bishop of Lincoln
who described it as a 'pore cownterfetyd cuppe'. It may
therefore be a copy of about 1554 of a fifteenth-century
cup. This possibility is supported by a rather graceful
style recalling the Renaissance rather than the Middle
Ages.

The group of seven cups with font-shaped bowls is represented by the most elaborate gilt example, that at Corpus Christi College, Oxford, which is embossed with a
pineapple pattern and whose finial is decorated with
foliage (plate 6). Similar cups have been used as chalices
although they were originally intended for secular use,
and their bowls are rather more everted, one standing on
three little gilt feet cast in the shape of dogs. The plainer
Campion Cup of 1500 (Victoria and Albert Museum) is
engraved with *Soli Deo Honor et Gloria* in Lombardic
lettering reserved on a pounced band (fig. 14).

The Studley Bowl (plate 4b) has a bowl everted like the
earlier font-shaped cups, but it stands on a pierced ver-

tical. foot-ring. The large gilt Foundress' Beaker (Christ's College, Cambridge) stands on a deep shaped vertical foot originally set with precious stones. Its body and cover are engraved with straps enclosing Tudor roses and portcullises and devices of the Foundress, Margaret Beaufort, mother of Henry VII.

Mazers. The principal interest of mazers, the most numerous of medieval drinking vessels, lies in the ornament which is found on their silver or silver-gilt mounts, round the lip, supporting the bowl itself, or on the raised circular disc, called the boss or print, within the bowl. From early times wooden vessels for food and drink preceded those of metal and pottery, and certain dense, smooth woods such as spotted maple, beech, and walnut were found to be particularly suitable because they were impervious and could be turned very thin. The lip-band offered an obvious field for ornamental engraving, generally of an inscription, though many examples are plain except for the typical edge (fig. 13c). Their diameters range from five to twelve inches; the earlier examples have deeper bowls and narrower lip-bands than the later examples, whose wooden bowls are shallow and their lip-bands deep; these may be represented by a transitional example of the latter half of the fifteenth century, the mazer belonging to Oriel College, Oxford (plate 4a). The Scrope Mazer (York Minster) of about 1400 was later raised up on three feet cast as female masks, while the Swan Mazer (Corpus Christi College, Cambridge) has an elevated print surmounted by a silver swan which conceals an amusing syphoning device that empties the mazer through its base if it is filled too full. The prints were religious or secular in character, the former decorated with sacred emblems or figures of saints, the latter with scenes of combat, coats of arms, or merchants' marks. They may be engraved, embossed, or enamelled, or set with crystals and other stones. Crystal was supposed to cloud on contact with any poison and was sometimes cut to form the vessel itself or set in the cup to warn the drinker;

similar properties were attributed to unicorn's horn (probably the horn of a narwhal) and other substances.

The large number of these vessels that were in use at least from the middle of the thirteenth century onwards – for a 'mazera' is mentioned in the will of William, Bishop of Chichester (1253) – and their later disuse is shown by monastic inventories. In 1328 the refectory of Canterbury Cathedral owned 182 mazers, in 1437 Battle Abbey owned thirty-two, and as late as the middle of the sixteenth century Westminster owned fifty-one.

Drinking Horns. Horn is another natural and common substance easily convertible into a drinking vessel, polished and mounted with a silver rim, two silver feet attached to a medial band, and a silver tip, sometimes with another foot, usually in the form of a human or animal mask. The finest of the five surviving specimens mounted in precious metal is that at Queen's College, Oxford, which dates from the fourteenth century. It stands on three very naturalistic claw feet and the bands are engraved between cable moulding and the vandyke edges; its cover is surmounted by the figure of an eagle which may have been added as late as the seventeenth century.

Coconut Cups. The impervious coconut, easily turned and polished, naturally forms a drinking vessel that was made additionally attractive by its rarity in England during the Middle Ages and by its reputed medicinal properties. Although they are mentioned in wills and inventories as early as the thirteenth century, the earliest remaining examples cannot be dated before the middle of the fifteenth century. Two particularly interesting examples are preserved at New College, Oxford; the mount of one is designed as a tree whose naturalistic trunk is surrounded by a fence and girded by a band of buckles, and whose seven straight leafy branches encircle the nut. The nut of the other is mounted with a deep everted lip-band, like those of the later mazers, which is engraved *Ecce ancilla Domini* in Gothic letters and supported within three broad vertical straps (cf. fig. 12a); its stem is imbricated and surrounded by an elaborate openwork cresting and is supported on three feet cast as figures of knights, each on a turret.

Other Materials Mounted as Cups or Bowls. Another rarity suitable for conversion to a drinking cup was the ostrich egg, described as a 'Gryphon's' egg in medieval lists. One example is listed as 'garnysshed wt silver and ouer gilt with a fote and a couercle'. The griffin is a fabulous beast with the head and wings of an eagle and a lion's body, but was nevertheless believed to lay eggs, while the now familiar ostrich was apparently unknown. No medieval example is known, but some have survived from later centuries.

The earliest example of mounted pottery is the Chinese celadon bowl of about 1500 (New College, Oxford), set in straps of openwork foliage, on which figure 12c is based. It has affinities with the ornament on the Richmond Cup and those of contemporary mazers.

Two or three vessels about 1525 show the combination of the surviving Gothic ornament and shapes with those of the new renaissance. The ivory bowl of the Howard Grace Cup (Victoria and Albert Museum) in its silver-gilt mounts of 1525 recalls the font cups and its deep lip-band inscribed in Lombardic letters VINVM. TVVM. BIBE. CVM. GAVDIO (Drink your wine joyfully) might seem to date back to the end of the fifteenth century. But the winged cherubs' heads, the setting of the jewels, and scrolled flowers, and foliage show the influence of neo-classical designers.

Beakers. Two rather small beakers in private possession complete the list of drinking vessels. The sides of the gilt example of 1496 are decorated with short vertical ribs, and the other, dating from 1525, is engraved with an imbricated scale pattern.

Salts. The most important and often the most elaborate piece of table plate during the Middle Ages was the standing salt. Various books of etiquette published in the late fifteenth and early sixteenth centuries instruct the page to set the principal salt on the right of the head of the house, the second at the lower end of the table, and the remainder on the other tables. Sir John Fastolf had eight large salts and a single small one of five ounces, and the Earl of Oxford sixteen large and four small salts.

Fourteenth-century inventories list salts in the shape of dogs, elephants, dragons, or lions. The Monkey Salt (New College, Oxford) seems to be the only extant English example; its circular foot and elaborate pedestal are supported by wild men seated on cushions, while on a large cushion sits the very life-like figure of a chimpanzee who balances the gilt-mounted crystal bowl for the salt upon his head.

With the exception of the Giant Salt, where the human figure replaces the animal as the principal feature of the vessel, the remaining ten medieval salts, which date from about 1490 to 1522, are shaped as hour-glasses, and almost every form of late Gothic ornament is represented, from the most elaborate to the comparatively plain. Warden Hill's Salt (New College, Oxford: plate 38) has many affinities with the bell-shaped cup there, which has been already mentioned, particularly in such features as the cresting and the fruit of the chestnut. Of about the same date is the hexagonal salt at Corpus Christi College, Oxford: each of its inclined planes is covered with a cast openwork panel of a pelican in her piety, the emblem of the college, among intricately interwoven foliage.

Ewers and Basins. Because forks were not used at table, hands were washed before, during, and after meals in basins which were brought round to each person by pages and were filled with hot or cold scented waters from ewers ornamented with similar motifs; another page brought a napkin. The same lavish ornament was employed on these vessels as on others; the central boss, which kept the jug from slipping, resembles on a larger scale the print of a mazer, being similarly decorated, e.g. with the *Judgement of Solomon* or with a *Wheel of Fortune*. The two or three remaining examples are unspectacular, their diameter being as much as two feet, and their weight anything between sixty and ninety ounces.

Spoons. From the departure of the Romans until the middle of the fourteenth century so few spoons survive that theories about their development during this millennium must remain unconfirmed. Isolated examples have been found, some approximately datable from accompanying material, others not. Although no reliable dating is possible until the striking of the earliest date letters, some spoons can be dated to the fourteenth century with reasonable confidence from external evidence. Therefore some kind of probable development between the Norman Conquest and the first of the Tudors can be outlined simply.

The important characteristics for dating purposes are the section and taper of the stem, the angles at which the bowl joins the stem, and the curve of the bowl. The development of the forms of the stem and the bowl are independent, but usually they coincide; sometimes one, but never both, is out of style for its date. The English national form appears to have lasted from about the middle of the fourteenth century until about 1475, and gradually to have merged into the early Tudor type. The form of the finial provides less evidence than might, at first, be expected.

The stem of the English national form is of slender hexagonal section at the joint and tapers towards the finial where it may seem, through wear, to be rounded. The bowl, seen in profile, may be compared to a crescent moon, turning up more sharply towards its front, which often cuts across an imaginary projection of the stem: seen from above, the two shoulders appear to leave the stem with little curvature and at an angle of about eighty degrees. Various devices at the end of the stem are known: acorn, moor's head, diamond point, wrythen, hexagonal, wodewose, ball, seal-head, lion sejant, owl, boar's head, slip-end, Gothic: many others are mentioned in inventories, particularly figures or objects which are related heraldically to the owner. Perhaps the best known are the figures of Christ and the twelve apostles, which combine to make a complete set of thirteen. Owing to division and loss, no complete set from before the sixteenth century is known. The mark is punched in the bowl near the stem. The finials and sometimes the whole spoon are gilt: many have been regilt.

The stem of the second type, about 1475–1525 (plate 60a), has wider lower and upper facets near the bowl, perhaps necessary after 1478 to receive the marks of the maker's punch, and the date letter: it tapers considerably. The bowl became fatter on plan and its rim more level; the angle at which the two sides leave the stem increases to more than ninety degrees. Numerous examples survive with provincial hall-marks, of which many have not yet been more than tentatively assigned to one of the small assay offices.

CHAPTER THREE

1525–1603: The Renaissance and the Reformation

THE amount of extant plate made from the accession of
Henry VIII in 1509 through the short intervening reigns
of Edward VI and Mary until the death of Elizabeth I (in
1603) exceeds by far that from the entire Middle Ages.
The personal extravagance of Henry VIII encouraged a
reckless over-expenditure at court, of which the Field of
the Cloth of Gold (1520) is the most celebrated instance.
Successive sovereigns ordered huge quantities of gold and
silver-gilt vessels, and jewellery for their own use, and for
presentation to foreign monarchs, as well as to their
ministers, advisers, and courtiers in return for the gifts
that these were accustomed to offer at the New Year. In
1558 Elizabeth I ordered payment of more than eleven
thousand pounds to Robert Brandon and Affabel Part-
ridge (both working 1549–69), her principal goldsmiths,
for 3,098 ounces of gilt plate at seven shillings and sixpence per ounce, which was given away as such gifts. In
Leningrad and Moscow much plate remains from successive gifts of Elizabeth I and James I. The wealthiest
nobles and prelates amassed large collections of plate;
indeed at one time the collection of Cardinal Wolsey was
estimated to rival that of his master in weight and
splendour.

Nevertheless, the great quantity of magnificent and impressive plate made is but feebly represented by what has
been preserved. Economic causes, changes in fashion, and
waste must have accounted for much loss even within this
period, but the principal reasons for the destruction of

almost all the plate, both ecclesiastical and domestic, belonging to the Church and its religious foundations were the ruthless suppression of the monasteries, and the Reformation.

It will be remembered that production in the silver mines in Germany and Central Europe increased considerably at the beginning of the sixteenth century and that from the middle of Henry VIII's reign both gold and silver were being imported from Spanish America into Europe in growing quantity. As the amount of available bullion increased, the prices of both metals began to fall.

The heavy war budget of 1523, and the king's lavishness exhausted the treasure accumulated by Henry VII, whose sources of income were again tapped. Even the introduction of a graduated scale of taxation to supplement the royal income was insufficient, and such was the rate of Henry VIII's expenditure that he determined to investigate the possibilities of two additional sources of revenue.

In 1526 an experiment was made in debasing the coinage, which had hitherto been constantly maintained at the sterling standard, by the abolition of the old Tower pound (see p. 281). But it was not until 1542 that the silver content of the coinage was reduced to eighty-three per cent; in 1544 it was further reduced to one-half, and in the following year to one-third. At that time the Mint contributed heavily to the royal treasure; by converting sterling bullion into coinage whose intrinsic value was so much less than its face value, Henry VIII succeeded in increasing his income substantially for the remainder of his reign. The silver content was slightly raised at the beginning of Edward VI's reign, but in 1551 it reached its nadir of only twenty-five per cent. In the following year, however, it was raised almost to the sterling standard, and very shortly after her accession Elizabeth I boldly called in all debased coins and paid for them with a new issue of currency of the old sterling standard at a rate somewhat below their nominal value. In this way the rapid inflationary trend was slowed, and confidence in the coinage was restored, and its standard subsequently maintained without a break until the present century. Because the sterling standard continued in force for all plate manufactured during these thirty-five years, the direct conversion of coinage into plate, and *vice versa*, was prevented and the sharp fall in the value of money and the almost doubling of prices had temporarily discouraged all but the very wealthy from buying plate.

The second potential source of wealth was the large group of institutions which served the Church. The monastic system, which had conferred so many lasting benefits upon Christendom during the Middle Ages, might have seemed to have outlived some of its purposes. Reliance on the manuscripts belonging to the religious houses for educational purposes had been superseded by the marvellous development of the printed book. Allegations of all kinds of misconduct were laid against their inmates, and their control from Rome was blamed for a number of injustices that were disliked by the king, and many of his ministers and people. At first perhaps Cardinal Wolsey honourably intended to reform them and to employ a large portion of their confiscated revenues to urgent state purposes, to more practical religious needs, and to the endowment of new colleges and schools. But in the event the parsimonious allotments to such purposes cannot hide the fact that a very large proportion of their property was confiscated into the hands of the king himself.

An opportunity to effect the dispossession of their inmates was afforded by Henry VIII's rift with the Pope. After a rapid visitation of the smaller houses, three hundred and seventy-six were dissolved and the proceeds from the sale of their property were given for the king's disposal. In the four following years the remaining abbeys and monasteries were suppressed by attainder or by voluntary surrender. The official charged with the despoliation of the shrine of St Swithin, at Winchester, wrote: .'About three o'clock in the morning we made a cud of the shrine here; the silver alone would amount to near two thousand marks', while three crosses, two chalices of gold, and some silver contributed to the total of 1,035 ounces of gold and 13,886 ounces of silver gilt. The shrine of St Richard at Chichester yielded 118 ounces of gold and 5,255 ounces of silver, as well as precious stones, and the shrine of St Cuthbert at Durham produced even more. While even from a place of comparatively small importance, such as Barking, 3,000 ounces of plate were surrendered. In spite of rebellious opposition, all this treasure was in the hands of the king by 1542.

Plans for the reformation of the Church were considered after the death of Henry VIII. The new prayer-book, published in 1549, introduced a simplified ritual in English. The logical culmination of this great undertaking was the removal of what were considered to be superstitious images from all churches and cathedrals and the replacement of all existing plate with new forms of communion vessels, though 'one, two or more chalices or cuppes according to the multitude of the people' were to be left – temporarily – so that services could be continued. The order initiating this protracted exchange, if it was contained in a document, has not survived, but the fact that one of the earliest of the new communion cups, engraved with arabesques (St Clement's, Oxford), bears the hall-marks of 1551 indicates that little time was lost.

Anthony Dericke, the last goldsmith to be appointed Engraver to the Mint, promoted several lotteries; the profits of the first, drawn in 1569 before the west door of St Paul's (400,000 lots at ten shillings with prizes of plate) were for harbour repairs. Others took place in 1586 (prizes of armour) and 1612 for the plantation of Virginia, in which the Grocers' Company won a silver-gilt salt and cover worth thirteen pounds ten shillings plus nineteen shillings and sixpence delivery fee, for tickets worth sixty-two pounds five shillings.

Except for the repetition of earlier provisions in the

Act of 1552, to which reference has been made in the previous chapter, no legislation directly concerning the goldsmiths was passed in the later Tudor period. But in about 1545 a fourth compulsory punch, the *Lion Passant* (fig. 17), was introduced. It is first found on plate assayed in that year, although it is not mentioned in any surviving statute, ordinance, or minute until the prosecution of two fraudulent goldsmiths in 1597, when it was described as 'Her Majesty's Lion'. It is thought that this mark (Appendix) showing a lion *passant guardant*, was introduced by the officials of the Goldsmiths' Company to indicate that the articles on which it was punched were of sterling silver and not of the low quality that was being used at that time for coinage. The fact that it was also stamped on gold plate, until alternative standards to eighteen carats were permitted at the end of the eighteenth century does not invalidate this theory, because at the time it might have been expected that the gold coinage would likewise be debased. The *Lion Passant* has since then been consistently stamped on sterling plate made in London, and has been used since 1719 by several other offices.

Figure 17
Lion passant mark
(1545 onwards)

STYLE AND ORNAMENT*

The gradual abandonment of Gothic motifs in favour of those inspired by the artistic remains of ancient Greece and Rome which were being studied and emulated in Italy with growing interest and admiration marks the first neo-classical revival in this country. It was the furthest ripple of a wave that began in the northern Italian city-states with the conscious attempt to achieve again the perfection attained in classical times. But it was not until the very end of the fifteenth century that the influence of the Renaissance passed beyond the Alps into Germany, France, and the Netherlands. Not only did northern

* See plates 5, 7, 8, 9, 16a, 17c, 18a, 21, 33a, 34, 35, 39, 60b, 60c.

painters, sculptors, architects, and designers travel to Italy to seek inspiration, but many Italian artists were persuaded to accept commissions and appointments in the north. France was successful in attracting Leonardo da Vinci, Francesco Primaticcio, and Benvenuto Cellini, to the chagrin of Henry VIII, who, not to be outdone, commissioned the Florentine Pietro Torrigiano, and other less famous sculptors and craftsmen, to work in his service. The first important works executed in this country by this fellow-pupil of Michelangelo were the tombs of Henry VII and his mother, Margaret Beaufort, on which work began in 1509. Moreover, those who travelled abroad were much impressed by the new styles and brought back accounts of them which seem to have stimulated those at home: again, many craftsmen trained in the principal centres of Germany, France, and the Low Countries came to work in England.

Nevertheless, the English goldsmiths seem to have been slow in accepting these new influences, and it is perhaps more than a coincidence that Renaissance motifs cannot be distinctly separated from Gothic until about 1526, the year when Hans Holbein the Younger came to London for the first time. Several of his designs for cups have been preserved, notably that for Jane Seymour, which was actually made in about 1536 at the King's order. Like many others in the royal treasury it was sent for disposal in the Netherlands in 1625 by Charles I and was melted. But it is well described in an inventory: 'Item oone faire standing Cup of golde, garnished about the Couer with eleuen table Diamoundes, and two pointed Diamoundes about the Cup Seventene table Diamoundes and one Pearle Pendent uppon the Cupp, with theis words BOVND TO OBEY AND SERVE, and H and I knitt together; in the Topp of the Cover the Queenes Armes, an Queene Janes Armes houlden by twoe Boyes under a Crowne Imperiall, weighing Threescore and five ounces and a halfe.'

Besides the presence of foreign goldsmiths and of foreign plate in England, a third influential source of design was the published pattern books and the many series of designs engraved in Germany, France, Italy, and the Netherlands. Not only did they furnish designs for the various forms of plate, e.g. the series of cups by the Master of 1551, and Hans Brosamer's *Ein new Kunstbüchlein*, but also ornamental details which might be engraved or embossed as space allowed. In England designers seem to have been comparatively inactive, for the only known engraved works are twenty-eight moresque patterns by the Fleming Thomas Geminus called *Morysse and Damsshime renewed and encreased very profitable for Goldsmyths and Embroders by Thomas Geminus at London Anno 1548*, one of which is reproduced as fig. 18, and Geoffrey Whitney's *Emblemes and other Devises,* published

Figure 18 – Moresque ornament (1548) by T. Geminus

at Leyden in 1586, on some of which the panels on the Vyvyan Salt (1592; Victoria and Albert Museum) are based.

In spite of the fine quality of most of the engravings available to them, the London and provincial engravers of plate seldom reached as high a standard as those working at the principal German centres, Nuremberg or Augsburg, and seem to have produced something similar to the patterns they followed, using them as sources of ideas rather than copying their minute details exactly. Sometimes they combined motifs or decorative compositions from different sources. The motifs employed on the set of six gilt and engraved dishes of 1573 in the Victoria and Albert Museum may be traced indirectly to two known sources, the roundels containing birds to Virgil Solis, and the marine subjects to the Antwerp artist, Adriaen Collaert, while the scenes depicting the *Story of Isaac* derive from a third, unidentified, source.

Apart from pictorial scenes representing episodes from the Bible, mythology, or allegory, the use of engraving was principally directed to border ornament. Panels of moresques (fig. 18), often combined with strapwork (e.g. plates 33a and 35), bands of scrolled foliage (fig. 22) relieved by the introduction of birds and animals, and friezes of hunting scenes are common, sometimes alternating with small medallions containing a head (cf. plate 35) or an animal. In the flattish bowl of a dish and between its central medallion and the border may be found radiating decoration of symmetrical scrolls and moresques. A simple pattern, often seen on Communion Cups, consists of rows of 'hit and miss' ornament (cf. the Henslowe Ewer, plate 35). Some coats-of-arms were engraved usually on a small scale in shaped or plain shields enclosed by neat plumage or strapwork. On the small number of pieces engraved with inscriptions, capital Roman letters or simple humanistic scripts are used. On the occasions when one piece of plate is decorated with both engraving and embossing, the two mediums are confined to separate areas.

The principal new technique introduced during the later Tudor period was the raising of small and intricate designs on thin plate by the *repoussé method* (see p. 55 above). The sides, covers, and feet of a variety of vessels are embossed all over in high relief with swags of fruit and foliage (plate 33a), or with medallions containing the heads of classical warriors (plate 35), grotesques, or animals separated by symmetrical strapwork that was often very complex, but quite different in character from Celtic interlacings (fig. 5). The flat ground between these raised ornaments was generally matted to contrast with their smooth and rounded surfaces. The finest examples of embossing in low relief are undoubtedly the few pictorial compositions, often based on engravings. Patterns of foliage, spiralling or radiating, were embossed in low relief (plate 7). In this too, the later designs became more formal, often consisting in no more than scrolled stalks flanked by a few indeterminate leaves and terminating in stylized flowers.

Tudor plate is generally of rather thin metal, and the strengthening wires soldered to the feet and rims of vessels were not at first very different from those of the Middle Ages, and billet (fig. 19a) and cross and dot moulding (fig. 13c) persisted until the end of the century. Perhaps the most characteristic design was the classical egg-and-dart (fig. 19c), presumably based on the shield and spear, in many variations; from about 1570 broader wires were stamped repetitively with larger and often quite intricate designs, a technique which continued well into the early Stuart period (fig. 24). Gadroons, in the form of both ribs and elongated ovolos, were applied and embossed on many vessels, both as principal and subsidiary ornament. On the Boleyn Cup they dominate the design, while on the Bowes Cup they are less obvious (plate 8).

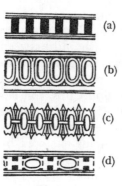

Figure 19
Stamped mouldings:
(a) billet, (b) ovolo,
(c) egg-and-dart,
(d) ovolo

Casting continued to be freely used, whether of classical or grotesque masks in low and high relief to be applied by solder (cf. plates 9 and 18a), of openwork foliate scrolls to form part of the stem or finial of standing vessels (plates 8 and 39), or of the more ambitious handles on the Italianate ewers derived from engravings such as those of Polidoro in emulation of antique models (plate 36). Figures of St George, Hercules, warriors, or naked women, with shield, sword, or spear commonly make the finial of standing salts or cups (plates 8 and 9). A very usual finial on tankards, mounted jugs, and covered cups is the turned baluster (plate 39), frequently set on a rayed platform (plate 18a).

It will be noticed that most plate of the Tudor period, and certainly all the important pieces, are gilt, very few domestic articles having been left white. The use of solid gold and of precious stones has been referred to; yet the earliest known piece of gold domestic plate dates only from the middle of the succeeding century, and the Howard Grace Cup cannot be considered to represent the highest quality of jewelled plate. The Vyvyan Salt (1592; Victoria and Albert Museum) introduces a refinement of an earlier technique, in that the circular medallions on the cover and the rectangular panels on the body are of painted glass, adaptations from Whitney's Emblems. The mounting of German and English pottery, Chinese porcelain and natural shells, as well as rock-crystal and glass, in precious metals continued a medieval tradition; the preservation of so large a number of these vessels, particularly of the so-called tigerware flagons, is no doubt due to the relatively small amount of metal used on them, which would barely repay the expense of melting them down.

PRINCIPAL ARTICLES OF DOMESTIC PLATE

Standing Cups. The continuity of shapes was broken, and the font-shaped bowl (plate 6) was virtually the only Gothic form which survived after 1525, a very late example having been made by Peter Peterson, the best known of the Norwich silversmiths, which was presented by him in 1575 to the Corporation there as a fine instead of undertaking the shrievalty. Such fines yielded considerable quantities of plate and money to guilds and corporations. Slender V-shaped or U-shaped bowls, deriving from continental sources, were among the most attractive of the early new forms. The latest covered cup to show Gothic features is of the first type, the elegant and slender Boleyn Cup of 1535 (Cirencester Church). Its cover bowl and stem are embossed with tapering ribs; the last feature may be compared with the lobes on the Richmond Cup. Another medieval feature is the finial with its pedestal and grotesque eagle, while the ornament of engraved running foliage and of embossed and applied acanthus leaves is unmistakably neo-classical.

Jane Seymour's Cup, already described, was one of the earliest of a type of large standing cup whose bowl may most simply be described as thistle-shaped (fig. 20). The most magnificent as well as the largest of these was presented by Sir Martin Bowes, Lord Mayor of London and Prime Warden, to the Goldsmiths' Company (plate 8). It is almost twenty inches in height and bears the hall-marks of 1554. The bowl is of rock-crystal, as is the polyhedron set in the stem and supported by four male figures which, if not remarkable for their modelling, show classical Italian rather than German inspiration. An unusually well-modelled figure on the finial holds a shield bearing the donor's arms. The very elaborate cast and embossed ornament is all of the highest quality. Another almost as elaborate dates from 1569 (Corpus Christi College, Cambridge: plate 9) and combines engraved with embossed ornament and a finial representing Hercules.

The Goldsmiths' Company possesses another, earlier cup (1545) with a fluted crystal bowl and a circular disc of crystal within the foot. While of less ambitious proportions and ornament, it ranks among the most beautiful designs of the age with its curved lip-band, gadrooned calyx, and vase-shaped stem.

A third and more common shape for large and small standing cups during the last three decades of Elizabeth I's reign is simpler. The cover and bowl together resemble an egg; the bowl is sometimes rather deep in proportion to its diameter, sometimes rather shallow (cf. plate 16a); their common feature is a baluster stem rising from a

Figure 20 – Form of a thistle-shaped standing cup
(mid 16th century)

spreading moulded foot. A small undecorated example of
1590 (Victoria and Albert Museum) has a height of less
than eight inches, while others are twice as large and are
often engraved all over with scrolling stems and flowers
(cf. fig. 22).

Another group of standing cups and covers follow a
contemporary German trend and have their bowls shaped
in imitation of melons or gourds, either on a stem representing a spiral stalk or a twisted tree-trunk – which in
one instance is being attacked by the diminutive figure of
a man with an axe – or on a baluster stem. The imbricated

ornament often found engraved in a vesica on their bowls presumably represents the seeds which the fruit contains.

Florence Caldwell's cup, of 1568 (Armourers' and Brasiers' Company), illustrates yet another form of bowl, shaped as it is like an upturned bell with a simple moulding a few inches below the rim, and the application of recurved scrolls to the baluster stem and below the finial, which represents Fortune standing on a globe.

A similar stem supports the Goodricke Cup of 1563 (British Museum) whose bowl was originally a coconut, now imitated in silver-gilt, mounted in straps partly stamped and partly cast as caryatids. Its cover is embossed with a frieze of animals running in the chase, and its finial is cast as a demi-lion. A coconut cup of about 1580 mounted with a silver lip-band, and simpler straps, stands on a stem constructed from two groups of three cast grotesques, one above the other.

A fine standing mazer, begun in 1523 and apparently altered in 1540, by Morett, the royal goldsmith, notably by the substitution of a silver for the wooden bowl and an additional flange to the foot, was presented in that year by Henry VIII on the occasion of the union of the Barbers' with the Surgeons' Company. Its cover, stem, and foot are chased most skilfully with floral scrollwork, not unlike that on the Corpus Christi College two-handled cup (plate 7), containing the royal emblems, while the cast finial represents the royal arms with supporters surmounted by a royal crown. From its lip-band four bells are suspended from lions' masks.

Mazers. No mazers with mounts hall-marked after the fourth decade of the sixteenth century seem to have survived. Belated medieval characteristics may be seen on the mounts of a standing mazer of 1529 at All Souls' College, Oxford, but the scrolled openwork cresting round the base derives from the neo-classical revival. Of the two mazers dating from the thirties in the British Museum, the Narford Hall Mazer, mounted in 1532, has engraved round its lip-band in a form of Tudor capitals the inscrip-

tion CIPHVS REFECTORII ROFENSIS PER FRATREM
ROBERTVM PECHAM, and the enamelled print represents
St Benet on a ground of green and red flowers that show
Renaissance influence.

Two-Handled Cups and Covers. The earliest example
of what was to become during the seventeenth and eighteenth centuries a very common form of drinking vessel to
be passed from hand to hand as a loving cup, or in reduced size a cup for wine or beer, is a cup of 1533 at
Corpus Christi College, Oxford (plate 7). The pear-shaped
body is set on a short foot-stem, which has a very graceful
stamped pattern on the outer moulding; its two cast
handles are of an unusual pattern, as are the tight foliate
spirals flat-chased against a matted ground.

Wine Cups. Standing cups and covers were at once imposing ornaments for the sideboard and capacious enough
to be handed round as loving cups; the wine cup is a small
vessel for the use of one person, being generally distinguishable by its size and lack of a cover from even the
smaller standing cups. A fine and very Germanic example
of 1567 (Victoria and Albert Museum) has a plain bowl
of Oriental agate mounted with a simple vandyked lip-
band that contrasts with the heavily ornamented calyx,
stem, and base. The cast lions' heads, lions' claws, and
dolphin-like foliage are typically Italian motifs, while
the cast snails and embossed swags are from more northern
sources.

One form, with a shallow curviform bowl and baluster
stem like those on some standing cups, may be illustrated
by the small gilt wine cup of 1587 (Goldsmiths' Company:
plate 16a); its bowl, stem, and foot are engraved with
scrolled foliage and flowers.

Beakers. The usual form assumed by the beaker in the
seventeenth century was presaged by Greek and Balkan
silversmiths of the fifth century B.C., though their horizontal lip-flange gave way to the more practical eversion
of the lip (plate 17c). The common type of beaker of
which examples date from the latter years of the sixteenth

century is a simple and unpretentious vessel, formed as a cylinder with a vertical seam and a flared top, in the bottom of which a circular disc was inserted and surrounded with a stamped flange and moulded band. It was generally employed as a secular vessel, but is sometimes used as a communion vessel in the reformed Churches of the Netherlandish community in this country. Moreover, the characteristic Elizabethan chalices are, for the most part, no more than such beakers raised on a stem and foot. One of the best examples comes from a group of four, formerly in the Dutch Church at Norwich, which are attributed to Peter Peterson and dated about 1595 (Ashmolean Museum: plate 17c). Each is unusually well engraved with the fine inscription THE GYFT OF MR RYCHARD BROWNE OF HEIGHAM and the characteristic scrolled foliage between straps from whose interlacings depend three spiral stems, each ending in a flower. This foliate motif can be expected on most beakers of this time, but few English examples are anything but coarsely engraved.

Tankards. During the last quarter of the sixteenth century the word 'tankard' gradually replaced 'can' as the current term denoting a new type of drinking vessel, perhaps of German or Scandinavian origin, which consists in a cylindrical drum with a hinged cover having a thumb-piece and finial and a large scrolled handle. A Norwich will of 1583 contains the entry 'one canne or Tanckerd of silver', and the 1589 inventory of the Master's plate at Peterhouse, Cambridge, lists the following:

Item a tankerd barred lipt and covered v ounces xxllljs. ljd.
Item a white horne tankerde with a cover barres and lipt double gilt vl ounces xxis.

The earliest extant example has indeed a horn drum mounted in silver-gilt in 1561. A tankard with a glass drum, its mounts hall-marked in 1570, belongs to Clare College, Cambridge; and in that year commences an unbroken series of tankards made entirely of metal, which continues, though in changing form and size, and with irregular frequency, until the present day. Corpus Christi College, Cambridge, possesses one of the first representative examples, made in 1571 (plate 18a). The drum tapers upwards from the flanged and moulded foot, which like the flange of the cover is composed of egg-and-dart and billet stampings. The domed cover is flat with swags of fruit and is surmounted by a rayed pedestal. The thumb-piece (or billet) is a cast and chased scroll, a forerunner of one common in the early seventeenth century (fig. 25). The billets take a variety of forms, among them entwined dolphins, winged heads, caryatid figures, or a mermaid holding in one hand her tail and in the other a bunch of fruit. The tapering hollow handle, of 'D' section, is scrolled and its side is chased with imbricated scales. They are all about seven inches high, though other examples may be less tapered or engraved or embossed with swags of fruit and strapwork; two prominent mouldings or, as in plate 18a, one (the 'barres' in the Peterhouse inventory) are applied round the drum. These seem to be vestiges of the iron hoops which held together the wooden staves of the rough vessels from which they derive: an example of 1784 showing the same motif is reproduced on plate 19d. Another form, of which the only example is dated 1597, perpetuates the same construction, though it more resembles a narrow beer barrel, or a black jack.

A third distinct but very rare form may be represented by the bulged tankard of 1567, '*The Gifte of Thomas Tyndale Bachelar 1574*' to the Armourers' and Brasiers' Company; it is seven inches in height and round its neck is engraved '*To Remembar the Poore*'. The difference of seven years between the date of its assay and that of its presentation is not unusual; many instances are known of a piece of plate being presented after it had already belonged to and been used by the donor or his ancestors for a considerable period. The value engraved beneath the foot (five pounds three shillings and sixpence) shows a considerable discrepancy from the twenty-four shillings at which the first of the Peterhouse tankards was valued, and is probably a later valuation.

Jugs of Rhenish Stoneware and other Pottery mounted in Silver or Silver-Gilt. Tyndale's tankard resembles in shape several dozen jugs of Rhenish stoneware with a mottled brown glaze that are preserved in silver-gilt or silver mounts made throughout the second half of the sixteenth century, and its engraved vertical straps show that it may well have been derived from them. The pottery (often called tigerware), originally imported from the Rhine Valley, but also made in England, was neither rare, nor does it seem specially attractive. Nevertheless, pots of this ware, as well as Wrotham ware, pottery with brown, purple, or turquoise glazes, Siegburg ware, so-called Rhodian ware, and glass, were commonly mounted in silver-gilt, or less commonly in white silver, not only in Germany and the Low Countries, but in England, where, outside London, the assay offices of Exeter and Barnstaple are sometimes represented. They range from six to ten inches in height, with mounts engraved, embossed, or stamped with contemporary ornament. One of the earliest, 1548, is in the British Museum, the body made of Venetian lace glass, and few date after 1590; the majority were not fully marked.

The top of the handle is usually about an inch below the rim of the jug, and the hinge of the domed cover therefore had to be raised on a box-like structure. A deep lip-band covers the inside and outside of the vertical neck. Sometimes a band of metal round the shoulder is attached to the foot-mount with four or more ornamental straps, which are secured in the normal way with locking pins at each end. Otherwise the foot-mount is secured by bent vandykes and sized plaster.

A similar form of mount was used on the taller 'canettes' of Siegburg ware, or *terre-de-pipe*, where they form so small a part of the whole that these vessels are often classified with ceramics.

Standing Dishes. The Italian word '*tazza*' is often applied to drinking vessels with a broad and rather shallow bowl mounted on a stem and foot (cf. plates 16a and b), though the word has in the past been loosely employed to denote salvers and dishes with upcurved edges and even to the patens used in church. The vessels here described are characterized by broad, shallow, saucer-like bowls, intended to hold fruit and other food on the table, rather than wine. In the centre of the bowl is usually an embossed print, and round it engraved ornament both radiating and concentric, usually of arabesques or moresques. The stem is an ornamental example of the common type that resembles a concave hour-glass with a large knop in the middle (fig. 21), very commonly found on the Eliza-

Figure 21 – Hour-glass stem

bethan communion cups. The known examples follow a standard form, that of 1584 belonging to the Goldsmiths' Company being unusual in having a cover, which is taller than the dish itself, the pedestal supporting the finial, a warrior, being more like the stem of a standing cup.

Plates. The only sets of plates that have been preserved from the later Tudor period are very finely engraved and emphasize the dependence of London goldsmiths on foreign decorative ideas. Each of the central depressions of a set of twelve in the Fowler Collection, Los Angeles, of which electrotype reproductions may be seen in the Victoria and Albert Museum, is engraved by Pieter Maas of Cologne with a scene from the Labours of Hercules, after designs by the Nuremberg designer, Hans Alde-grever. In the same museum are preserved a set of half-a-dozen gilt plates of 1573, whose decoration and its sources were described above on p. 91.

Ewers and Basins. It has already been remarked that forks were not used at table in England until after the Restoration. If one was not expected to keep the hands clean at table, at least provision was made to wash them from ewers and basins. Tudor ewers may be divided into three types, and distinguished by the shapes of their bodies and handles. The first has a thistle-shaped body with a scrolled handle resembling those on the contempor-ary tankards and an opposing wedge-shaped spout. An example of 1562 (Winchester College: plate 35) stands on a plain reel stem and decorated foot, and the lowest part of the bowl is sharply bulged and flat-chased with strap-work. Two engraved bands of moresques encompass both spout and bowl; the hinged and embossed cover is domed and surmounted by a raised medallion enamelled with the arms of the college. The military trophies are a some-what uncommon motif, of classical origin, on English plate. Round the flange is engraved MANERS MAKET MAN QVOTHE WYLLYAM WYKEHAM. Its accompanying basin is ornamented *en suite* with an unusually intricate and finely engraved inscription round the flange. A variation of octagonal section, the sides being alternately plain and engraved with arabesques, the handle of angular form, and the stem being replaced by an everted and moulded foot on a circular base is represented by Arch-bishop Parker's ewer of 1545 (Corpus Christi College, Cambridge: plate 34). Its cover is embossed with spiral gadrooning about a central medallion enamelled with his arms. Its basin is decorated to match.

A continental, perhaps Italian, origin must be given to the second category, which is distinguishable by a baluster-shaped body, with a narrow neck and stem, a prominent spout, and a tall cast scrolled handle, to the many elab-orate designs of which much care was given. An example of 1583 in the Victoria and Albert Museum, about thirteen inches in height, has a demi-lion at the junction of the handle with the neck; the flat-chased band of aquatic motifs, such as waves, grotesque dolphins, and reed-maces, is comparable with many oval cartouches similarly decorated during the last two decades of the sixteenth century and the first two of the seventeenth century (cf. plates 20 and 33). A very elaborate example of two years earlier, set with agates, together with its ewer *en suite*, belongs to the Duke of Rutland.

A third kind has a long spout, usually supported by a stay, and seems to derive from the Chinese wine jug. Of the ceramic examples mounted in silver, two blue-and-white porcelain vessels in the Victoria and Albert Museum, others of Turkish ware in the British Museum and the Fitzwilliam Museum, and two of Siegburg ware, one in the Lee of Fareham collection, are representative of the variety. In Moscow are larger and later examples entirely in silver-gilt.

The most remarkable of the basins that have survived without their ewers belongs to the Goldsmiths' Company (plate 33a). The rim is meticulously engraved with three rows of moresques within interlacing straps between four panels of embossed strapwork; the raised centre is embossed with two patterns repeated alternately round the enamelled arms of Legh of Lyme, which represent the family that originally owned it.

Salts. Although the symbolic importance of the standing salt on the table in no way diminished during the sixteenth century, none of the fantastic and splendid items listed in contemporary royal inventories remain. Perhaps many of them had been preserved from the Gothic period and were already out of fashion. Nevertheless, several dozen salts still exist in a corresponding variety of sizes and designs.

A number of large covered salts of good proportions and the best workmanship are derived from architectural designs. Of these the finest is the gilt Gibbon Salt of 1576

(Goldsmiths' Company: plate 39), a miniature baldachino in the centre of which a figure of Neptune is enclosed in a cylinder of rock-crystal. An Ionic column is placed in the centre of each side, and the finial consists of a large vase surmounted by a piered castor on scrolled brackets.

A greater number of salts comprising a cylindrical drum, with or without feet, and a domed cover surmounted by a variety of finials were made between 1554 and 1626, and they range in height from six to twelve inches. The Tudor examples are commonly embossed all over with conventional strapwork and swags of fruit, though a solitary example of 1601 (Goldsmiths' Company) is made from a drum of rock-crystal containing a parchment painted with the arms of the Company. Archbishop Parker's Salt of 1562 at Corpus Christi College, Cambridge, has a flask-shaped finial and four feet in the form of tortoises. The Queen Elizabeth Salt of the same year (Tower of London) is embossed with figures of *Faith, Hope*, and *Charity* after Peter Flötner's engravings of the *Eight Virtues*.

From the same set of designs are figures representing *Patience, Justice*, and *Temperance* and a figure of *Venus* from Flötner's series of planetary deities, which are embossed on a fine large regilt salt of 1569 (Vintners' Company). This may be taken to represent a similar, less common, series with generally analogous characteristics but of square section. The finial is a female figure holding a shield, this time engraved with the arms of the company, and the four feet are cast as sphinxes. Of very similar design is the Vyvyan Salt (Victoria and Albert Museum) of 1592, whose height of about sixteen inches is accounted for by the four scrolled and cast brackets that support the cover above the depression for the salt. Each side frames a panel of glass painted with, for example, a branch of grapes with a scroll inscribed RVDENTES VINO ABSTINENT, based on Whitney's *Emblems*; the four circular glass medallions on the cover are painted with portrait busts of Ninus, Cyrus, Alexander, and Julius Caesar, the four great founders of empires. Above, the finial figure represents *Justice*.

Of both the circular and square salts several smaller versions of broader proportions and more standardized ornament are known.

At the end of the sixteenth century a new shape was introduced and lasted for about a generation. It may roughly be likened to two bells, a smaller imposed upon a larger and surmounted by a small pierced ball, which is a castor (plate 40). While no examples of the bell salt are listed in the royal inventory of 1574, there are five in that of 1596. An example of 1594 in the Victoria and Albert Museum is flat-chased with straps, foliage, and conventional flowers and stands on four ball and claw feet, while an example of five years later (Goldsmiths' Company) is engraved with bands of arabesques and laurel wreaths. They are generally gilt, and range in height from 7 to 13 inches.

A few smaller salts of square, circular, or triangular section exist; they are about three inches high and are sometimes without covers. Although of generally inferior quality and ordinary ornament, their existence is important because they foreshadow in size and use the several varieties that were to prevail in the following centuries. Mention has already been made of castors incorporated in the structure of large salts. A few independent castors are known from as early as about 1540, but they have more affinities with some of the Adam and Regency periods than with the larger types that were common during the later Stuart and early Georgian periods.

Spoons. During the sixteenth century the stem was made flatter, wider and with little taper, perhaps to give space for the four punches in force after 1545. The bowl dips less sharply from the stem, and, without increasing in area, thus has a greater capacity (plate 60b); shoulders become more curved and the angle at which they leave the stem is increased to about 105°. The general decline in quality of the casting and chasing of the finials is per-

haps due to worn moulds – the same moulds, and casts
from them, seem to have been used over and over again,
leading to a general deterioration in modelling, especially
of the figures. Some it is thought are from the same moulds
as the figures on the pastoral staff at Corpus Christi College, Oxford (plate 2b).

It might be expected from the mass of plate manufactured during this period that other articles of domestic
plate would have been preserved, but though a number of
vessels and utensils have been preserved in single examples, many more are only known from their description
in inventories.

An orange-strainer weighing four ounces is listed in the
royal inventory of 1520 and six in that of 1574. The latter
includes 'oone fountaine of silver and guilt having vi
pillars and a pipe, standing upon the toppe a woman
holding a cluster of grapes in her hands'.

A candlestick in the royal inventory of 1532 was accompanied by a steel, a chain, and snuffers engraved with
H and K, a rose, and a pomegranate. Such a snuffer of
about 1550 (Victoria and Albert Museum) has a heart-
shaped box chased with the royal arms in an oval shield
and flanked by the letters E and R; the scissor-like stems
are engraved GOD SAVE THE KYNGE and a cast female
mask and a seated Oriental figure are applied at either end.
In the advertisement of the state lottery held in 1567 may
be seen two candlesticks with sockets, wide greasepans,
short stems and spreading bases that are not greatly dis-
similar from the rare silver example of 1634 (cf. fig. 33),
the shape of which may have been derived from the
Middle East. But the earliest silver English candlestick,
probably made during the last quarter of the century,
comprises a gilt stem decorated with eagles and satyrs
supporting a crystal cross bar to each end of which is
attached a socket. Silver wall-sconces seem to have been
used in the royal palaces in considerable numbers. George
Cavendish, in his description of Wolsey's reception in
1527 of the French Ambassador at Hampton Court, not

by then completed, noted 'the plates that hung on the walls to give light in the chamber were of silver and gilt, with lights burning in them'.

A small embossed scent flask (1546), rather less than five inches in height, with a fitting design of strapwork, and swags of fruit, and a later engraved crest, may be seen in the Victoria and Albert Museum. A small bowl-shaped casket of mother-of-pearl, in silver-gilt mounts (cf. fig. 22), dating from about 1600 is in the same museum.

CHAPTER FOUR

1603–60: The Early Stuarts and the Protectorate

THE first years of the reign of James I (1603–25) mark only a gradual development of the trends noted in the reign of Elizabeth I, neither the change of dynasty nor the advent of a new century in themselves upsetting the existing order and prosperity.

Yet the Goldsmiths' Company, together with the other corporations and their members, were on several occasions pressed for loans on behalf of the king. In 1618 the members were surprised to find that no less than £14,000 had been charged against the Company for alleged arrears of rent upon the Statute of Chantries over a period of sixty years. Fortunately the Attorney-General, Sir Henry Yelverton, had recently become the tenant of a garden belonging to the Company and wrote, 'If my place may turn to your advantage you shall have no tenant more pliable to your requests than myself . . .'

Some idea of the number of goldsmiths working in 1620 may be gathered from the fact that 767 persons were ordered to pay quarterage in that year. But the number of London makers' marks listed by Jackson from 1600 to 1639 inclusive is only about 340. Of these about ten per cent show only devices (cf. fig. 9), the proportion gradually decreasing towards the end of the period. Some makers used devices resembling merchants' marks, others their initial letters alone: the great majority used two initial letters with some distinguishing devices. A few incuse (i.e. without relief) marks are found; the remainder are in plain or shaped shields, or in punches shaped as hearts, ovals, diamonds, or, later, circles, sometimes indicated by dots.

The Company continued to exercise its right of search and punishment, even, it appears, through the Civil War and the fighting in the forties. For example in 1609, one John Brooke, having been found guilty of practising deceit in making bowls, was fined twenty pounds and put in the stocks with the bowl hanging round his neck; in 1617 a goldsmith as far away as Dorchester was fined.

In 1622 the King declared, through both the Lord Mayor and the Lords of the Council, his great dislike of the mixture of mean trades with the goldsmiths in Gold-smiths' Row in Cheapside, and required speedy 'reforma-tion and that the houses and shops there should be furn-ished and supplied with goldsmiths for the continuance of the beauty and ornament of the chief street of this our city and to restore it to its former splendour'.

The same year the lack of bullion metal available for both the Mint and the manufacturers led to an enquiry into the waste of silver, for which seven reasons were adduced:

i. The immoderate use and waste of foreign plate; there had been a number of complaints by the goldsmiths in recent years that Nuremberg plate, in particular, had been much imported to their great loss.
ii. The neglect of the true making of English manufactures.
iii. The disproportion of the monetary value of gold and silver coins as compared with the prices of gold and silver bul-lion was unfavourable to silver.
iv. The sale of bullion by the reformers was not in accordance with the statute of Henry VII's reign, which required that bullion should be of sterling.
v. That the bullion merchants were selling neither to the Mint nor to the goldsmiths as the same statute required.
vi. That too much gold and silver bullion as well as English coinage was being exported.
vii. That the use of gold and silver for spangles and such-like was excessive, it being estimated that the expenditure on such ornaments was more than one hundred thousand pounds per annum.

In 1628 the Lord Mayor requested the Company to pay nearly £1,500 to the Chamberlain as the portion of a sum demanded for the king's use, and six years later they paid £66 ship money, in spite of John Hampden's protest and imprisonment in 1627.

In 1637 the Goldsmiths' Company was appointed, by order of Parliament, to consider the patents lately granted to Henry Rich, 1st Earl of Holland, of the office of His Majesty's Exchanger. The revival of this ancient office had been proposed on several occasions, but strong opposition on the grounds that the holder was entitled to a monopoly of the bullion trade had hitherto prevented its re-inauguration. The committee's report was unfavourable, finding among other things that the Earl's deputies had not always ready money to pay for even small amounts of the bullion offered to them; that they discriminated unfairly in their prices between those ignorant of its value and the experts; that they had taken no bullion to the Mint, so that it was open to suspicion how they had disposed of what they had purchased, especially as they had kept no account books, and that they had deputed their duties to unworthy persons, reserving a rent. It seems that the lack of confidence in the office was prejudicial to trade in general, more particularly to the importation of bullion on which the Mint wholly relied – for the amount produced in these islands was negligible – and therefore to the daily business of goldsmiths and the bullion merchants.

The autocratic tendencies of the first Stuart king and of his son Charles I (1625–49) were politically unacceptable to so many of their subjects that by 1640 there was considerable unrest. Merchants had long been accustomed to deposit their money at the Mint in the Tower of London; but after Charles threatened in 1640 to seize the bullion there, estimated at £120,000, they turned to the goldsmiths of Lombard Street, who, already equipped with safe means for keeping valuables on their premises, now began to take in deposits from their customers, allowing interest at five per cent and lending out the money at higher rates limited to eight per cent by an Act of 1623. These 'running cashes' developed into the modern banking system, and goldsmiths' notes began to circulate which could be exchanged for cash on demand, forerunners of the notes issued by the Bank of England on its foundation in 1694.

When in 1642 the court was established in Oxford, King Charles asked the sixteen then existing colleges to hand over all their silver and gilt plate on loan until they should be repaid at the end of hostilities. Twelve colleges complied and some 1,600 lb. of plate was subscribed, as well as a considerable amount from the King's supporters in the neighbourhood: only essential chapel plate, a few pieces of sentimental importance (such as founders' plate), or vessels of other substances mounted in silver or in silver-gilt of such small weight as to have but little breakdown value, have survived this sacrifice. In like manner the supporters of each side throughout the country gave, or were encouraged – even forced – to give their plate. The Stoke Prior Treasure, which was found in the winter of 1891 beneath a hedge near Leominster, Herefordshire, and purchased as treasure trove for the Victoria and Albert Museum two years later, consists of seven pieces of plate dating between 1578 and 1640 and may well have been hastily buried by its fleeing owner or by some looter during the trouble.

In 1643 the Lord Mayor asked the Company for a loan of £3,500 for the safety and defence of the City. Such a long and turbulent upheaval could not but directly affect the goldsmiths. Not only was established trade upset in that the goldsmiths were politically divided amongst themselves, but some of the foreign goldsmiths established in London returned to the Continent. Moreover, the demand for new plate must have diminished, even if bullion had been available after both armies had commandeered all they possibly could. Consequently the production of plate fell; indeed, so little was manufactured from 1643 to 1646, that Sir C. J. Jackson had some difficulty in finding even seven pieces bearing the date letters for these four years.

During the Commonwealth bullion once more became available; but many of the richer royalists, who in more normal times would, together with the monarch, have been the most important patrons of the goldsmiths, had left the country. Widespread financial difficulties might at first have limited the number of those who could afford to buy plate. At the same time a reaction against earlier extravagances was fostered and encouraged by the Protector and his supporters. Yet during the fifties these considerations became of less importance as prosperity returned and the influence of puritanical factions diminished. Already before the Restoration of 1660 there are signs that the skill of the goldsmiths was emerging undiminished after nearly two decades of hardship.

STYLE AND ORNAMENT*

The choice of the year 1603 as a boundary between the chapter dealing with the later Tudor plate and the present one is unfortunate for the considerations of style, as it might be taken to infer a break in their smooth and imperceptible development which continued for another generation. The influence of the German pattern-books declined and indeed virtually disappeared, giving place to that of the Netherlands, whence several thousand Protestant refugees had arrived during Elizabeth's reign. This too was in its turn swamped about 1630 by purely English designs which were not made on the Continent. Not until as late as 1650 can a baroque influence from the Netherlands and France be seen; that of the latter gradually increased in strength and maintained its lead until the middle of the eighteenth century. In short, after the decline of the foreign influences of the High Renaissance, there elapsed a period, artificially prolonged by the civil war with its consequent economic difficulties to about

* See plates 10, 12a, 16b, 16c, 16d, 18b, 20, 33b, 36, 40, 41, 50a, 60d.

thirty years, when native talent was forced to rely largely upon itself until a further outside stimulus was received from the Continent.

A tendency for the minute embossing in high relief, learned from the German silversmiths, to be gradually superseded by the lower and coarser designs of the Netherlands and England itself has already been shown; the em-

Figure 22 – Engraved scrolled foliate ornament

bossing of small swags of fruit, of masks, both human and animal, became less carefully studied and meticulous. These naturalistic patterns themselves gave way to more stylized patterns of formal circular flowers that formed the centres of spirals of continuous foliage (fig. 22), flat-chased or embossed in such low relief as to be almost indistinguishable from flat-chasing. They were outlined and reserved against a pounced or granulated ground (plates 20 and 21) or, less commonly, pounced against a plain

Figure 23 – Engraved guilloche ornament (about 1600)

ground. Several variations based on guilloche mouldings are flat-chased in this way (fig. 23). Such ornaments lasted from about 1595 to 1615. From about 1615 to 1625 a low-embossed calyx of acanthus leaves ended in a tight scroll (plate 16c) is characteristic on the bowls, or, inverted, on the steeply domed feet of taller drinking cups. Until about 1630 continued use was made of monstrous fishes and reed-maces either on oval panels (plates 20 and 33b), or in continuous bands.

During the reign of James I, the bowls of many wine cups, except for a narrow band at the lip, were ornamented with closely punched lozenges which produce a diaper pattern not unlike the fine network of opaque white lines enclosed in the transparent metal of *façon-de-Venise* glasses and other objects (plate 16b). At any rate it is another example of the simple repetitive, geometrical patterns which lasted from the reign of Charles I until, and in a few instances after, the Restoration. Objects made of thin plate, especially small wine tasters, were indented with dotted patterns, by means of circular punches of various sizes, which were raised on the inside of the vessels, and usually consist in a circular stylized flower of several petals surrounded on the side of the bowl by a number of identical or alternating panels containing, for the most part, a simple upright plant often reminiscent of a tulip (plates 16c and 50a). Although the general effect of such work on small items is not unpleasing, the larger the article the more elaborate had to be the pattern and the more careful the execution. Its use on any but small objects is rarely successful.

One characteristic feature of many English standing cups and salts from the 1590s until about 1630 is the steeple or obelisk (plate 10). It was perhaps derived from the stone pinnacles commonly used on Gothic churches, and occurs on many important buildings, e.g. the Library of St Mark's, Venice (1536), the town hall of Leyden (1579), Wollaton Hall, Nottinghamshire (1590), and, internally, on the screen in the hall of Wadham College, Oxford (1610–13). It is of either triangular or square section, sometimes pierced, and often raised at each lower corner on a cast scroll and surmounted by a variety of small finials.

The flanges of feet and covers continued to be ornamented with repetitive patterns stamped in low relief, especially various ovolo or egg and tongue stampings (cf.

figs. 19b and d, p. 92). Very broad stamped bands were used until about 1625 as hoops on tankards: the same pattern recurs on the mounts of two notable examples, an alabaster casket and a serpentine tank-ard, both of about 1620 (Victoria and Albert Museum); on the second of these there is a remarkable broader one, near-ly three-quarters of an inch across, simi-lar in style to that shown in fig. 24.

Figure 24
Broad stamped
repetition pattern
(about 1600)

During the middle of this period the thinness of many of the beaten sheets of silver partly explains the use of embos-sing to add to its strength. Much plate was left entirely plain, especially wine cups of all kinds, tankards, and two-handled cups. Engraving was often rather feeble and scratchy, even where it was directly copied from an existing and much-used pattern, and especially where the engraver relied on his own inventions as on some of the armorial bearings engraved on tobacco boxes.

The use of gilding decreased and is seldom found after the beginning of the Civil War. Some small items, such as sweetmeat boxes or watch-cases of English manufacture, are ornamented with niello directly copied from continen-tal ornament prints.

PRINCIPAL ARTICLES OF DOMESTIC PLATE

Standing Cups. The most characteristic and at the same time the most imposing variety of standing cup that was made throughout the reign of James I depends for its spec-tacular effect on the steeple or obelisk that surmounts it and gives it several inches of extra height. This feature, of triangular or rectangular section, is usually ornament-ally pierced, or at least engraved; each corner is supported on a cast grotesque scroll, itself raised on a shallow circu-lar pedestal. The steeple itself is sometimes the support for a cast figure of a warrior, an obelisk, or a turned finial. From the earliest (1599) of more than seventy surviving examples to the latest imitation, they are surprisingly constant in form, though they vary in height from thirteen to twenty-six inches; an exceptional example (St Ives Corporation) measures nearly three feet. An example of 1613 (Wallace Collection; plate 10) illustrates the essential features – the flattish dome of the cover, the almost straight sides of the bowl that curve sharply underneath, the short length of baluster stem, usually between two collars of stamped work to which, on the examples after 1610, elaborate cast scrolls are applied, and finally the tall flaring bell-like, and often waisted, pedestal which is raised on a narrow stamped band surrounded by a stamped flange. The bowl and cover are usually embossed in low relief with a calyx of acanthus leaves ending in a tight embossed roll in higher relief (cf. plate 16c), the remaining spaces being often engraved with scrolls. Imbricated scales, peacock's feathers (as on the Election Cup, plate 5), shells, flowers in a spiral of foliage (*rinceaux*), all part of the widespread revival of classical motifs, as well as friezes of stylized flowers or of the chase, and the sea-monster motif, are conspicuous among the other embossed, chased, and engraved ornaments used. Another group of cups from the same period show similarities in general design and ornament but lack the steeples, which were either intentionally omitted or subsequently removed.

An analogous but more gracefully curved form of bowl may be seen on two particularly fine and almost identical gilt standing cups and covers of 1611 by a silversmith whose cypher was, apparently, ?YZ (Victoria and Albert Museum, and Christ's College, Cambridge). The flattish cover, of two moulded stages, is surmounted by a vase of flowers; the stem consists of a large vase with cast scrolls, mounted on two domes, one above the other. The cover, bowl, and stem are each ornamented by three bands of an elaborate pattern of applied filigree work on a matted ground; between those on the bowl are engraved two friezes of hunting scenes, perhaps after Virgil Solis. A salt attributed to him is illustrated in plate 41.

A few cups with gourd-shaped bowls and twisted stems protract till as late as 1619 a German tradition that dates back to about 1570. Tudor strapwork and swags of fruit are embossed on the bell section of the foot, and the bowl and cover are decorated with the curving straps and panels typical of the fifteen-nineties. A small cup made of the rind of a gourd, lacquered and mounted in silver, dates from about the same time (Victoria and Albert Museum). A similar conceit is illustrated by a few coconut cups; the nuts are set in the usual three straps with a tall lip-band with such contemporary ornamental details as small steeples or engraved repetitive bands. An elaborately emphasized motif occurs in the mounted ostrich-egg cup at Exeter College, Oxford (about 1610): a life-like figure of an ostrich surmounts the cover, and the bowl is supported on a stem consisting principally in three ostrich legs on a bell foot. Other quaint members of this ornithological group deserve mention: the five Cockayne Cups (1605: Skinners' Company) in each of which the bowl and cover together represent a cock, with stiffly indicated feathers; and the cup in the form of a peahen with three chicks which was given to the same Company by Mary, wife of James Peacock. But with these amusing examples, elaborate fancies seem to have disappeared from the silversmiths' repertory for more than half a century.

After the unproductive interlude of the Civil War a new design for standing cups became, with few exceptions, standard until the end of the seventeenth century, though it had been foreshadowed by examples in the thirties. The tub-shaped body, practical and solid, with straight sides, sometimes a little everted, and a flattish base, stands on a sturdy baluster stem with a wide-spreading foot. They are of simple construction, and usually without ornament though sometimes gilt, pounced, or engraved. The cover is stepped and curves to a pyramid with a platform for a finial, often figured. Many are without covers and it is

doubtful if they were always supplied. They are represented by an elaborate example of the later Stuart period
(plate 11).

Two-Handled Cups. Only a few two-handled cups date
from the earlier part of the period; their number increases
rapidly during the fifties. An early survivor, though examples are recorded before 1600, of a form often known
as a 'college cup', dates from 1616 (cf. fig. 32). The body is
bulged with a plain everted rim, flanked by two hollow
ring-handles. They are principally found with later hall-
marks as 'plates', 'tuns', or 'ox-eye cups' at five Oxford

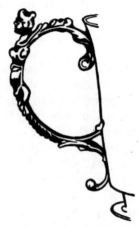

Figure 25 – Grotesque cast handle (mid 16th century)

colleges, though a few have gone into other ownership. A
similar cup of 1619, only two and a half inches high with
slightly shaped sides, is embossed with four conventional
flowers resembling tulips and its base is punched with a
flower of six petals; its handles are plain scrolls. Of the
many later varieties, one in particular (plate 12a) may be
noted as a forerunner of the bulged cups, embossed with
more naturalistic foliage, flowers, or fruit, which derive
from Netherlandish patterns, and are most common
during the first decade of the reign of Charles II (plate
12b). The shapes and the decorations had not yet become

standardized, though the finish of the grotesque handles with projecting scrolls and female heads (fig. 25) is often more elaborate and more carefully finished than during the succeeding period. In the Victoria and Albert Museum may be seen a cup of mother-of-pearl (*c.* 1650) with these handles, silver mounts, and a flared plain foot. Other smaller cups, of many shapes, may be the pounce pots or maudlin cups, or pots, for mead, referred to in contemporary sources.

Wine Cups. Some hundreds of wine cups and goblets, in height between five and ten inches, remain from this period. Most of them, in several varieties, were made before the Civil War; the smaller number of goblets remaining from the late forties and fifties tend to follow the design of the larger standing cups. For the most part plain baluster stems on spreading feet support the various kinds of bowls, of which there are more than a dozen shapes, but the greater number can be classified in five categories:

(*a*) A broad shallow bowl, whose elevation is almost a regular segment, usually plain, but not infrequently punched with the diaper pattern of lozenges (plate 16b).

(*b*) A bell-shaped or conical bowl, plain or embossed.

(*c*) A straight-sided bowl, often octagonal, with a flattish base and a very slender stem, embossed on each facet with a panel of a tulip-like flower on a matted ground, or with the tightly rolled acanthus (plate 16c).

(*d*) Goblets with a fuller bell-shaped bowl, generally plain, but sometimes embossed.

(*e*) Goblets with tub-shaped bowls, usually plain, with slightly flaring or, later, almost straight side. Occasionally a trumpet stem is found (plate 16d).

Beakers. The form of the beaker has already been described and illustrated (plate 17c). To a gilt example of 1604 are applied two horizontal moulded bands and between them, cast in relief, three maidenheads, emblems of the Mercers' Company. In the Ashmolean Museum is a pair of undated horn beakers with silver mounts, to the sides of which are fastened a cast double portrait of Charles I and Henrietta Maria in profile in the same style.

Tankards. The principal Tudor pattern (see plate 18a) continued into the reign of James I, and began to be replaced about 1620 by one with a plainer and more truncated drum. The finial on the cover is retained in the surprisingly few surviving examples of the twenties and thirties. During the third decade a new pattern came into fashion. The lowest diameter of the drum is almost as great as its height, and its sides taper slightly towards the top; the plain flat cover, sometimes engraved with concentric rings, is hinged on to the handle, which is a

Figure 26 – Early Stuart tankard (about 1630)

plainer version of the Tudor kind, and a simple thumb-piece shaped like a section of a breaking wave (fig. 26). Some are of serpentine in undated mounts. The form lasted until about 1650 when the so-called Puritan or Commonwealth Tankard (plate 18b) with a moulded and skirted base, a flattish stepped cover, and a thumb-piece in the form of twin lobes appeared. This form, without the skirt, lasted until the end of the century, and with modifications for another hundred years. A fourth pattern, which was principally made in this country on the North-East coast, derived from a type common in Scandinavia and the Baltic area. Its distinguishing features are three feet, usually in the form of balls or round fruit such as pomegranates, and flat cover with rounded edges (plate 19a). As it did not appear until shortly before the Restoration, it will be more fully described in the next chapter.

Spout Cups. Found also in ceramics, they are no more than a tankard or two-handled cup of one of the forms described below, to the side of which is soldered a narrow vertical tube ending in a curved spout. Their true purpose is conjectural, for they would appear to be too heavy and capacious for invalids. It is not impossible that they were used as tea pots or coffee pots before the new forms were introduced in the seventies and eighties, or for serving, or even imbibing, the whey from milk curdled by various additions.

Flagons. Although two main types of these tall vessels were made during the last decades of the sixteenth century and some examples survive from them, they are more characteristic of the Early Stuart period. Both forms have in common the S-scrolled handle, sometimes surmounted by a button, and are similarly ornamented. They may be plain, gilt, engraved, or chased in low relief. The first important form (plate 21), an enlargement of the bellied cans in North European pictures of the fifteenth century, did not outlast the reign of James I. To some of these are fitted spouts resembling those on some ewers mentioned above (p. 103).

More important as the prototype of the standard form used thereafter, the straight-sided flagon (plate 20) is an enlargement of the common tankard. During the fourth decade a skirted base resembling that on the Puritan tankard (plate 18b) was added.

Punch Bowls. An enlarged version of the two-handled cup and cover seems to have been the precursor to the punch bowl. Sir Charles Chitty's bowl and cover (1640) at King's College, Cambridge, has lobed sides with almost flat base on three pear-shaped feet; its flattish cover is embossed with radiating gadroons; its low reel-shaped finial enables it to be used as a salver. A similar but later vessel, nearly sixteen inches in diameter with a capacity of three gallons, has two scrolled handles and stands on dolphin feet. It was given to Stamford Corporation in 1685, and is accompanied by a ladle with the same blackberry finial. A smaller but less finely finished vessel of the same sort is the posset pot with three pear-shaped feet and a handle like that of a tankard (fig. 27).

Wine Tasters. Among the more common small vessels to be found are the two-handled wine tasters, shallow bowls with a raised centre and almost vertical sides, in diameter from three to six inches: the handles are often plain wire scrolls. The decoration, if any, is generally a number of panels round a central rosette made up of punched dots or lines. It is probable that when the raised centre is absent they were not used solely in the wine trade as they had been certainly since the fourteenth century,

Figure 27 – Posset pot or skillet

but domestically as cups of a less expensive nature for brandy and other spirits. Another vessel with a shallow bowl and vertical side, often bulged with a narrow vertical flange, to the rim of which is soldered a single horizontal handle, shaped and pierced with simple designs, is commonly called a bleeding bowl in England and a porringer in the United States, but it may also be described as the lid of a skillet (cf. fig. 27).

Dishes and Bowls. An unusually well-made fruit bowl of 1649 (plate 50a), about ten inches in diameter, has a flat border with a shaped edge of twenty-two little flowers in dotted and chased circles, and in the centre eight straps and stylized plants on a matted ground, enclosing a seeded rose in the middle of which is engraved a small coat-of-arms. Smaller sweetmeat dishes, like circular or oval saucers with two opposed scallop handles, are not uncommon.

Ewers and Basins. Ewers of the baluster kind were still made with varied ornament into the third decade of the century, but only isolated examples remain. The gilt ewer made in Norwich in 1617 (Norwich Corporation) has a large figure composition embossed round the drum representing tritons and mermaids (plate 36). An embossed dish eighteen inches in diameter matches it: the rim has six panels of boys, alternating with masks, separated by festoons of fruit. Within is a continuous frieze showing Nep-

Figure 28 – (a) Ewer (1624), (b) Ewer (1635)

tune and other marine mythological figures; in the centre is a medallion of Christ washing the feet of His disciples. A more typical, gilt, basin of 1605 (Merton College, Oxford) is one in which the normal motifs of grotesque sea monsters, bunches of fruit, and strapwork are conspicuously illustrated (plate 33b).

Two other types of ewer, both unrelieved by ornament, require brief notice. The first resembles a large Restoration communion cup with a scrolled handle, on the top of which is a small button thumb-piece; the spout springs from near the base and ends in a hooked lip (fig. 28b). The second shares certain characteristics with those last described, having the same kind of handle and stem, but a helmet-shaped drum with a broad lip (fig. 28a).

Salts. The imposing salts of earlier times were not made after the third decade, except in some special circumstances which will be noted later. The bell salts already described above (p. 105) may be represented by one of 1613 (Holburne of Menstrie Museum, Bath: plate 40).

The pedestal forms, both round and square, continued into the fourth decade; sometimes their domed covers, with

Figure 29 – Pulley-salt with three scrolls

steeple finials, were raised up on scrolled supports above a second shallow container. A small group of particularly fine gilt salts which has some analogies with this category are about ten inches high, and chased with bands of scrolling vines in the individual manner of the maker (?YZ) of a group of standing cups about 1610. The example illustrated is from Woburn Abbey (plate 41).

A new variety was the pulley-salt, waisted like the medieval hour-glass salts, but much lower in proportion to its diameter. A rare square example in the Ashmolean Museum (1632) has engraved spandrels round the central depression instead of the more usual three or four scrolled members intended to support a dish (fig. 29).

A small triangular salt with vertical sides (1607) seems

to herald the many varieties of trencher salts which have continued until the present day. It will have been noticed that even on the largest of the examples illustrated the depression for the salt was comparatively small. It is clear that some small salts existed long before this date, but were valued too little to merit preservation. The triangular example may have been adapted from German designs of the sixteenth century, when comparable examples were made. Circular or polygonal shapes are known, as are some with sloped sides that are very like a type common in the first decades of the eighteenth century.

Silver Baskets. The rare baskets remaining from the Tudor period are circular with high sides pierced in contemporary style. A basket of 1656 is more ambitious: its widely everted side is pierced and embossed with rather naturalistic flowers and fruit in the style most common about 1660, and pierced with arcades containing acanthus leaves an an oval cartouche of punched and chased ornament.

Boxes and Caskets. The Dyneley casket (Victoria and Albert Museum) consists of a drum of alabaster set in stamped gilt mounts, on three ball-and-claw feet, with a hinged domed cover surmounted by a rayed platform and a spiked baluster finial. By the same maker as the serpentine tankard – his mark was a trefoil slipped in a shaped punch – it has the same stamped pattern combining ovolos and Tudor roses and a similar pointed finial. In the Ashmolean Museum are two of the several known caskets with covers in the form of shells: the lid of one is in fact a large cockle shell and its base a scallop shell, both mounted in silver. The lid of the other is shaped like a cockle, and is entirely of silver.

Candlesticks. A few candlesticks remaining from the middle decades show a general resemblance to those illustrated in the Lottery advertisement of 1567, as well as to some of the contemporary delft supports. They consist in a short plain column with thin mouldings above a broad circular grease-pan which, overhanging a wide expandi⁻

foot or inverted bowl, serves to protect the hand (fig. 30). Of two important large gilt pairs by the anonymous maker, the symbol in whose punch was a hound *sejant,* that of 1654 (Staunton Harold) shows some of the ornament of Dutch baroque plate such as volutes, shells, and heads in relief superimposed on the antique quadruped form of candelabrum.

Flat Plate. There was no considerable change in the form of spoons, and the bowls became somewhat more oval

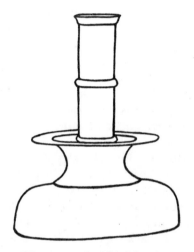

Figure 30 – Candlestick (1634)

(plate 60d). From 1657 the Innholders' Company required the gift of a spoon on admission, and these bear the figure of St Julian the Hospitaller, and examples continue until 1685. Another innovation of the seventeenth century is the so-called Buddha knop, a kneeling hooded figure. They are mostly of provincial origin and this fact alone would weigh against any Oriental connexion: the figures have also been identified with other Oriental deities, e.g. Krishna and Vishnu. In the reign of Charles I the so-called Puritan spoon (plate 60e) began to appear; it differs from the slipped-in-the-stalk type, which it superficially resembles, because the bowl is almost a regular oval and the stem is not attached but belongs to the same piece of metal, being a plain strip of flat section. The fact that some French examples antedate any known English example would indicate at least a continental origin for a type of spoon that differs so much from the traditional patterns.

The use of forks at table does not seem to have been generally introduced into this country until after the Restoration, and the experienced traveller Fynes Moryson (1617)

observed a custom in all those Italian cities and towns through which I passed that is not used in any other country that I saw in my travels, neither do I think that any other nation of Christendom doth use it, but only Italy. The Italians, and also most strangers that are commorant in Italy do always at their meals use a little fork when they cut their meat ... their forks being for the most part of iron or steel, and some of silver, but those were used only by gentlemen. The reason for this their curiosity is because the Italian cannot endure by any means to have his dish touched by fingers, seeing that all men's fingers are not alike clean.

By 1652, Peter Heylin mentions in his *Cosmography* 'the use of silver forks with us, by some of our spruce gallants taken up of late'.

In 1692 'Belted Will' Howard, of Naworth, purchased ten silver forks for £3 13s 6d. In fact the earliest known silver table fork of 1632 (Victoria and Albert Museum) has two prongs, and its stem resembles that of a Puritan spoon (plate 60e). Recently a combined spoon and fork of the same period was found under the floorboards of Haddon Hall.

Smaller items include a tiny sweetmeat box (Victoria and Albert Museum) of eighteen square and eight triangular facets, each with beautifully scrolled floral ornaments reserved against a niello ground, a small engraved terrestrial globe of 1652, a handbell whose handle takes the form of a wolf's head erased, and a staffhead of the

Blacksmiths' Company which takes the form of a hammer engraved *'By hammer and hand all arts do stand: 1659'* and surmounted by a phoenix rising from the flames above a coronet.

Among the unusual items of plate mentioned in the records of the Goldsmiths' Company are the following: beer bowls, *aqua vitae* dishes, a strong-water cup with a tunnel in it, a tobacco stopper, boxes for sweet powders and antidotes, perfuming pans, cases for beard brushes, children's corals with bells and whistles, a little windmill, funnel cups, fork-spoons, ink horns, napkin hooks, tinder boxes, pictures of the late king, and many more.

CHAPTER FIVE

1660–97: The Restoration

THE thirty-six years from the Restoration of the Stuarts in 1660 until the *New Sterling Act* came into force in 1697 form a convenient period for examination. The first date marks not only an event of prime political significance, but also the full flood into England of important new forms and ornaments for plate. Plate in the predominant styles of the sixties appeared shortly before the Restoration, and occasional examples of earlier patterns were made after that event. This vigorous and productive period embraces the reigns of Charles II and James II and ends in the middle of the joint reign of William III and Mary II. The *New Sterling Act* was of enough importance in the history of the manufacture of plate in London, and subsequently throughout the country, to merit a separate chapter about its provisions and effects, although for stylistic considerations the divisions may be considered untidy.

More than nine out of every ten pieces of plate made in the British Isles that remain from this period emanated from the workshops of the London goldsmiths. Around the busy port of the wealthiest and largest city in Europe both traders and manufacturers were engaged in extending their activities not only at home and in Europe, but in the distant continents of America, Africa, and Asia. The mercantile companies were importing new commodities from beyond the seas; exiles returning from the Netherlands and France, immigrants, and foreign visitors were responsible for an infusion of new ideas in both the intellectual and the scientific spheres. The monarchs themselves set a standard of luxurious living that was quickly and readily copied by their immediate entourages of noble and wealthy families and imitated to the best of their ability by the prosperous merchants. Changes are apparent in most activities and in every station of life: the arts and sciences, food and drink, apparel and manners, all reflect in some degree the importance of the new influences which have been preserved in the works of Newton and Boyle, Dryden and Locke, Purcell and Lely, Wren and Grinling Gibbons. In short, a somewhat sober and restrained way of life was leavened by the refinements and splendours which had been tasted in the courts of Louis XIV and William of Orange.

The manufacture in increasing quantities of cheap new crystalline glass, the gradual introduction of the use of forks at table, and the popular acceptance of three new beverages, tea, cocoa, and coffee, had important effects on the forms of plate. Now that the exigencies of the Civil War and the Protectorate had passed, a general prosperity created a vast demand for plate of all kinds for ecclesiastical, ceremonial, and domestic use, not only to replace that which had been surrendered, lost, or damaged during the previous two decades, but to comply with the prevailing fashion.

In 1670 Prince Rupert was sent an account from Alderman Backwell for 272 ounces of plate, with fashion and engraving included, that comprised a dozen dishes, four plates, three pairs of candlesticks, a pair of gilt candlesticks, five dozen plates, a sweetmeat stand, two tankards, six sconces, two dozen spoons and the same number of forks, two sugar casters, a dozen salts, a pepper box, a mustard pot, two cruets, two snuffer pans and pairs of snuffers. All this cost £960. From Messrs Childs and Rogers the Earl of Devonshire received an account in 1687 as follows:

	£	s	d
forr a greate silver cisterne, weight 3,496 oz, at 7s per oz	1,223	12	0
ffor a case	6	10	0

forr a suger-box, weighing 32 oz, at 7s per oz .	11	3	3
ffor graveing a bason and ewre	1	15	0
ffor boyleing the plate, which I sauld at 5s 8d per oz	1	0	0
ffor a greate jarr, 2 flower potts, 4 little jarrs, a bottle with a spoon, weight 255½ oz, at 6s per oz	76	13	0
forr a pair of andirons, 143 oz 12 dwt, at 7s 2d per oz	51	9	0
ffor the iron worke	0	12	0
ffor 2 ffigures on pedestalls, 154 oz 10 dwt, at 6s 8d per oz	49	7	0
ffor 2 branch candlesticks, 172 oz 14 dwt, at 6s per oz	51	16	0
ffor 1 dozen and ½ of silver guilt plates, 475 oz, at 8s 6d per oz, is	201	17	6

From the enormous quantities of magnificent plate in the royal palaces to the silver tankards in the taverns, the abundant and widespread use of silver is one of the most remarkable manifestations of this period. In 1695 the Grand Jury of Middlesex represented that the frequent and common use of silver basins, monteiths, silver tankards, bowls, cups, and tumblers in public houses and taverns had occasioned many burglaries and murders, and prayed the bench to apply to Parliament to seek means to prevent such common use of silver in these places. In compliance an Act was passed forbidding publicans to use publicly or expose any wrought or manufactured plate whatsoever, with the exception of spoons.

A most unjust action by Charles II ruined many goldsmiths and, with them, their customers. The goldsmith bankers were accustomed to lend their clients' money to the Exchequer at the rate of five or six per cent; Alderman Backwell had more than a quarter of a million pounds invested there. The King wished to raise money but without the need of going to Parliament to obtain its aid. Accordingly he promised the office of Lord Treasurer to whomsoever should suggest the means; Sir Thomas Clifford, whom Lord Ashley told of the idea, mentioned to the King that the closure of the Exchequer and suspension of all payments from it would meet his purpose. More than a million pounds was seized in 1672 and, although the King intended to reopen it in a year, neither principal nor interest was paid until 1677, when for six years interest was paid out of excise and was then stopped.

Towards the end of the century this huge production of plate began to interfere with the supplies of bullion for the mints, for the metal imported from abroad was largely consumed by the goldsmiths, and coins, too, being of the common sterling standard, were readily converted into plate. A smaller, but readily welcomed, source of metal was provided by the illegal practice of coin-clipping.

STYLE AND ORNAMENT*

Plate was once again made in all qualities, and of all weights. The lighter gauges of silver often required to be strengthened by embossing, for which designs were derived from the Netherlands. The most clearly recognizable style of ornament, which more than any other is characteristic of the decade from about 1658 to 1670, comprised embossed floral motifs. Tulips, irises, poppies, carnations, and other flowers less easily identifiable, appear amid a profusion of scrolled or spiralling foliage. Sometimes fruits, and almost as frequently such animals as lions, bulls, horses, unicorns, dragons, or bears were included in the scheme; and on occasion turkeys, peacocks, and other birds. This embossed work, which may often seem to have been coarsely executed without direct observation of the natural forms, owes its effectiveness to the bold and broad treatment it received and to the judicious balance between it and the plain surfaces.

These motifs originated in the Netherlands and were the direct ornamental derivatives of the large number of fruit-pieces and flower-pieces, the painting of which had been fostered by an intense and widespread interest in

* See plates 11, 12b, 13a, 17a, 17b, 17d, 18c, 18d, 19a, 24a, 26a, 43a, 48a, 56a, 56b, 60e, 60f, 60g, 60h.

botany and biology. Carved and inlaid furniture, textiles, and plate reflect this direct interest in floral ornament as opposed to the largely imaginative attention paid to it in previous centuries.

Netherlandish decorative artists also produced another clearly distinguishable ornamental style, a baroque manifestation made popular in Northern Europe in the forties by the Utrecht goldsmiths Adam and Christian van Vianen, and the Amsterdam goldsmiths Jan Lutma and his son of the same name. Christian van Vianen was employed in London by Charles I from about 1637 to 1644 and was again in England for about four years after 1652. This style consists in embossed lobular scrolls of indefinite, though sometimes symmetrical, forms, from which parts of the decoration appear to assume the shapes of grotesque masks of human beings or animals. From its resemblance to the gristle of the human ear the style is variously referred to as the *Ohrmuschel-* or *Knorpelwerkstil*, from which it has acquired the English translations of auricular and cartilaginous. Perhaps on account of its eccentricity, however, it achieved little vogue in this country and scarcely lasted as a decorative form beyond 1670. In some respects it has features in common with the rococo style of the mid eighteenth century, though a comparison quickly reveals that the idioms and their execution are fundamentally different.

Though so little of the magnificent plate wrought in France at this time survived the meltings under Louis XV and at the Revolution, its influence on English plate is unmistakable. The massive plate with its delicately wrought ornament made early in the reign of Louis XIV (1643–1715) found much of its inspiration from the classical remains of Italy. Not only was plate of French manufacture imported, but after the Revocation of the Edict of Nantes (1685) many skilled Huguenot goldsmiths came to work in England.

A form of ornament, usually embossed, in the repetitive classical pattern of vertical or radiating acanthus leaves, which can be noticed especially on tankards, tumblers (plate 17a), and two-handled cups from about 1670 until about 1685. The application of this rather limited and stylized decoration was restricted to the surbase and cover; their finials were often formed as a cluster of burgeoning acanthus leaves, either almost closed or widely opened. The motif itself is of some antiquity, being most familiar as the sculpted decoration around Corinthian capitals, as well as being widely used in Greek and Roman ornaments and friezes. Its rediscovery during the Italian renaissance naturally led to its employment on both continental and English plate during the sixteenth century, and it is never entirely lost to view during the seventeenth and eighteenth centuries.

Another form of embossed surbase derived from Roman sarcophagi, is composed of vertical, oblique, or spiral flutes, concave alternating with convex and ending with a punched quatrefoil or similar simple pattern. Commonly referred to as the 'William and Mary style', it was employed from about 1685 until well into the Britannia period.

On more massive ornamental plate, garnitures, and furnishings, extremely elaborate embossed work is found during this period, directly derived from French designers. *Rinceaux*, spirals of foliage, especially of acanthus leaves, predominate and surround figures of boys in playful attitudes, masks, or plaques with mythological or religious figure-scenes in low relief, while garlands and drapes are also incorporated into the schemes.

A casing of embossed open work in similar style was fitted over the plain drums of several two-handled cups and covers, or to such a standing cup as the Pepys Cup of 1677 (plate 11). A contrast was made by placing a gilt casing over a silver body, or *vice versa*.

Heavier gauges of metal do not lend themselves so easily to embossing, nor do they require it for structural strength. Goldsmiths therefore relied more on pure form, alone or embellished with engraving or applied ornament, to produce their effects. The Parisian goldsmiths in particular effected a monumental elegance in their productions which is due to an admirable harmony in the relationship between the shape of the article with its finely conceived line and the forms of applied decoration. Perhaps the most attractive of these applications is cut-card work, a term used to describe flat patterns of sheet metal applied to the body of the object to be decorated;

Figure 31 – Harp-shaped handle

trefoils or multifoils applied within the corners of rect-angular surfaces, a repetitive band of leaves, sometimes extremely elaborate, applied round the lower part of a cup at its junction with the base of stem to form a calyx (plate 13a); plain or elaborated stars or ovals, sometimes a smaller superimposed upon a larger and more ornate, to form the platform for a finial or to mask the junction of a handle with the body (plate 28). Other forms of applied ornament typical of this style are bay-wreaths, bound reeding, or gadrooned edging. Handles were often chased wires coiled into the shape of a serpent, or cast into the shape of a harp (fig. 31). Such handles were often orna-mented with graduated beading, acanthus husks, or an applied leaf. These motifs were used in moderation on plain curving surfaces, a combination which has resulted in some of the most graceful vessels of any period. English goldsmiths often selected some of these devices to ornament plate of a purely English character such as tankards, or combined them with decorative motifs from other sources. Such mixtures were not always unpleasing in effect.

It is interesting to note that French ornamental motifs and designs for plates, while they do occur occasionally in the sixties and seventies, did not achieve any prominence until the two following decades. This may be partly explained by the decline of Netherlandish art, and by the effects of the revocation of the Edict of Nantes in 1685. The strong commercial ties between England and Holland were not completely disrupted by the second war (1665–7), or by the vacillating policies designed to overcome simultaneously the economic competition from that country and the threat of French political supremacy in Europe. In spite of the fact that after the successful landing at Torbay and the flight of the King, William of Orange and Mary were accepted as joint sovereigns, the artistic influence of the Dutch had ended. The persecution of the Huguenots in France caused more than a quarter of a million skilful and industrious artisans and merchants, including some well-established goldsmiths, mostly provincial but some from Paris, to seek asylum in the more tolerant or Protestant countries of North-West Europe and America, particularly in Holland, Germany, England, and Ireland. The influence of these Huguenots was out of all proportion to their relatively small numbers, and resulted in changes as profound and lasting as those from Germany in the sixteenth century, and far more so than those from Holland at the Restoration.

From imported Chinese porcelain wares, which arrived in this country mostly by way of Holland, are derived the shapes of some of the earliest tea pots and of the massive garnitures of vases and flasks which will be described below. But a more important oriental influence is to be found in the decoration, both engraved (plate 18d), embossed or cast in relief, consisting of human figures as well as birds, trees, and flowers which seem to have been imitated or copied from Chinese lacquer-work rather than ceramics. These *chinoiseries* began to appear on plate in about 1670, and from their quaint and agreeable conceptions have retained their popularity in some forms to the present day.

Yet these foreign influences, although remarkable for their variety and attractiveness, did not stop the manufacture of plain and simple plate. Fashioning was then, as now, a question of money. When Pepys was presented with two flagons costing about a hundred pounds, he wrote: 'Weighed my two silver flagons at Steven's, they weigh 212 ounces, which is about £50 at 5s per ounce, and they judge the fashion to be worth about 5s per ounce more, nay, some say 10s an ounce the fashion; sorry to see that the fashion is worth so much, and the silver comes to no more.' Much of the plate produced during this period, as during every other, is utilitarian and lacks ornament which was not necessary to the construction of the article itself or to its use. Examples of this simplicity may be seen in the tankards, tumbler cups, and spoons, among the articles of domestic plate, and in communion cups, patens, and alms-dishes among the ecclesiastical. Indeed by far the greater part of the church plate made after the Restoration comes within this category. Although the addition of ornament might have increased the cost almost indefinitely, its absence by no means resulted in ugly, unattractive, or ill-finished designs: in some instances the contrary is true, because more attention was paid to the form than to the often superfluous ornament, which often distracts attention from an ungainly shape.

Many earlier decorative techniques continued with little change. Matting (pouncing) was used, either by itself in plain panels over the surface of the object, as on

the tea pot of about 1685 in the Ashmolean Museum
(plate 26a) or as a ground to embossed ornament. A much
coarser type, almost akin to granulation in appearance,
but produced by punches and not by application in the
strict sense, may be found on large decorative plate. Embossed figure scenes of high quality are not uncommon
on both church and domestic plate, the subjects being
appropriately chosen from well-balanced and lively compositions. The figures are rendered with great skill and
delicacy which compare favourably with the best embossed
work of any period, and the landscape and architectural
backgrounds are equally assured. Little is known of the
sources from which many of the compositions are derived
or of their executants: it may be that they were Dutch
workers who had been trained in the workshops of the
Van Vianens or others specializing in such work. English
painters and engravers of the period were little concerned
with any form of subject pictures, while a number of
similar embossed subjects have been conclusively or reas-
onably attributed to continental silversmiths.

A very large proportion of the plate made in this period
bears engraved decoration in the form of armorial bearings (plates 18c and 13a), inscriptions (plate 18c), or, less
frequently, decorative patterns of scrolled foliage (plate
17a), *chinoiseries* (plate 18d), or figure scenes. The shield
itself is generally plain, sometimes oval or shaped. It is
usually contained within some form of foliate ornament,
two crossed branches of palms or laurel leaves tied below
with a ribbon, or between two stylized ostrich feathers
which often reached exuberant size when the space allowed. Supporters, crests, mantling, and mottoes were
sometimes added to complete the blazon. An interesting
example of elaborate armorial engraving is provided by
a rose-water dish of 1672 belonging to St John's College,
Oxford, which is not only exceptional in its design and
quality, but signed (an extremely rare occurrence) by the
engraver L. King. On more restricted grounds a crest
alone sufficed, or the initials of the owner in Roman capi-

tals; for example, $*^s_w{}^*_A$ might stand for William and Anne Smith, husband and wife. On other pieces, the shield may contain an elaborate and often incomprehensible cypher or monogram of several letters, probably taken from pattern books.

On much plate, especially that belonging to churches, colleges, corporations, or other bodies, inscriptions commemorate the donor and the occasion of the gift. For the most part they are in English, except on that belonging to the colleges of Oxford and Cambridge, when they are often in Latin, and on rare occasions in Greek. Some examples (plates 11 and 18c) show that the formation of the letters and the use of abbreviations follow those on contemporary monumental inscriptions. The lettering is in non-cursive italic script rather than in Roman. The capital letters are often elaborately and decoratively looped and scrolled. The spacing, both of the whole inscription in relation to its ground, and of the letters and words to each other, is on the whole well balanced. Although the handling of the graver was generally bold and the incisions deep, there are some very unskilled scratchings. Some vessels have rather elaborate pictorial engravings: three tankards are known with small panels, depicting the burial of plague victims and the Great Fire of the following year. Another has a view of Pontefract Castle, dated 1680, and another is engraved all over with flowers very skilfully observed.

The gilding or parcel-gilding of domestic plate, except of ceremonial or presentation pieces, was infrequent. The use of solid gold was, to judge from the fact that only about a dozen pieces survive, only occasional.

PRINCIPAL ARTICLES OF DOMESTIC PLATE

Standing Cups and Covers. With the exception of a small number of specially designed cups, some of which will be described below, the principal pattern was the simple and stately vessel already noted (p. 117). The bowl is tub-shaped, similar to that of the so-called porringer (plate 13a) and surmounts a sturdy baluster stem on a flattish spreading foot (cf. plate 16d), whose shape was often repeated in the cover. The finial, mounted on a small pedestal, is either turned or takes the form of a figure, human or animal (plate 11). These standing cups are often gilt, and are devoid of ornament except matting or engraving. They seem to have been made for presentation to City companies, municipal corporations, or colleges, in whose possession the majority are still to be found (plate 11). They were made during the second half of the century and vary in height, including their covers (some of which have disappeared), from about eighteen to twenty-four inches.

The Royal Oak Cup, presented by Charles II to the Barber-Surgeons' Company in 1676, is a fanciful extravagance commemorating his hiding-place in the Boscobel Oak, and might be mistaken for a curious hybrid of the nineteenth century. Its gilt bowl and cover have outer casings embossed to represent oak leaves, and it stands on a trunk-like stem at the foot of which are snails and lizards, reminiscent of those on Germanic cups of earlier date. On either side of the embossed cartouche containing the commemorative inscription hang festoons of oak leaves, and suspended from the branches are four acorns which serve as bells. The cover, surmounted by an arched royal crown, gives it a height of almost seventeen inches.

Another ornate gilt cup, taller by six inches, was given to the Clothworkers' Company by Samuel Pepys in 1677 (plate 11). Beneath a plain band round the lip, the outer casing is pierced and embossed with acanthus leaves among which appear birds and sheep, and bands of acanthus are applied to the baluster stem. The urn-shaped finial is surmounted by the cast figure of a ram *couchant*, the emblem of the Company.

Two-Handled Cups and Covers. Although these are generally described as porringers, caudle cups, or posset cups, these terms have come to be associated with a particular form rather than to denote the beverage which they were intended to contain. All the vessels in this group show the same basic characteristics – a deep bowl with two opposed handles and, usually, a detachable cover. That they were used to contain a beverage is evident from their traditional names. The term porringer does not seem to be connected with the word porridge, but is a corruption of the earlier word potager, i.e. a container for potage or soup. Caudle is a warm gruel of wine flavoured with spices and sugar, and posset is a hot drink made from milk curdled with wine or ale and likewise flavoured with spices. While some small examples contain an amount which can be comfortably taken by one person, the largest ones hold as much as a gallon and measure fifteen inches across the handles. These presumably were meant to be passed from person to person at table as a loving-cup, or to be used like punch bowls or monteiths.

Two-handled cups survive in considerable numbers and can be classified into four types. The first, usually referred to as a caudle cup (plate 12b), is a gourd-shaped vessel beaten up from thinnish metal and embossed in the floral or auricular styles. The cover is domed and has a small horizontal flange, and the two handles are cast in many shapes, usually rather grotesque and uncomfortable to hold because of their smallness and the scrolls and knobs (fig. 25). The finials on the covers are usually balusters or something more elaborate; occasionally they take the form of a reel-shaped foot-handle which enables the cover to be used as a salver as well. Not a few cups of this form are plain, or decorated only with matted panels, and their handles are curved strips, plain or reeded.

The second type, generally called a porringer (plate 13a), is more substantial. The sides of its tub-shaped bowl taper slightly towards the foot and then curve sharply underneath to produce an almost flat bottom supported on a shallow moulded base. The removable cover is surrounded by a narrow flat flange and the central portion is stepped and slightly domed, rather like the cover of the common form of tankard (plates 18c and 18d). The finial is usually

turned in the form of a baluster, cast as a flower or burgeoning acanthus, sometimes open, sometimes closed, or
replaced by three cast feet shaped as scrolls (plate 13a) or
the heads of animals, so that the cover may be inverted
and used as a salver. In some cases a separate salver was
provided *en suite*. The greater size and the more elegant
shape of their cast scrolled handles make them more attractive and more comfortable to hold. Their decoration
takes a variety of forms, cut-card work, embossed acanthus
leaves, or engraved *chinoiseries*, with rope-moulding or
gadrooning. This form of two-handled cup is principally
confined to the seventies and eighties. A small gilt pair
in the Ashmolean Museum, hall-marked as early as 1664,
is ornamented in the French style with cut-card work,
rope-moulding, and handles in the form of coiled serpents.
Some much simpler examples, usually found without a
cover, have a plain bowl with a flattened base and no
foot; the two handles are scrolled from thickish wires.

The third type, of which the drum-shaped body has
vertical sides, stands on three decorated ball feet, recalling
the Scandinavian form of tankard (plate 19a). They are
generally of elaborate design and of fine workmanship,
the handles being very ornamental and the gilt drum
covered with a casing of embossed openwork. Between
seven and eight inches in height, they date from the late
sixties to the eighties. One belonging to the Goldsmiths'
Company and dated 1669 stands on three bun-and-claw
feet; the casing is pierced and embossed with scrolled
foliage amidst which are two phoenixes; the cover has a
similar casing. On another, dated 1685, in the Victoria
and Albert Museum, a turkey is embossed amongst the
foliage, and the casing is fitted between two moulded
bands. Its cast finial is in the shape of a phoenix rising
from the ashes and the three feet are also cast in the form
of birds.

The fourth type, which foreshadows the massive two-
handled cups and covers of the first half of the eighteenth
century, has a somewhat taller body with a rounded base

supported on a low-waisted stem and moulded foot (plate 13b). The handles are larger and of a simpler tapering line; the cover is domed in tiers. The ornament as well as the shape is clearly derived from France: applied cut-card work, bands of braided laurel leaves, graded acanthus husks or drops applied to the handles, and gadrooning. This form began to appear in the eighties and is matched by an analogous type of thinner metal which was common throughout the reign of William III; the decoration was principally provided by embossed vertical or spiral flutes on the lower part of the body and on the cover (plate 13b).

Wine Cups. Although English crystal drinking glasses came into common use after 1673, a few silver wine cups remain from this period. One of 1670, with its bucket-shaped bowl, trumpet stem, and a decoration of punched foliate patterns and matting, is a survival of a type made during the previous thirty years.

Beakers. The standard form of beaker continued to be made. Small plain beakers, about three or four inches in height, are not uncommon. At some Cambridge colleges they are called stoups. Some of the larger ones, about six inches in height, are embossed all over in the floral manner (plate 17d), while others have a surbase of acanthus leaves.

A bell-shaped beaker with a small reeded foot also occurs. An example, of gold, about three and a half inches in height, was made by George Garthorne in 1685; it is plain with armorial bearings. A plain beaker with two grotesque cast handles, about four inches in height, seems to be peculiar to Exeter College, Oxford. Large ornamental beakers are included in the later section on garnitures (p. 159).

Mugs. Several varieties of mugs with a single handle were made. One, which seldom occurs outside the plate of Wadham and Brasenose Colleges, Oxford, has a bulbous body with deep vertical reeded neck and a reeded loop or S-handle. A similar, though slightly larger, variation has an everted neck (plate 17b): on the example reproduced the lines are engraved as zig-zags, scarcely visible, by a hand found on several other vessels, which seems to derive from the coarser wriggle-work on pewter. A third variant, again slightly larger, has a small body with a shouldered bulge and a rather tall expanding neck. A fourth type, similar to the last, was commonly made in Scotland and is often called a thistle cup. A fifth type, like the second in outline, but with two hollow rings opposed at the neck (fig. 32), has already been mentioned; examples vary considerably in proportion and size, ranging from three to seven inches in height. They are commonly known as college cups from the fact that they are chiefly to be

Figure 32 – Ox-eye college cup

found among the plate of colleges at both Oxford and Cambridge, where they are given such names as 'tuns', 'plates', 'silver potts with ears', and 'ox-eye cups' (see above, p. 118). A large number were made after the Restoration and their production has continued sporadically up to the present day, either for presentation to the colleges where they are customarily used or as souvenirs.

Tumbler Cups. This simple cup was beaten up from a single circular sheet of metal so that the thickness at the rounded bottom provides sufficient weight to bring the vessel back to an upright position after it has been tilted over, even after its side is horizontal. Examples are usually between two and four inches in height and rather greater in diameter. By reason of their shape they offer little scope for decoration, except with the graver, although the sur-base is occasionally embossed with acanthus leaves (plate 17a). Examples from the seventeenth century are much less common than those from the eighteenth, and they continued to be made up to the present time; modern examples are more often spun than beaten.

Tankards. The shape of tankards developed in several ways in the second half of the century. The most common size holds a quart and is about seven inches in height: they vary in capacity from one to eight pints and in height from five to eleven inches; the plain drum tapers slightly towards the top and the side may be a little bowed. Round the base is a small moulding. The changes are principally on the cover: the slight projection of the flange opposite the handle is usually larger and is often serrated; the flattish central platform raised on a step becomes higher until by the end of the century it takes the form of a moulded dome of two or more stages (plate 18d). The thumb-pieces are usually twin cusps, double scrolls, or volutes (plates 19b and c); some are cast in the form of an animal, in allusion to a bearing on the arms, or for the sake of its decorative value alone. Among these are lions, *couchant* or *sejant*, and hedgehogs. More occa-sionally tankards are raised on three or four feet cast in animal form.

Most tankards of this period are plain, with only en-graved arms or inscriptions opposite the handle, though there are examples with elaborate engravings. In the seventies and eighties, the surbase is frequently embossed with a band of vertical acanthus leaves, and the cover with a rosette or whorl of the same. Cut-card work also appears in the same places – at the junction of the handle, or flanking a horizontal moulded band round the centre of the drum.

At York, Hull, and Newcastle, and sometimes in Lon-don, the Scandinavian type of tankard was made (plate 19a). Its tub-shaped body stands on three ball feet, often cast as pomegranates, and attached to the drum with cast scrolled leaves. The cover is rounded like the base of the drum and is almost flush with the side, with little or no projection, and a narrow bezel fits inside the rim of the body. The thumb-pieces are cast after earlier types or as double fruits.

Monteiths. The monteith is a variant of the punch bowl, from which it is distinguished by its scalloped rim. The first mention of this large vessel is made by the Oxford antiquarian, Anthony à Wood, in 1683: 'This yeare in the summer time came up a vessel or bason notched at the brim to let drinking glasses hang there by the foot, so that the body or drinking place might hang in the water to cool them. Such a bason was called a "Monteigh", from a fantastical Scott called "Monsieur Monteigh", who at that time, or a little before, wore the bottome of his cloake or coate so notched ᴜᴜᴜ.' It does not seem to have been a vessel for private domestic use and many of the examples known have always belonged to the corporate bodies which now possess them. The earliest examples, of 1666, belong to the Salters' Company. Their diameter is about thirteen inches, some have drop-handles on either side. They were made most frequently between about 1685 and 1705.

Wine Fountains. From among these large urns which were filled with wine for banquets, the gilt Coronation Fountain of 1660 in the Tower of London is not only the earliest but one of the finest. A niche in each side of the octagonal bowl contains a figure of Neptune or a sea nymph; the domed base is supported by four mermaids and the finial is a female figure holding snakes, perhaps a representation of Medusa.

Wine Cisterns. These massive vessels were likewise for use at banquets, and contained the bottles rather than the decanted wine; they are not unlike small baths standing on four heavy cast and chased feet with carrying handles at either end, often a drop-handle suspended from the mask of a lion, a heraldic beast, or a female bust. One of the most magnificent of these belongs to the Duke of

Rutland and was made in 1681; four feet in length and eighteen inches in height, it weighs no less than 3,000 ounces. Its body is bulged and embossed with large lobes, while the shoulders are decorated with acanthus leaves; the interior is engraved with the Rutland arms and the two handles hang each from a finely modelled peacock. A smaller example is shown in plate 24a.

Tea Pots. Tea was on sale in London at least two years before the Restoration, and by 1669 Rugge could write in his *Diurnal* that it was sold in almost every street in London, either in the leaf or as a drink. It was nevertheless very expensive and seems to have been brewed in the Chinese manner in porcelain pots, some examples of which are in silver mounts dating from about 1660.

The earliest known silver tea pot (Victoria and Albert Museum) was not made until 1670, and it will be shown below that this preceded the earliest coffee pot, for which it would now be undoubtedly mistaken were it not for the engraved inscription which makes it quite clear that it was made as a tea pot. Its body is a tall tapering cylinder with straight sides; the conical cover, surmounted by a small baluster finial, is hinged to the top of the loop handle, which is partly covered by leather; between the straight spout, which is set at right-angles to the handle, beginning about two-thirds of the way up the side, is a full contemporary blazon of arms and the inscription. Next in point of time seems to be a melon-shaped tea pot made by Charles Shelley, which on the evidence of the arms engraved on it was made before 1679; it has a wooden handle pinned into two silver sockets and a narrow recurving spout. It is certainly the earliest specimen of the shapes accepted for tea pots, and superficially resembles two gilt examples of about 1685, one in the Victoria and Albert Museum, and the other in the Ashmolean Museum, Oxford (plate 26a). The shape of their bodies seem to be based on the Chinese wine pot, although the scrolled handles, finials, and other decoration are of more local design; both are rather less than six inches in height and are divided into vertical panels which are matted. Some have spout-caps attached by chains.

Coffee Pots. Though Evelyn mentions the beverage in 1637, the first coffee-house of the long succession that were such important meeting-places does not seem to have been established before 1650. Oldys, the antiquarian, mentions that in 1652 a 'Mr Edwards, a Turkey merchant, brought from Smyrna to London one Pasqua Rosee, a Ragusan youth, who prepared this drink for him every morning. But the novelty therof drawing too much company to him, he allowed his said servant . . . to sell it publicly, and they set up the first coffee house in London, in St Michael's Alley in Cornhill. The sign was Pasqua Rosee's own head.'

Early examples are similar in shape to the tea pot of 1670 mentioned above, and presumably are copied from the similar metal vessels in which coffee is made in the Near Eastern manner. One in the Victoria and Albert Museum (1681) is over nine inches in height; its leather-covered handle is like that of a contemporary tankard; the straight spout is directly opposed; the conical cover is hinged and surmounted by a button finial. This is typical of the form made during the penultimate decades of the century and refined into more sophisticated shapes during the Queen Anne and early Georgian periods.

Chocolate Pots. Chocolate, too, was introduced during the Protectorate; and the fact that these two beverages were sold side by side would go far to explain the similarity in shape of the vessels used to contain them; in fact the only distinguishing feature is the second very small cover fitted to the top of the principal cover; into this was inserted the swizzle-stick (molionet) for stirring up the liquid into an evenly thick consistency. The earliest example was made by George Garthorne in 1685. An example of a later and rather unusual form, clearly deriving from France, made in 1695 by Pierre Harache, has a pear-shaped body, with a small short curved lip and a single turned wooden baluster handle at right-angles to it: it stands on three hooved feet; the cover which extends forward over the spout has a gadrooned edge, while the small swizzle-stick cover is surmounted by a baluster finial and swivels horizontally on a pin.

Plates and Dishes. While the greater number of plates and dishes were made of pewter or glazed earthenware, many services were made from silver. For example, Prince Rupert purchased five dozen plates from Alderman Backwell in 1670 and in 1680 Prince George of Denmark bought two dozen plates and the same number of trenchers; each of the former weighed 17–18 ounces, the latter 21 ounces, and they cost 5s. 8d. per ounce for silver and fashioning together. Pepys mentions that he owned two dozen and a half. Although the extant examples are neither numerous nor especially remarkable for their forms, there can be no doubt that they were widely used by the wealthier families. Since such utilitarian articles offered little scope for variations in decoration and design, those that are not completely plain are given gadrooned borders, or are engraved with more or less elaborate armorials, usually on the flange. Standing dishes, on the other hand, are more decorative. The series of standing dishes, after a considerable gap, starts again just before the Restoration with a new type, a plate raised on a trumpet foot with a plain centre and a flange embossed in the Dutch floral manner. These are sometimes directly associated with two-handled cups *en suite.* Flattish or saucer-shaped dishes are found in several varieties, on turned baluster stems with slightly domed bases, either plain, matted, or with gadrooned borders. A more elaborate pair (Ashmolean Museum), closely resembling those belonging to the Calverley toilet service, is embossed with four classical deities reclining in the clouds, within an oval border (plate 48a).

Ewers and Basins. The slow introduction of the fork did not oust the ewer and basin; they were used in toilet services and for decorative purposes. The most common form of ewer during this period is somewhat awkward and heavy in design, differing but little from those described in the previous chapter (fig. 28a). The body is squat with curved side and rounded bottom, the low stem rising from a domed foot; the lip is no more than a narrow eversion of the rim; the opposed handle is generally cast in the shape of a harp. Examples of this pattern are seldom gilt, and are remarkable for the relative lack of ornament, which may consist of a moulded band, a small quantity of cut-card work or gadrooning, and some engraving. The accompanying basins are similarly plain, although the engraving on a dish of 1685, perhaps by John Ruslen, is remarkable for its quality and for the fact that it is signed by L. King.

Near the end of the reign of James II, the French helmet-shaped ewer already foreshadowed (fig. 28a) was introduced into this country, and continued as the fundamental form until in the middle of the eighteenth century the manufacture of ewers was practically discontinued. The body resembles a deep circular, but occasionally oval, inverted helmet to which is attached a handle shaped like a harp, sometimes of exceedingly elaborate and skilful workmanship (fig. 31); the stem is turned and the foot moulded. The reproduction on plate 37 is from the Treby toilet set by Paul de Lamerie (Ashmolean Museum; 1724) which differs little from some of the best examples of about 1695 onwards.

Salt Cellars. 'Cellar' is a corruption of the obsolete word 'saler', and anglicization of the French '*salier*', salt box. It has already been explained that the large ceremonial standing-salt was no longer used domestically during the period under discussion, partly because its social importance had dwindled, and partly because it had been superseded by more convenient smaller forms, prototypes of which were examined in the previous chapter. Nevertheless, examples of ceremonial decorative salts from the late Stuart period do remain. The most notable group consists of twelve gilt salts kept in the Tower of London, which are believed to have been made for the coronation banquet of Charles II and to have been used subsequently on similar occasions. There are three types. The first closely resembles the earlier pattern of bell-salt (plate 40) standing on four feet in the form of lions *couchant*; the lower part of the body is embossed with a band of acanthus leaves above auricular embossing; a detachable cover is supported above the depression for the salt by three grotesque scrolled members and is surmounted by an equestrian figure of St George.

The second type, of which there are four, is about sixteen inches in height, and of the earlier waisted shape (plate 38); it is similarly embossed with acanthus leaves and surmounted by an almost identical cover. The salts from the third set, of 1660, are somewhat smaller, being ten inches in height, and take the form of a slightly waisted drum embossed with tulips and other flowers amid foliage. The Exeter salt, about eighteen inches in height, the last of this group, is of a completely different and more imposing character, being fashioned as a castle with a circular keep surmounted by a royal crown.

The Goldsmiths' Company possesses the famous Seymour Salt which was surrendered to them in 1693 by Thomas Seymour as a fine instead of undertaking the office of touch warden. Pepys records how he 'visited the Mayor, Mr Timbrell, our anchor-smith of Portsmouth, who showed us the present they have for the Queen (Catherine of Braganza), which is a Salt Sellar of silver, the walls of Christal, with four eagles and four greyhounds standing up at the top to bear up a dish; which indeed is one of the neatest pieces of plate I ever saw.'

The last of these great salts, made in 1698, may be conveniently mentioned here. It is the Eddystone Salt (City Museum, Plymouth), a model, seventeen inches in height, of the original lighthouse which was swept away by a storm in the following year. It is most ingeniously constructed; in the open upper gallery was placed the salt, while the lantern above is perforated for powdered sugar; the remainder of the structure consists of three detachable containers, one of which is also pierced for pepper.

Perhaps the most common of the various types of smaller salt was reel-shaped (fig. 29) with a shallow depression in the upper side, from which three scrolls rise to support a dish, or to serve as handles. Although some writers have conjectured that these scrolls supported napkins, and there are earlier confirmations of this, there seems to be no doubt on the evidence of the passage quoted above from Pepys' *Diary* as well as from contemporary Netherlandish still-life paintings, that after the Restoration they were in fact used to support plates and dishes. Variations of this elevation are found on square and octagonal plans, with four scrolls. More usually the salts are symmetrical and plain; they are often decorated with moulding, cabling, or embossed gadrooning at the foot, centre, top, or round the depression.

The second main type is the trencher salt, usually circular and little more than an inch in height and about three inches across. They are of polygonal section, as well as oblong with cut corners; their sides are generally moulded or embossed into a number of lobes.

Castors. In previous chapters it has been remarked (pp. 105, 124) that pepper castors were attached to the larger salts, the most common example being the small perforated balls which surmount the bell-salts. With the Restoration independent castors appear in greater numbers, whether singly or in sets of three or more. The earliest extant specimens are two of about 1670, perhaps a pair, belonging to Queen's College, Oxford; they are about five inches in height. Characteristic features are the vertical sides, sometimes fluted, the bayonet joint to fasten the detachable cover, and the simple foliate and geometrical piercings of the cover. The ornament and size may vary from specimen to specimen, but otherwise the example reproduced (plate 43a) is typical for the period.

Sweetmeat Dishes. Often referred to as strawberry

dishes, few late-seventeenth-century examples are known; the shallow bowls, variously decorated, are usually flanked by two handles. One, dating probably from about 1665, is embossed in the centre with a swan, round which radiate fluted segments; its handles are in the form of coiled serpents. Another, standing on three ball feet, has its segments alternately plain and embossed with floral designs, and the two cast handles terminate in herons' heads. A third, rather greater in diameter, is without handles; the flattish dish is divided by ribs into about thirty segments and anticipates the many similar dishes of the early eighteenth century.

Sugar Boxes or Sweetmeat Boxes. These small caskets – their precise purpose does not seem to be beyond doubt – are not common. They are shallow oval boxes standing on four feet with a hinged and hasped cover, in the centre of which is usually a handle. An example of 1664, belonging to the Ironmongers' Company, stands on volute feet applied to cut-card cinquefoils; the body of the box is considerably bulged and its low cover domed in three tiers; the handle is in the form of a coiled serpent mounted on a pattern of cut-card work. The sides and cover of an example of 1670 are embossed, while it is otherwise very similar to the earlier specimen. The cover of a third casket, of 1670 (Christ Church, Oxford) has a broad flange, and the whole is plain except for an engraved coat-of-arms. Another of 1683 (Victoria and Albert Museum) has a bulged body and domed cover; both are engraved all over with *chinoiseries*.

Flat plate. Occasionally sets of apostle spoons and seal-top spoons were made after the Restoration, but they show no marked deviations from the forms of those made earlier in the century. The so-called Puritan spoon seems to be the starting-point for more decorative developments. The plain square end was hammered out into a thin leaf-shaped blade which is most commonly notched on either side of the pointed end to form a simple trefoil (plate 60f); such spoons are therefore described as 'trefid' (or 'trifid'), a more appropriate name than '*pied-de-biche*' (hind's foot) which has been used by earlier writers. The bowl is an almost symmetrical oval with a level rim, and a longish fluted tapering wedge (rat-tail) runs from the handle along the back of the bowl to strengthen the junction of the two parts (plate 6og). Generally they are plain, sometimes gilt or engraved with running foliage (plate 6of); on more ornamental varieties the back of the bowl and the upper end of the stem and trefid are stamped or cast and chased with delicate designs of foliate scrolls in low relief. The trefid is often engraved with a crest or more commonly with initials. There seem to be two principal sizes, the smaller about $6\frac{1}{2}$ inches long, the larger from $7\frac{1}{2}$ to $8\frac{1}{2}$ inches; the larger weigh about $1\frac{1}{2}$ ounces, the smaller about one ounce.

Larger trefid spoons with the same characteristics, but a much longer stem, are found; sometimes half the bowl is pierced with small holes so that they can be used for straining. Smaller examples, of the same pattern as the dessert spoon, are about three or four inches long.

The silver table fork now began to come slowly into common use, although the English lagged far behind the French and Italians in their adoption of this utensil. The stem of the fork was made in imitation of that of the spoon. The three prongs were curved, unlike the two prongs of the sucket fork; at Cotehele is a set of a dozen such forks made in 1667, which seem to be the earliest now extant. In 1670 Prince Rupert purchased two dozen, probably of this pattern, at 5s. 8d. the ounce, to which was added a charge of 2s. 6d. for the fashioning of each (cf. plate 61d). The four-pronged fork, with which we are most familiar today, was seldom made at this time and the earliest example dates from 1674. Many people still carried their own cutlery when they travelled, in a small case (*étui*) fitted with a knife, fork, and spoon, usually rather smaller, often much smaller, than the normal table cutlery. An example of 1693 contains a steel knife and two-pronged steel fork, each with a silver handle in the form of a cartridge case, while the spoon follows the trefid form. The case was generally made of black or green shagreen decorated with silver, or of silver openwork.

Canteens. Typical of the canteens that were used on military service is an example of about 1690 (Victoria and Albert Museum). A stout leather case contains two plain oval dishes, two round bowls, as well as a small box divided into two compartments for salt and pepper; in other sets occur a beaker, knife, fork, and spoon, toothpicks, marrow-scoops, corkscrews, nutmeg-graters, and other items.

Candlesticks. More domestic candlesticks remain from the later Stuart period than from all the previous periods combined. For the most part they are built up of hammered sheet metal, but after the eighties cast patterns are common. They are generally found in pairs and are seldom gilt. The pricket seems to have been almost entirely confined to church candlesticks. The architectural form of the single fluted Doric column (plate 56a) was well suited to its essential requirements; there is usually a broad platform round the socket; the column is commonly mounted on a high plinth, waisted below and rising from a large foot of square, octagonal, or circular shape, whose width was as much as two-thirds of the height of the whole to give it stability. The hand guard so prominent before (fig. 30) has become rudimentary, and has disappeared in the types to be described next.

Many candlesticks are considerably more elaborate, being built up with variously ornamented cast or embossed members ending in a short section of clustered column to contain the socket. Two unusual kinds may be mentioned; the first, dated 1673(?), stands on four feet embossed as scallop shells, a motif which is repeated elsewhere on the stem between cast scrolled members that support a clustered column (plate 56b). The second, more properly described as a candelabrum of three branches, is unmarked, but is thought to date from about 1680. The stem takes the form of a draped female figure standing on a tripod base and supporting above her head the three branches, which are constructed from continuous strips of acanthus leaves soldered together, an attractive and unusual feature.

The later form of cast candlestick with its baluster stem is found from about 1680 onwards and is the forerunner of the type found in a less severe form during the Queen Anne period (fig. 33). It has affinities with the bobbin-

Figure 33 – Candlestick

turning on furniture at this time, particularly in the reel-shaped socket.

Snuffers. This requisite, which served either to trim the wick of the candle or to extinguish its flame, resembles a pair of scissors; to the longer blade is soldered a small box, open on the side opposed to the shorter blade, into which the dead wick is gathered. It is usually held vertically in a stand on a foot of rectangular shape or later laid flat on a dish with a handle fixed midway along one of the sides.

Taper sticks. Examples do not occur in silver until the later part of the period and are generally miniature candlesticks. Their purpose was to hold the taper for melting sealing-wax, and they are therefore often found in conjunction with standishes (see below), especially during the eighteenth century.

Wax Jacks. The wax jack, an analogous device, is a simple framework supporting a horizontal reel which revolves to feed a length of taper up through a central nozzle. Examples of brass are much more common than those of silver and the details of their construction vary considerably. A series of examples principally of the eighteenth century may be seen in the Victoria and Albert Museum.

Sconces. That silver wall sconces were widely used during the later Stuart period is to be assumed rather from references to them than from the small number of extant specimens. The simplest consist of a flat vertical plate which acts as the reflector for a candle fixed before it in a socket at the end of a scrolled branch. This panel was usually in the form of a plain oval tablet, but sometimes engraved with arms or a cypher, or embossed, while the shaped border might be embossed with flowers and foliage, acanthus leaves, or floral swags with cherubs' heads.

In another example a mirror framed in silver serves as the reflector; on others Biblical or mythological scenes are embossed in low relief; sometimes the reflector was replaced by a richly decorated console. The more usual form of branch may be varied by one representing a human arm in whose hand is held the socket, or by a socket fixed in a bowed tray below the reflector.

Chandeliers. They were never extensively used, but in Hampton Court may be seen a very fine example with twelve branches which was made by George Garthorne in the late nineties.

Inkstands. Until the beginning of the nineteenth century an inkstand was usually called a standish. The so-called Treasury inkstand is an oblong rectangular box with two covers hinged back to back along the spine, to which was attached a loop handle. An example of 1681 stands on four ball feet, and their ornament is usually limited to mouldings, cut-card work, or heraldic engraving. One lid covers three divisions, for the ink-bottle, the sand which was sprinkled on the ink to dry it, and the wafers; below the other lid a long compartment held the quill-pens. A similar arrangement of compartments is sometimes covered by a single lid.

Penners. The penner was a convenient portable writing apparatus, presumably derived from similar instruments used by itinerant scribes in the Near East. Two similar specimens in the Ashmolean Museum can be ascribed to the eighties from the evidence of the arms on one and the form of the makers' punches. Much alike, each consists of a bell-shaped inkpot, filled with a rag impregnated with ink; into the pen is screwed the end of a cluster of three hollow columns, each to hold a short quill with a slip-on cap bearing an oval disc on which is engraved a seal; when in use the column is screwed into the base of the inkpot so that this may be conveniently held upright in the free hand.

Furniture. In the dressing-room of the Countess of Arlington at Goring House, Evelyn noted 'silver jars and vases, cabinets, and other so rich furniture as I had seldom seene', and in the house of the Duchess of Portsmouth, 'massy pieces of plate, whole tables and stands of incredible value', and 'great vases of wrought plate, tables, stands, chimney furniture, sconces, branches, braseras, etc., all of massive silver, and out of number'. But of all this wealth not many examples remain today. In the state apartments at Windsor Castle stand two silver tables. Such furniture is not, as might appear from these descriptions, of solid metal, but of wood covered all over with plates of silver embossed with a profusion of foliage and other motifs, all of the finest workmanship. Fire-irons, andirons, and braziers, were, on the other hand, made of iron because they are to be exposed directly to the flames, but have handles and much prominent and elaborate ornament in solid silver. Good examples may be seen at Ham House, Knole, Windsor, and elsewhere.

Although no examples survive from this period, Pepys

records that in 1669 Captain Beckford presented him with a noble silver warming pan 'which I am doubtful to take or no'.

Garniture. Vases, jars, and beakers, usually made in pairs or in sets of three, were much used in the decoration of chimney pieces in very large houses. Their shapes were derived from Chinese porcelain jars, though perhaps more immediately from Dutch earthenware copies of the Chinese vessels. Although they stand from about twelve to eighteen inches in height and look to be made of massive plate, they are in fact surprisingly light in weight. Their ornament, splendid in design and execution, is usually of French inspiration, with embossed acanthus *rinceaux*, ovolos, entwined ribbons, *putti*, or engraved *chinoiseries*. Some very fine examples of 1675 may be seen in the Victoria and Albert Museum, but the greater number have remained in the possession of the descendants of their original owners, at Welbeck, Belvoir, Knole, and elsewhere.

Toilet Sets. Evelyn wrote that he saw 'her Majesty's rich toylet in her dressing roome, being all of massie gold, presented to her by the King, valued at 4,000 l', as well as the Queen's 'great looking glasse and toilet of beaten and massive gold at Hampton Court'. A superb French toilet set, known as the Lennoxlove, in the Royal Scottish Museum, Edinburgh, was made in 1674 and belonged to the Duchess of Richmond and Lennox.

The best known English toilet set of this period is the Calverley set of 1683 in the Victoria and Albert Museum, which comprises thirteen pieces: an oblong mirror decorated at the top with an embossed figure scene in a roundel; a pair of footed circular salvers whose centres are embossed with four classical deities reclining among clouds; an oblong casket on scrolled feet; two large and two small circular caskets; two covered bowls; a pair of small covered vases; and finally a pin-cushion shaped as a truncated pyramid on scrolled feet. Each of the last pieces is embossed with exquisitely conceived patterns of scrolled acanthus foliage, flowers, and fruit, amongst which *putti* play.

The contents of each set differ in detail as well as in design, and include pots for pomatum, glue, patches, powder, unguents, cosmetics, comb boxes, pin cushions, salvers, brushes, bells and ewers, candlesticks, snuffers, and, most outstanding, a mirror.

Toys. All the articles described were reproduced in miniature as children's toys, often by makers who specialized in such things. The earliest belong to the beginning of this period both in date and in the style of the articles which they reproduce. They are widely assorted in their variety, ranging from furniture and fire-irons on the one hand to spoons and forks on the other, but their size relative to each other does not accurately reflect the difference in the size of the real objects. Their decoration and workmanship, while reproducing the essential elements of the object and its ornament, was necessarily rather clumsy on account of the difficulties of soldering and embossing such small things.

King John's Cup. XIV century. H 15 ins

I

a. Pastoral Staff. About 1370.
D of crook 7½ ins

b. Pastoral Staff. About 1487–1501.
D of crook 5 ins

a. Detail of volute from plate 2*b*

b. Detail of niches from plate 2*a*

3

a. Mazer. Later xv century. D 8 ins

b. Studley Bowl. xiv century. H 5½ ins

4

Election Cup. About 1554. H 17¼ ins

5

Font Cup. 1515. H 7¾ ins

6

Two-handled Cup. 1533. H 7¼ ins

Bowes Cup. 1554. H 19½ ins

8

Cup and Cover. 1569. Bunch of Grapes. H 21 ins

9

Steeple Cup. 1613. H 23 ins

Pepys Cup. About 1677. H 23 ins

11

a. Two-handled Cup and Cover. 1657. A.M. H 6 ins

b. Two-handled Cup and Cover. 1664. I.W. H 6¼ ins

12

a. Two-handled Cup and Cover. 1675. T.M. H 5¼ ins

b. Two-handled Cup. 1699. Joseph Ward. H 7¼ ins

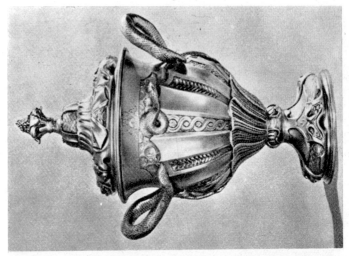

b. Two-handled Cup and Cover. 1737.
Paul de Lamerie. H 15 ins

a. Two-handled Cup and Cover. 1730. Paul de Lamerie. H 7 ins

14

a. Two-handled Cup and Cover. 1785.
Daniel Smith and Robert Sharp. H 18 ins

b. Brighton Cup. 1805. John Emes.
H 17¾ ins

15

a. Wine Cup. 1587. I.N. H 5¼ ins

b. Wine Cup. 1603. Three
Bells. H 5 ins

c. Wine Cup. 1616. H.S.
H 7¼ ins

d. Wine Cup. 1637. W.C. H 6¼ ins

a. Tumbler Cup. York, 1680.
George Gibson. H 2¼ ins

b. Mug. 1692. I.C. H 4¾ ins

c. Beaker. Norwich, about 1595.
Orb and Cross. H 7 ins

d. Beaker. 1664. S.R. H 5 ins

a. Tankard. 1571. Dove. H 6¼ ins   *b*. Tankard. 1653. A.F. H 6¼ ins

c. Tankard. 1679. T.C. H 7¼ ins   *d*. Tankard. 1683. Anthony Nelme. H 6¼ ins

a. Tankard. Hull, about 1689.
Thomas Hebden. H 8 ins

b. Tankard. 1703.
Samuel Wastell. H 8 ins

c. Tankard. 1717.
Humphrey Payne. H 9½ ins

d. Tankard. 1772. Louisa Courtauld
and George Cowles. H 8 ins

Flagon. 1616. E.L. H 12¾ ins

Flagon. 1598. I.D. h 13½ ins

a. Monteith. 1700. Francis Garthorne. D 12¼ ins

b. Punch Bowl. 1735. John White. D 12 ins

22

a. Punch Bowl (George Boothby) and Ladle (William Fordham). 1727.
D 15 ins

b. Punch Bowl and Ladle. 1814. Paul Storr. D 12½ ins

a. Wine Cistern. 1694.
George Garthorne. H 13 ins

b. Wine Cistern. 1697.
Pierre Harache. H 7 ins

24

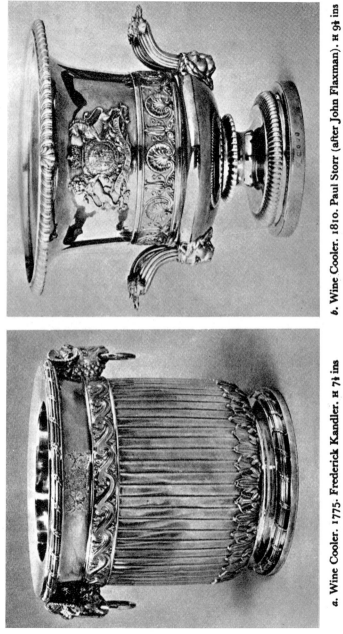

b. Wine Cooler. 1810. Paul Storr (after John Flaxman). H 9¼ ins

a. Wine Cooler. 1775. Frederick Kandler. H 7½ ins

25

a. Tea Pot. About 1685. Benjamin Pyne. H 5¼ ins

b. Tea Pot. 1718. James Seabrook. H 6 ins

a. Tea Pot. 1735. Paul de Lamerie. H 5¼ ins

b. Tea Pot. 1785. Daniel Smith and Robert Sharp. H 5 ins

27

Coffee Pot. 1702. William Lukin. H 10 ins

Coffee Pot. About 1735. Charles Kandler. H 8¼ ins

a. Jug. 1718. Thomas Parr. H 3½ ins

b. Jug. 1740. William Gwillim.
H 3½ ins

c. Jug. 1750. John Pollock. H 3¾ ins

d. Jug. 1785. Robert Hennell.
H 7½ ins

a. Tea Canister. 1759. William Shaw & William Priest. H 5 ins

b. Tea Canister. 1761. A.S. H 5 ins

c. Bowl and Tea Canisters. 1752. Samuel Taylor. H 5⅜ ins and 5¼ ins

Tea Kettle and Stand. 1727–37. Charles Kandler. H 13¼ ins

a. Basin. 1556. M. D 17½ ins

b. Basin. 1605. W.I. D 18¼ ins

Parker Ewer. 1545. Maiden's Head. H 8¼ ins

Henslowe Ewer. 1562. H 8½ ins

35

Ewer. 1617. I. V. H 13¾ ins

36

Ewer. 1724. Paul de Lamerie. H 8¼ ins

Warden Hill's Salt. About 1490. H 19½ ins

Gibbon Salt. 1576. Three trefoils. H 12 ins

Bell Salt. 1613. I.M. ʜ 10 ins

Pedestal Salt. About 1610. ? TY. H 10 ins

41

a. Salt Cellar. 1712.
Paul de Lamerie. D 2¾ ins

b. Salt Cellar. 1726.
Anne Tanqueray. D 3¼ ins

c. Salt Cellar. 1737.
Paul de Lamerie. D 3 ins

d. Salt Cellar. 1770.
D. & R. Hennell. H 1⅞ ins

e. Salt Cellar. 1799.
John Wren. H 2¼ ins

f. Salt Cellar. 1805.
Robert Garrard. D 3¼ ins

a. Castor. 1683.
Francis Garthorne. H 5¼ ins

b. Castor. 1703.
Richard Syng. H 7¼ ins

c. Set of three Castors and Stand. 1735.
Paul de Lamerie. H 8 ins

a. Soup Tureen. 1723. Paul de Lamerie. W 11 ins

b. Soup Tureen. 1754. Peter Archambo & Peter Meure. H 11 ins

a. Sauce Tureen. 1778. Carter, Smith & Sharp. H 5 ins

b. Sauce Tureen. 1819. Paul Storr. H 7⅛ ins

45

a. Sauce Boat. 1730. H 3 ins

b. Sauce Boat. 1764. V$_\text{L}^\text{I}$W L 7¾ ins

Centre Piece. 1811. Paul Storr (for Rundells). H 21¾ ins

47

b. Salver. 1724. Paul de Lamerie. w 5 ins

a. Salver. 1686. W.I. D 9 ins

b. Salver. 1753. William Peaston. D 12¼ ins

a. Salver. 1750. Paul de Lamerie. D 9¼ ins

49

a. Fruit Dish. 1649. E.S. D 10¼ ins

b. Tray. 1799. ? Thomas Robins. L 23¼ ins

a. Fruit Dish. 1734. Paul de Lamerie. L 8¼ ins

b. Tray. Dublin, 1705. Joseph Walker. D 17 ins

a. Sugar Bowl. 1728. Samuel Laundry. D 5¾ ins

b. Sugar Vase. 1805. Digby Scott & Benjamin Smith. H 6¾ ins

Sugar Vase. 1810. Benjamin & James Smith. H 8 ins

a. Basket. 1731. Paul de Lamerie. L 14¾ ins

b. Basket. 1744. Paul de Lamerie. L 15 ins

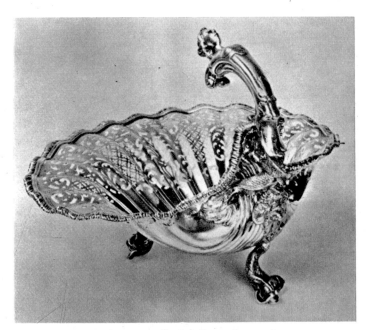

a. Basket. 1747. Paul de Lamerie. L 14 ins

b. Basket. 1783. Charles Aldridge & Henry Green. L 17¼ ins

55

a. Candlestick. 1673. I.B. H 10¾ ins   *b*. Candlestick. 1673. T.D. H 10 ins

c. Candlestick. 1715. John Broake.
H 6¾ ins

d. Candlestick. 1700–2. Joseph Bird.
H 9¼ ins

56

a. Candlestick. 1729. James Gould.
H 6½ ins

b. Candlestick. 1741. John Jacob.
H 9½ ins

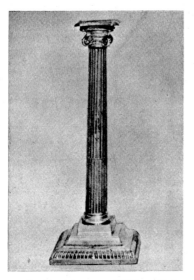

c. Candlestick. 1770. William Abdy.
H 13 ins

d. Candlestick. Sheffield, 1791.
Maker's mark overpunched with
that of William Robertson of
Edinburgh. H 12 ins

57

Candelabrum. 1816. Benjamin Smith. H 57 ins

Candelabrum. 1823. Paul Storr. H 29 ins

a. Apostle Spoon (St John). 1504. A plant. L 7¼ ins – *b*. Apostle Spoon (St Simon). 1555. I.F. L 7¼ ins – *c*. Apostle Spoon (St Jude). 1601. C enclosing W. L 7 ins – *d*. Seal Top Spoon. 1635. E.H. L 7 ins

e. Puritan Spoon. 1669. Lawrence Coles. L 7¼ ins – *f*. Engraved Trifid Spoon. 1695. Indistinct mark. L 6¼ ins – *g*. Trifid Spoon with Lace ornament. 1691. T.Z. L 7¼ ins – *h*. Pointed end with Lace pattern. Provincial, about 1695. R.S. L 8¼ ins

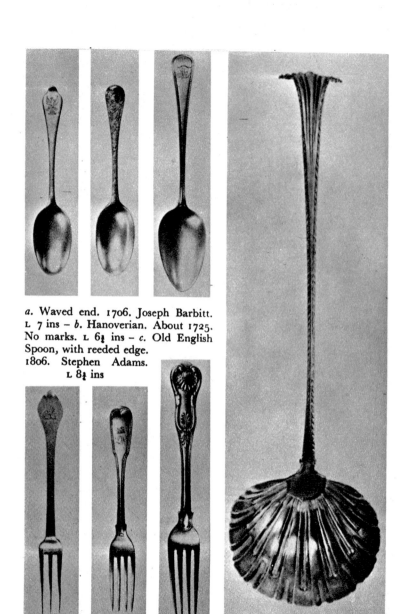

a. Waved end. 1706. Joseph Barbitt.
L 7 ins – *b.* Hanoverian. About 1725.
No marks. L 6¾ ins – *c.* Old English
Spoon, with reeded edge.
1806. Stephen Adams.
L 8¼ ins

d. Three-pronged Trifid Fork. 1689. I.C. L 5¼ ins – *e.* Four-pronged Reeded
Fiddle pattern Fork. 1810. Eley, Fearn & Chawner. L 6¼ ins –*f.* Four-pronged
King's pattern Fork. 1837. John & Henry Lias. L 8 ins – *g.* Ladle. 1769.
T. Evans. L 13¼ ins

61

a. Inkstand. 1735. Paul de Lamerie. L 12½ ins

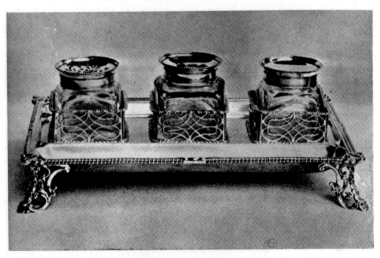

b. Inkstand. 1773. AF. L 10 ins

a. Dish Ring. Dublin, about 1770. D 8 ins

b. Wine Coaster. 1814. Paul Storr. H 5¾ ins

63

Queen's Cup. 1953. R. Y. Goodden. H 15 ins

CHAPTER SIX

1697–1719: The Britannia Standard:
'William and Mary' and 'Queen Anne' Styles

THIS chapter opens towards the middle of the reign of William III (1695–1702) with the introduction of the 'new sterling' or 'Britannia' standard, embraces the reign of Queen Anne (1702–14), and ends in 1719 during the reign of George I (1714–27) with the reversion to the 'old standard'.

The circumstances which led the government to raise the standard of silver alloy used in the manufacture of plate may be briefly recounted. In 1560 Sir Thomas Gresham recommended that the debased coinage be restored to the sterling standard, which was maintained until the *Coinage Act* of 1920. This equality was not a matter of principle but one of convenience which permitted the masters of the mint to convert bullion and plate into silver coins without the intermediate processes of refining and alloying to another standard of fineness. On the other hand it equally enabled silversmiths to reverse the process and fashion melted coins directly into articles of plate of the standard required for their assay. After the Restoration the demand for plate increased and became too great to be met by the amount of bullion available, and the shortage would not allow an unlimited manufacture of plate as well as the minting of enough coins to meet the growing need for more money in circulation. This situation gave rise to more general recourse to the running cashes and credit systems of the goldsmith bankers, so that whereas the smaller merchants and tradesmen had formerly been content to keep their capital in coins on their own premises, it was at this time more convenient, and safer, to deposit it with a goldsmith who not only would guarantee its safe custody but also pay interest at a high rate. This system of credit had also the effect of restraining the increase of coinage in circulation.

Manufacturing goldsmiths were unable to satisfy their clients' orders from bullion purchased in the normal way of trade and were, therefore, glad to accept small parcels of metal from other sources, such as melted plate or coins already in the country or newly imported bullion. Fresh encouragement was given in this way to the practice of coin clipping. Confidence in the coinage dropped and some coins were returned to the mint light by as much as a fifth of their proper weight. In these circumstances an obvious way to prevent the easy conversion of coins into plate without greatly affecting the administration of the mint, was to require the amount of pure silver in each pound (Troy) to be increased by 8 dwt, viz. from 925 to 958 parts fine per thousand.

The Act for encouraging the bringing in of wrought plate to be coined came into force on 25 March 1697, after which date

no goldsmith, silversmith, or other person whatsoever, shall work or make or cause to be wrought or made any silver vessel or manufacture of silver, less in fineness than that of 11 oz 10 dwt of fine silver in every pound Troy.

All the marks were changed so that the two standards could easily be distinguished:

the worker's mark to be expressed by the two first letters of his surname, the marks of the mystery or craft of the Goldsmiths, which, instead of the Leopard's Head and the Lion, shall for this plate be the figure of a woman, commonly called *Britannia* and the figure of a *lion's head erased*, and a distinct variable mark to be used by the warden of the said mystery, to denote the year in which such plate is made.

While recognition of the Company's marks is not difficult, even when considerably rubbed, or, as on the stems of spoons, distorted, it is sometimes hard to distinguish between those of the makers. For example Jackson lists no less than nine marks having the letters CO with various devices and outlines, of which some are so alike as to lead to confusion. On the other hand, the records of the Company enable most marks after 1697 to be ascribed with certainty to definite makers. Some scanty biographical details are now known, such as their addresses, and the dates of their admission to the Company.

The Act thus introduced a completely new series of marks in order that the new and old standards could be readily distinguished. But it was found that no reference had been made to the provincial and Irish assay offices. 'Whereas', to quote from the preamble of the Britannia Standard (Provincial Offices) Act of 1700

the goldsmiths, silversmiths and plateworkers of this Kingdom remote from London are under great difficulties and hardships in the exercise of their trade for want of assayers in convenient places to assay and touch their wrought plate ...

it was enacted that a company of goldsmiths be incorporated at York, Exeter, Bristol, Chester, and Norwich, cities where mints had recently been established to recoin the silver money of the kingdom. Each company, consisting of the makers resident in the respective cities, was authorized to elect two wardens annually, each being

... an able and skillful man experienced in assaying of gold and silver ... from whom it shall be lawful to detain eight grains only from every pound troy of silver [that] he shall assay, four grains whereof shall be put into the box of dyett, and the other four grains shall be allowed him towards his waste and spillings in making the said assays.

The diet-boxes were to be locked with three different locks and their respective keys kept by the wardens and assayer of each company. These diet-boxes ought to have been taken annually to the mint in the Tower of London, if the Lord Chancellor or Keeper of the Great Seal of England so required, for the diet to be tried as the 'pyx of the coin of this kingdom is tried'. The diet-box of the Chester Company, for example, was sent to London in 1707, though in 1773 the Assay Master from Chester said in evidence before a Parliamentary Committee that in his time the diet had never been required.

This Act further provided that all plate, 'except such things as by reason of their smallness are not capable of receiving a touch', manufactured after 29 September 1701, shall be punched with marks similar to those used in London, but with the addition of the arms of the city to denote the goodness of the work.

Bristol seems never to have taken advantage of its privilege, and the Norwich office hardly continued beyond 1701. Newcastle upon Tyne, however, was not mentioned although an assay office had operated there regularly since 1658. The petition of its goldsmiths that they were in 'danger of losing the greatest part of their trade, which chiefly consists of plate bespoke to be wrought up in a short time, and they cannot have it returned from York in less than a fortnight's time', led to the statutory establishment of the Newcastle Assay Office in 1702.

None of these three Acts applied to Irish assay offices where the Britannia standard has never been used at any time, nor to those of Scotland, because the Act of Union did not take effect until 1707. The Act of 1719 (see p. 184 below), passed after the Union, made the standard optional in Scotland.

Opinions differed in the craft about the working qualities of metal of the new standard, as compared with those of the old. Some thought that the old standard was a better medium, and that its greater hardness gave the finished articles a longer life. As soon as the urgency for restricting manufacture to safeguard the mint had passed, a Bill was drafted for reducing the standard of wrought Silver Plate, and laying a duty thereon. But the following broadsheet put forward arguments for retaining the new standard, and at the same time, against a proposed tax on plate.

THE CASE

OF THE WORKING GOLDSMITHS

In relation to a Bill *now depending in the Honourable* House of Commons, *for reducing the Standard of* Wrought Silver Plate, *and laying a Duty thereon.*

I. IT must be acknowledged by all who are Workers of Silver Plate, that the New Standard of 11 *oz* 10 *dwt* is of much finer Colour, and better adapted for curious Work, than the Old Standard of 11 *oz* 2 *dwt* which will not stand the Fire to receive proper ornaments; so that Foreign Courts (where a coarser Alloy is used) give frequent commissions for their most valuable plate to be made in *London,* to the great Profit of this Kingdom. But should the Standard be altered, as by the Bill is intended, it would be impossible for the finest Artist, to finish so compleat a Work in Silver of the Old Standard, as it is now performed in the New Standard. Besides that, there are some instances where Plate of the Old Standard will require more Silver than the same piece of Plate, were it made of the New Standard.

II. THAT the laying a Duty will ruin the Goldsmith's Trade is apparent: for where a Duty is laid on any Manufacture, the Consumption of which is not absolutely necessary, the Consequence must be the Sinking or Destroying that Trade; because every Person is at liberty to use or refuse it. And if 6d *per* oz be laid on Plate, the Manufacturer must, for all weighty Plate, pay as much, or more, than he receives for the Fashion; (besides the Loss to the Buyer, at every time of exchanging such Plate). And it must be further observed, that the Old Standard, with the Duty, will be 3d *per* Ounce dearer than the New Standard now is; whereby so great decrease will be made in the Trade, that not only the Duty will fall short of what is expected from it, but many numerous Families will be deprived of their Subsistance.

III. THAT the Liberty given to Officers for searching, as well in the Night as in the Day, will be very burdensome to the Subjects, and be attended with many ill Consequences; for that the Goods of a Goldsmith being Valuable, of small Bulk, and the Property easily to be altered, evil disposed Persons may be tempted by such an Opportunity to personate Officers, and not only rob the Goldsmiths of their own Plate, Jewels and Cash, but that also of Noblemen and Gentlemen intrusted with them, whose Plate will likewise be liable to Seizure, as well for the Duties in Arrear, as also for the Penalties incur'd by the Workmen; even tho' it should happen through the Carelessness or Design of their Servants, who will have it in their Power to ruin their Masters, and make all the Plate in their Shops liable to Seizure, whosoever are the owners thereof.

IV. THAT the business of the Workmen generally require Dispatch, to get their Work to *Goldsmiths-Hall* to be Assayed and Mark'd; but if this Bill pass, which obliges them to keep it — Hours to be Surveyed, it will often happen that they will be hindred from getting their Plate mark'd till next Hall-Day; wherby they will lose the Benefit of Fairs, and other Sales, to the ruin of their Families. And their Plate also, by lying some Hours exposed in an open Shop, will be liable to be stolen or imbezell'd; whereas, now, so soon as finish'd, the Worker locks it up under his own Custody.

V. THAT by this Bill a Duty being laid on all small Plate (capable of bearing a Mark) amongst which Snuff Boxes, Watch Cases, Sword Hilts, Shoe Buckles, and other small Toys are supposed to be included, the Workers whereof chiefly live in Lodgings, and work in Garrets, in the utmost Skirts of the Town; and by which some Thousands of Families are maintained (should this Bill pass) will find very few, or none, that will enter them; because of the great Disturbance which will be given to their Landlord, by the Officers coming to survey their Work, especially in the Night-time. Besides, the Danger of such Officers being personated by Rogues, who never stick to make Use of any Opportunity to perfect their wicked designs.

VI. THAT should the Manufacturing of Silver decay in this Kingdom (as certainly it will, should this Bill pass) the Government will be deprived of those Advantages receiv'd by wrought Plate; which it hath formerly experienced when *Bullion* was wanting.

VII. THAT granting (as some People Alledge) Plate is unnecessary, and an Excess, Whether it is not more to the Advantage of the Government, to allow of an Excess in Plate, which will be always in the possession of the Subjects of the Kingdom; and consequently may be, upon any Exergency, of greater Use to the Public Service, than to permit the Use of any Foreign Trifles, which export our *Bullion*, and are of no real Worth or value.

All which is humbly submitted to the Consideration of this most Honourable House

In deference to the arguments put forward by both sides, a compromise was reached in the *Wrought Plate Act*, 1719:

Whereas it is found by experience, that the SILVER vessels, plate and manufacture of silver, which were made according to the old standard of 11 oz 2 dwt of fine silver ... are more serviceable and durable than [those] which have been made according to [new standard]; be it therefore enacted ... that the said old standard ... made after 1st June, 1720, shall be restored, revived, and take place instead of the said new standard...

The Act provides that no goldsmith shall be obliged to work according to the new standard or be restrained from working in the old standard; in other words, from that date the choice of standard became, and still is, free. Most silver wrought after 1720 was made in the old standard, in spite of the tax.

The softer metal may have presented some slight technical difficulties at first, because the temperature of soldering and melting were lower and because the metal had a different feel; on the other hand, though many have asserted to the contrary, there is no perceptible difference between the two colours when polished. In any case the skilled craftsmen quickly overcomes difficulties, and if there seems to be less plate extant from the five years after the introduction of the Act, this may be attributable to the genuine scarcity of metal and the success of the Act.

STYLE AND ORNAMENT*

There were three distinct styles of ornament in concurrent use at the turn of the century, of which the 'William and Mary' soon dropped out, leaving only the 'Queen Anne' style for domestic use and the very ornamental and magnificent 'Louis XIV' style for the more important objects ordered by clients of royal and noble households, or for presentation to municipal and other corporations. Little plate falls between the chaste simplicity of the 'Queen Anne' style and the decorated splendour of the last-named style.

While the popularity of the 'William and Mary' style lasted for about twenty-five years, at about the turn of the century, as was foreshadowed in the previous chapter, its use gradually diminished and only occasional pieces of this fashion, often of provincial make or perhaps for a particular order, are to be found in and after the second decade.

On domestic plate of the more common kinds it was slowly replaced by the 'Queen Anne' style, which from about 1705 until about 1720 was supreme in this field. Its outstanding feature is the lack of applied ornament, the objects relying for their beauty on their carefully designed proportions and accurate execution. Not only was the gauge of the metal for the most part so much more substantial that embossed ornament was unnecessary for strengthening its structure, but also a far greater use was made of casting for such articles as candlesticks, or for spouts and handles.

Although English drawings and engravings for plate of this period are rare, the general similarity of the articles of any particular use by different makers is so great that some pattern-books must have been available. Most of the

* See plates 13b, 19b, 22a, 28 ('William and Mary'); 19c, 26b, 30a, 42a, 43b, 51b, 56c, 61a ('Queen Anne'); 24a and b, 56d, 61b ('Louis XIV').

surviving pieces in this style are by English silversmiths, but in spite of the Dutch and German connexions of the succeeding sovereigns, it is clear that the Huguenots exercised a disproportionate influence, and were responsible for most of the highly-finished ornamental plate. Pierre Harache, David Willaume, Pierre Platel, and Paul Crespin are names that often recur, though the names of the English makers Benjamin Pyne and Anthony Nelme are connected with many important pieces, particularly of royal and corporation plate, during the early part of the period.

The full strength of the Huguenot influence began to be felt at the beginning of the century, and so it will not be out of place to review their position, and account for their success. In 1703 the company's court was thanked for having forbidden a member to bring goods made by foreigners to the Hall to be assayed and touched. It was also advised that 'there are severall ffrenchmen, not free of this City, who are now endeavouring to get their freedom of the same by redemption', that is, by paying a fine. In 1711 a number of working goldsmiths presented another petition against the 'intrusion of foreigners', in which they complained 'that by the admittance of the necessitous strangers, whose desperate fortunes obliged them to worke at miserable rates, the representing members have been forced to bestow much more time and labour in working up their plate than hath been the practice of former times, when pieces of workmanship were much greater'. From this it may be assumed that, although the Huguenots were always far outnumbered by native goldsmiths, their competition was a serious threat.

A few prominent goldsmiths from the first generation of Huguenots whose works can be seen in several public collections may be singled out. Pierre Harache the Elder, whose work in London dates at least from 1695, made plate of the highest quality, the Barber Surgeons' wine cistern of 1697 (plate 24b) being an imposing example. He apparently died in 1700 and was succeeded in business by his son of the same name who also produced many fine vessels.

David Willaume the Elder and Pierre Platel the Elder came to London about 1687, became free of the Goldsmiths' Company a few years later, and produced work of high quality until 1720 and 1728 respectively. In 1705 Paul de Lamerie was apprenticed to the latter goldsmith and seven years later punched his own mark for the first time in a long career which, lasting until 1751, earned him the greatest reputation of any eighteenth-century London goldsmith, and resulted in his becoming the subject of the first monograph to be devoted to the works of a goldsmith. A representative assemblage of his products is shown in the Ashmolean Museum, and a number are here reproduced (plates 14a, 27a, 37, 42a, 42c, 43c, 44a, 48b, 49a, 51a, 54a, 54b, 55a, 62a). Other outstanding Huguenots were Isaac Liger (working 1704–30), Simon Pantin (working 1699–1728), and Louis Mettayer (working 1700–20).

The prominent English goldsmiths of the period are Anthony Nelme and Benjamin Pyne. The former worked at the 'Golden Bottle' from 1685 until 1722, and was one of the principal exponents of the 'Queen Anne' style. The latter, principal goldsmith to successive sovereigns, specialized in corporation regalia and show plate from 1684 until after 1724. Plates 18d and 26a show examples of their work.

The engraved work of this period is almost limited to lettering, armorial bearings, and the varied and often elaborate ornamental frames containing them. A specially good example is on a salver of 1717 in the Victoria and Albert Museum, one of a few signed (rarely done) by Joseph Sympson. William Hogarth (1697–1764) was apprenticed to a silver plate engraver for the firm of Ellis and Gamble; but by 1719 he had declared his boredom with this work and his intention never to take to it again; nevertheless, his name is widely associated with the ornamental designs engraved round coats-of-arms, and while it can hardly be possible that he did not work in this common style, no piece by his hand has so far been authenticated.

The art of penmanship was aided by many writing masters' books which must have been consulted by the engravers of lettering. George Shelley's *The Penman's Magazine* (1705), and *The Accomplisht Clerk* by John Ayres (1700) contain many typical scripts. Cyphers are perhaps due to Colonel Parsons' *A New Book of Cyphers* (1704), or S. Sympson's work of the same title.

PRINCIPAL ARTICLES OF DOMESTIC PLATE

Standing Cups and Covers. The manufacture of large standing cups was much diminished, probably as a result of the introduction of hot drinks requiring monteiths, punch bowls, or of the increasing capacity of two-handled cups. While some examples of the mid-seventeenth-century pattern were made as late as 1720, the Huguenots introduced more ornamental and slender examples, such as the chalice of 1699 by John Chartier (Christ Church, Oxford) and the similar but larger cups of 1705 (Pewterers' Company) and 1720 (City of London Corporation) by Benjamin Pyne. There are ornamented with gadrooning and applied palm-leaf or cut-card ornament. A set of four plainer examples by Humphrey Payne (Salters' Company) dates from 1716.

Two-handled Cups and Covers. Often described as loving cups or grace cups, they are here more prosaically classified. The diversity of patterns found during the preceding period gave way to two principal types. At the turn of the century the body became taller and less dumpy, curving round less sharply underneath; it is sometimes supported on a shallow stem above its moulded foot; the cover, like that of the tankards, acquired a pronounced dome, and the handles are more graceful and solid, tapering towards the lower junction with the body. The lighter vessels are embossed with vertical or swirled flutes and gadroons in the 'William and Mary' style, the upper end of each outlined with a narrow band of matting and emphasized by a punched trefoil or similar small device (plates 13b and 19b). The dome of the cover is often similarly treated. Sometimes a cable-moulding is embossed below the rim, and an embossed oval tablet in a baroque cartouche (perhaps after engravings by Stefano della Bella) often chased with imbricated scales, cuts into the surbase ornament between the handles, which having lost their grotesque protuberances and being of a thicker hollow section, are proportionately more graceful. Some small examples with a slightly everted rim and without a moulded foot-ring or cover, only a few inches in height and of small capacity, were made into the twenties. But more common between 1690 and 1710 are the larger covered cups about eight inches in height surmounted by a turned or gadrooned finial.

Already the heavier and more graceful French type of cup and cover had been introduced, the finest examples of which rank among the most notable achievements of the London goldsmiths of the early eighteenth century. The bowls, of most elegant line, often encircled by a moulded band, are set on low stems and moulded feet; the heavy cast handles are scrolled or shaped as harps, and the domed covers surmounted by large finials. Many earlier examples are ornamented with elaborate applied cut-card work and gadrooning, the later examples with an elongated arcading that has affinities with some varieties of sixteenth-century egg-and-dart variations (fig. 19c), palm leaves, or other variously shaped vertical patterns. Examples may be seen in the Victoria and Albert Museum (R. Bayley, 1719), and Ashmolean Museum (John Chartier, 1699, and Pierre Platel, 1705). Some in silver-gilt and gold were awarded as Race Cups, e.g. for the Newmarket Stakes of 1705 – and began a tradition of presenting silver cups as prizes that has lasted for more than two centuries.

Some cups with shallower and broader bowls and

smaller cast handles, perhaps for soup or vegetables, correspond in their ornament with these drinking vessels. Furthermore, the *écuelle,* a similar French vessel with two opposed flat handles, somewhat resembling the Scottish quaich, but with a domed cover, was introduced early in the century.

Tankards. The height of tankards, as of cups, began to increase in proportion to their diameter, and the curvatures of the handles became more graceful than on those of the previous century, often being cast in two reversed sections which were soldered together.

The cover retained at first the flattish top with a low step, and later the central space was gradually heightened into a dome (plates 19b and 19c); serrations on the flange are seldom found after the reign of Queen Anne. Some-

Figure 34 – Mug

times smaller plain mugs were made without covers (fig. 34). Some tankards hold as much as a gallon; more usually they have a capacity of two or three pints and measure between six and eight inches in height. One set of three, the largest holding a gallon and the smaller pair holding each two quarts, are twelve inches and nine inches in height respectively; they are unusual in that the handles are cast as double scrolls and the covers surmounted by a turned vase-shaped finial, which is more common on flagons and American tankards. The 'William and Mary' style is imposed by the embossing of fluted panels, or alternate flutes and gadroons, both on the drum and on the cover (plate 19b).

As the bulged shape began to appear it was applied to tankards and mugs, a group by the Edinburgh maker Colin McKenzie being among the earliest (1709–11). They are further distinguished by the baluster finial and a graceful 'Onslow' thumb-piece (cf. the termination of the ladle handle in plate 61g) strengthened with a triple scroll.

Monteiths and Punch Bowls. A typical monteith (plate 22a), which has a salver *en suite*, is that of 1700 by Francis Garthorne (Tallow Chandlers' Company); it is twelve and a half inches in diameter. Diameters vary about three inches either way, and weights range from sixty ounces to more than twice that amount. It seems that the elaborate rim was troublesome and that, though the form was preserved – eight notches separated by pairs of scrolls surmounted by heads – it was very often made separately so that it could be detached. In this way the punch bowl appears to have evolved. As a result there may be doubts whether some so-called punch bowls with fluted sides are not, strictly speaking, monteiths that have been separated from their rims. Though monteiths usually have two drop-handles, which punch bowls often lack, the presence or absence of such handles is perhaps a less sure guide than the type of ornamentation. Most punch bowls are plain except for mouldings though many are engraved with inscriptions, relevant pictorial subjects (plate 23a), or, more commonly, coats of arms. Many monteiths and punch bowls still belong to corporations though some have been presented later to churches for use as christening bowls.

Bottles. These massive containers, sometimes called flasks, were used to hold wine; their stoppers and chain distinguish them from the purely ornamental flasks described in the previous chapter. Though their ultimate origin may have been oriental, similar vessels in ceramics and silver, used as pilgrims' flasks, were made in France and Italy. In London they were nearly all made by the

Anglo-French goldsmiths; they are of oval section and measure as much as twenty-one inches in height and 250 ounces in weight. Perhaps the finest and most elaborate pair by Pierre Harache (1699; Eton College) have heavy ornamental chains attaching the stopper to points above the boldly cast human masks which were applied to either side. There is gadrooning on the moulded feet and stopper, and flowing guilloche and ovolo cut-card work applied to the neck and surbase. The arms, however, were engraved more than a century later. A smaller undated example, perhaps about 1710, by Pierre Platel is in the Victoria and Albert Museum.

Tea Pots and Kettles. About half-way through the reign of Queen Anne tea pots became much more common, and those made in London were of two principal types, the pear-shaped, either circular or polygonal (plate 26b), and the globular (plate 27a). Most of the former types, generally from five to eight inches in height, were made during the first twenty-five years of the century. They have a hinged domed lid surmounted by a baluster or knobbed finial entirely of metal or with a wooden knop to protect the fingers. The wooden handles, of elegantly carved shapes with a small thumb-grip, are pinned into circular sockets. On some earlier tea pots the handle was set at right angles to the spout, though it was more frequently opposed. The spout, of shaped or faceted section rather than circular, springs from the middle of the bulge and tapers in a double curve towards the mouth, which may be covered with a small hinged flap, or often is shaped rather like a duck's head, as on the coffee pots. The bodies seldom have applied ornament of any kind, but sometimes straps are applied to the cover or surbase, or small cut-card patterns round the sockets of the handles.

A painting of about 1728 in the Victoria and Albert Museum shows three persons at tea with a tea pot like this mounted on a stand with four cast legs and bun feet between which is supported a small spirit lamp, which can be lifted by a turned wooden baluster handle.

The globular tea pot, standing on a narrow moulded ring base, is seldom spherical, but flattish at the top, the lid being sometimes flush, sometimes slightly moulded, with a small finial. The handles generally are of wood, springing from a horizontal lower socket and curving down into the upper socket. The opposed spout is generally a straight tube tapering from a moulded joint at about 45 degrees, its mouth slipped horizontally. In Scotland a spherical tea pot with straight spout, moulded

Figure 35 – Spherical Scottish tea pot (with handle of mid 18th century)

foot and finial, seems to have predominated (fig. 35), though the example shown has the later double-scrolled handle.

Large tea kettles of pear-shaped form, circular or occasionally polygonal, were made during the first three decades. They differ from tea pots in having a large swing handle with a wooden grip hinged in front of and behind the cover, a moulding at the base of the spout, and a large base area over the flame of the lamp which was supported beneath on a three-legged framework.

Coffee Pots and Chocolate Pots. From the simple vessel

described in the previous chapter, the developments in the forms and shapes of the coffee pot followed the general contemporary trends. The chocolate pot is only distinguished from it by a second small covered aperture in the lid for the insertion of the swizzle-stick (molionet).

The most common form retains the circular drum with

Figure 36 – Octagonal coffee pot

straight sides, and is varied by octagonal or polygonal plans (fig. 36); it tapers from its moulded base to its mouth and has a domed lid surmounted by a small finial. The spout, occasionally at right angles to the handle, springs from near the base of the vessel and tapers in a double curve to a head shaped somewhat like a gargoyle. The wooden handle is either scrolled or looped; occasionally it is leather-covered and overlaid with a strap of cut-card work. Beyond simple horizontal courses of moulding and coats-of-arms engraved in ornamental frames, they lack elaborate decoration. A number made about 1700 have flaming cut-card ornaments at the junctions of the handle and spout, with fluting on the cover, and a thumb-piece. An example of 1702 by William Lukin (Burrell Collection: plate 28) shows most of these features. They range in height from eight to twelve inches, with a capacity of a pint upwards, and weigh 15–40 ounces.

The second type is characterized by the curving of the side out over the narrow moulded foot, which corresponds to that on tankards and mugs of the same period (cf. fig. 34).

As on some tea pots, a hinged flap covers the mouth of the spout; occasionally a thumb-piece is applied to the lid.

An uncommon third type, clearly of French origin, has a pear-shaped body standing on three cast feet, with a wooden baluster-handle set at right angles to the pronounced pouring lip.

Tea Caddies. 'Canister' was the accepted word for such a container until the late years of the eighteenth century when it was replaced by the word 'caddy', which seems to be a corruption of the Malay word 'kati', a weight equivalent to rather more than a pound, used in the tea trade.

An early canister of 1699 (Ashmolean Museum) is almost an exact cube of $3\frac{1}{8}$ inches, with matted panels on each side and a circular slip-on cap. The common type of canister of the Queen Anne period retains the vertical sides but is taller and thinner, sometimes hexagonal or triangular, more often rectangular or octagonal (eight-square), on a moulded base with a hinged domed cap and horizontal moulding. A sliding panel through which to fill it was sometimes fitted in the base or top. Even before 1720 the slightly bulged sides, already mentioned in connexion with other vessels, was applied to canisters. They were generally made in sets of two or three, to contain two different kinds of tea (such as green, bohea, or hyson), and lumps of sugar. These sets were kept in boxes of wood covered with leather, shagreen, tortoiseshell, or mother-of-pearl, and fitted with silver mounts and with a lock, a precaution warranted by the high prices of both tea and sugar.

Ewers. Decorative ewers in the French style for toilet water were made, sometimes with a salver to match. The ewer consists of a deep helmet-shaped container with a high curved and everted lip opposite a cast ornamental handle, and stands on a knopped stem and moulded base. The decoration is usually elaborate and provides particularly good material for the study of Anglo-French ornamental design during the first quarter of the century as well as the high standard of execution attained by the best goldsmiths, principally Huguenots, by whom such works were made. Ewers usually stand about eight to fifteen inches in height. A gold pair is known. The plainer examples have a moulded band which follows the line of the lip, a surbase of applied straps, and a heavy curved handle on the top of which is an applied leaf. More ornamental examples may have gadrooned feet and knops, double straps or cut-card work below and arcaded moulding with shells and other ornaments, a cabled girdle with an applied female mask below the lip, and an elaborate handle cast solid in the form of a female torso curved back over the bowl. In the space below the lip may be found a coat-of-arms in a finely engraved ornamental surround.

Candlesticks and Tapersticks. There are five principal varieties to be considered. The first retains the form of the fluted column but is embossed on the hand-guard, stem, and foot with fluting and gadrooning in the 'William and Mary' style. The second, less common type retains the same characteristic base and hand-guard, but is cast and its turned stem is surmounted by a bell-shaped socket. This is a transitional form from which the third and most common variety derived during the last two decades of the seventeenth century and continued till about 1725. Cast in one piece or in sections, there are many minor variations in design of the principal characteristics, a reel-shaped nozzle on a distinct neck, and a shouldered stem with one or two knops below, set on a moulded circular or polygonal foot, sometimes depressed, sometimes domed (fig. 33). During the second decade the nozzle, the edge of the foot, and other members are faceted with triangles (plate 56c). The fourth kind, of French origin, which appears early in the reign of George I, is somewhat larger, about eight or nine inches in height, and, while similar to the third, is generally of circular section with a pronounced shoulder and knop, and is chased with gadrooning, palmettes, strapwork, and other raised designs. While more ornate and of excellent finish, they are generally less graceful. Heavy tripod candlesticks were made in sets of two or four in the Italian baroque style, which derived ultimately from ancient sources, at this period; the set in the Ashmolean Museum (plate 56d) is accompanied by wick trimmers held vertically in a tripod stand *en suite*.

Tapersticks are generally miniature versions of the candlesticks described. A small variety with pierced foot was made about 1700–5, either in the conventional columnar form or like a chamber candlestick. An example of the former (Victoria and Albert Museum) is pierced 'QUEEN ANNE 1702'.

Wall sconces in pairs or sets consist of a cartouche with a central portion reserved for engraved armorial bearings, surrounded with pierced and embossed scrolls, fruit or foliage flanked with figures of boys and topped by an urn, basket of fruit, or similar ornament. A single recurving arm holds the socket and grease-pan (Victoria and Albert Museum). Another kind has the reflector shaped as an arched tablet with the socket fixed on a projecting curved ledge.

Inkstands. Inkstands designed as boxes were replaced by those consisting of a tray fitted with three sockets for detachable inkpot, pounce box, and wafer box. In front was a long trough for the pens, though sometimes a drawer was fitted for them beneath the tray. This is the standard form which, decorated and shaped according to successive fashions, lasted into the nineteenth century. A hand bell and a taperstick were occasionally added to the group.

Furniture. After the turn of the century, more silver furniture was made than the few existing items indicate. A plain table about 1715 engraved with the coat-of-arms, with no less than seventy-two quarterings, of Edward Harley, second Earl of Oxford, belongs to the Duke of Portland. In the Kremlin is preserved the throne and footstool made by Nicholas Clausen in 1713: it is probably the richest and most elaborate surviving monument of goldsmiths' work of the period.

Silver fire-dogs and andirons were still made, but the increasingly widespread use of coal fires led to their disuse.

A single warming-pan of this period, preserved at Buckingham Palace, was made in 1715 by Seth Lofthouse, for the Princess of Wales, later Queen Caroline.

Flat Plate. Shortly after the introduction of the new standard, the pattern of both spoons and forks began to change fundamentally, presumably through the influence of the Huguenots. A thicker and more graceful stem with a waved end curves smoothly into the egg-shaped bowl which is backed by a rat-tail (plate 61a).

This pattern was made until about 1720 when the 'Hanoverian' rat-tail spoon, similarly forged in one piece, with a longer and more pointed bowl began to be made. Its stem has a pronounced central ridge and curves forward into a fattened and rounded end (plate 61b). It is bent forwards because the spoon was laid with its bowl downwards on the table in the French manner, the reversal of which usage required the tail to be curved backwards in order to allow the engraving on the flat surface to be seen.

At this time the distinction between the two principal sizes, the large table spoon and the smaller dessert spoon, becomes clearer, and the weight of the former correspondingly increased to about two or two-and-a-half ounces.

Tea spoons of like patterns are found, and are shown in use on a spoon-tray in the painting mentioned above (p. 175). Later some small changes were made to the rat-tail, which became structurally unnecessary, and therefore was continued as an ornamental feature in the form of lobes or drops. The handles of forks, as well as the technique of their manufacture, with three, and occasionally four, prongs, followed the fashion of the spoons, though they seldom survive in sets of equal numbers as in modern canteens.

The bowls of some small spoons are ornamentally pierced and the stems shaped as long and tapering spikes. Their use has been much discussed: the more probable view is that their bowls were perforated for straining the fragments of leaf from the cups and their stems spiked to move the pieces of leaf which were large enough to clog up the perforated strainer at the entry into the spout, for at that period the leaves were not so finely shredded before sale as they are now. The fact that one of these so-called mote-skimmers is associated with a composite tea service of 1735, mostly by Paul de Lamerie, provides evidence for this view.

Marrow scoops or spoons are found stamped with early-eighteenth-century hall-marks. At one end is a short scoop, like a narrow spoon bowl, which is separated by a rounded collar from a narrower scoop about half the length of the whole implement. Some examples have the bowl of a rat-tailed spoon with the stem grooved to form the scoop.

Miscellaneous. Much of the other domestic plate reflects such lack of ornament or such simplicity of construction that only brief references to a few objects are required. Strawberry dishes from six to eight inches in diameter were both oval and circular with scalloped edges, each division being separated by embossed ridges that either taper away towards the centre or are joined to those on either side to make a continuous arcade. The flat central area is very often engraved with armorial bearings.

Standing dishes take the form of a plate with slightly

upturned sides, the traditional formula, set on a trumpet
foot or a stem with moulded base, and the borders either
moulded, cabled, or gadrooned. Arms were usually engraved in the centre.

Plates in sets of up to several dozen are still preserved
and occasionally used. They are about nine or ten inches
in diameter; the engraved arms are as a rule crammed into
the flat border between the edge and the central depression. Even the larger dishes, oval or circular, are seldom
of interest; but some very fine and massive chargers
splendidly engraved with coats of arms and with gadrooned edges are preserved. They are sometimes called
voiding dishes because they were used to hold the scraps
removed, or voided, from the table. An unusual octagonal tray, made in Dublin and engraved with an elaborate
coat of arms, is shown on plate 51b.

CHAPTER SEVEN

1719–70: George II and the Rococo Style

THE arguments brought forward in the *Case of the Working Goldsmiths* (above p. 165) were not convincing enough to prevent the passage of the *Wrought Plate Act*, but only to modify its proposed provisions. Experience showed that plate made according to the old, or sterling, standard was more serviceable and durable than that made of the new, or Britannia, silver. The old standard was therefore revived from 1 June 1720 and the new standard was retained as an alternative, 'without obligation or restraint'. Moreover, the Act imposed on wrought silver a duty of sixpence per ounce, which was removed in 1758. A like tax was imposed in 1729 by the Irish Parliament on certain articles of gold and silver, to raise funds for agricultural improvements there; its payment was receipted by a new mark, the figure of *Hibernia*. When this mark is worn it may be confused with that of Britannia, though their resemblance is only superficial and the dilemma can usually be resolved by reference to other accompanying marks.

Several London goldsmiths, including Paul de Lamerie, complained that, notwithstanding previous Acts of Parliament and charters, 'great frauds are daily committed in the manufacturing of gold and silver wares for want of sufficient power effectually to prevent the same'. The resulting *Plate Offences Act* (1738) reaffirmed the two standards of silver and that of gold at 22 carats, and exempted jewellery (except mourning rings) not only from marking but from compliance with the standards. Among the small objects specifically mentioned are chains, lockets, buttons, thimbles, coral sockets and bells, pipelighters, small nutmeg graters, sliding pencils, cases for toothpicks, tweezers, pencils, and needles, and other things which could not be marked without damaging their appearance. The only specific fraud dealt with was the use of too much solder, but nevertheless every goldsmith throughout the country, those in the jurisdiction of the York, Exeter, Bristol, Chester, Norwich, and Newcastle assay offices being specifically mentioned, was required to have the punch for his old mark destroyed and to have a new one made of a different 'character or alphabet'. No continuous series of marks has been compiled for the Bristol office as for the others. The Norwich office seems to have been already closed.

From what has been said it will be apparent that many makers will have punched three different marks during the present period: moreover, the damage through wear or accident to these punches or the need for punches of different sizes may have resulted in many more being registered in the name of one maker. The first group of makers' marks, from 1720 to 1738, resemble those of the Britannia period, a wide variety of alphabets, emblems, and outlines being used. After 1738 there was a tendency to simplification among the younger makers, who often used no more than their initials in a rectangular or oval outline.

Some makers combined together in partnerships, if only for short periods, for the manufacture of plate. Thomas Whipham who entered his mark in 1737 joined with William Williams from 1740 until 1746 at the 'Spread Eagle', Foster Lane, and from 1757 to 1775 worked with Charles Wright in Ave Maria Lane. William Shaw and William Priest went into partnership as working goldsmiths from 1749 until 1758 at the sign of the Unicorn. Samuel Herbert entered his mark in 1747, and three years later founded a company in Foster Lane that continued until 1760.

There are signs that makers began to specialize in the production of wares other than flat plate, e.g. John Cafe (working 1740–60) and William Cafe (working from 1757 until his bankruptcy in 1772) specialized as candlestick-makers. Another Huguenot, Nicholas Sprimont, was trained at Liège and entered his mark in 1742 in London, and in the following year made a pair of oval dishes decorated with naturalistic models of shells, coral, insects, and stones in a manner reminiscent of Bernard Palissy's large centre piece and several pottery dishes of the later sixteenth century. A pair of gilt salts of 1742–5 at Windsor Castle, similarly inspired, were cast from crab, whelk, and other shells. His interests passing to ceramic art, he founded in 1750 the Chelsea porcelain factory (under the patronage of the Duke of Cumberland and Sir Edward Fawkener) where his taste for modelling after nature was continued in the manufacture of porcelain centre pieces. Paul Crespin (working 1720–57), his neighbour at the 'Golden Ball' in the same street, borrowed this idea and produced in 1743 a shell-shaped inkstand covered with coral and shells (Chatsworth).

In 1761 the Goldsmiths' Company had a membership of three hundred; a Prime Warden and three other Wardens, with ninety-eight Assistants, and a livery of one hundred and ninety-eight members, who paid a fine of twenty pounds upon admission.

STYLE AND ORNAMENT*

There was no sharp change in style or diminution of production in the years after the *Wrought Plate Act* took effect. A gradual and general trend, already started, towards more elaborate ornament reached its peak in the mid thirties with the earliest use of motifs and designs taken almost exclusively from the rococo ornamentists (cf plates 31, 32, 49, and 54). The almost undecorated plate of 'Queen Anne' style had for about fifteen years been produced side by side with more expensive items in the

* See plates 14a, 14b, 22b, 23a, 27a, 29, 30a, 30b, 30c, 31a, 31b, 31c, 32, 37, 42b, 42c, 43c, 44a, 44b, 46a, 46b, 48b, 49a, 49b, 51a, 52a, 54a, 54b, 55a, 57a, 57b, 61b, 62a, 63a.

Régence style which was employed by few plate-workers other than Huguenots of the first generation. The Régence in France lasted from the accession of Louis XV in 1715 until 1723. The two styles, one common to all domestic plate in widespread use, and the other principally reserved for display and infrequent use in the richer houses, seem almost to merge during the third decade and to take on a purely English character that can seldom be mistaken for anything made on the Continent at the same time.

The most characteristic decorative technique of the twenties and early thirties is flat-chasing of ornamental borders on spaces that would have previously been left plain or engraved (plates 48b and 49a). In the former case, only the details of the arms and the crest in each corner are engraved. Oblong border panels, filled with diaper patterns, are separated by shells or medallions containing masks or other designs, and in the centre, or other suitable position, would be chased a coat-of-arms in an elaborately designed frame-work. Sometimes the finer lines of hatching were engraved, but a skilled craftsman was able to chase even these satisfactorily. Where the surface is much worn it may be possible to distinguish between the two techniques only by the slight ridges that the chasing. tools have driven up on the opposite side.

The rich and varied symmetrical designs of straight lines and delicately modulated curves are executed with an amazing precision and consistency and are fitted into the space to be decorated with a remarkable sense of pro-

Figure 37 – Carved ornament in low relief from a jewel-casket (1724)

portion. These designs seem to originate from French and German ornamentists of the early eighteenth century, on whom the English silversmith still largely depended (fig. 37). Few English engraved pattern books or even single designs for metal work have survived. The political tension between the British and the French and the resultant colonial rivalries did not prevent the styles prevalent under Louis XV (1715–74) from being eagerly accepted in this country. Though less imaginative and less clearly understood than in France, their application in London was more restrained and in better proportions than in the provinces, or even in the Netherlands and Germany.

The early panels of simple rectangles developed by about 1730 into very elaborate patterns of interlacing and recurving lines, filled with diaper designs, which gradually during the next decade gave way to the extravagant rococo repertoire of harmonious but complex scrolls with *rocaille*, flowers, and leaves (plates 49a and 54b).

Even during the late seventeenth century a trend was noticeable in Genoa towards the lightening of the heavy symmetry of the baroque. It is not without significance that Gilles-Marie Oppenort (1672–1742), Thomas Germain (1673–1748), and Justin-Aurèle Meissonier (1675–1750, admitted a master goldsmith by the brevet of young Louis XV), the leaders of a group of designers who began to tire of the symmetry of the Régence and late Italianate baroque, had all spent several of their formative years in Italy. The unpredictable and seemingly inexhaustible asymmetry of rock formations which yet managed to result in a harmonious whole without any repetition of detail seems to have provided the inspiration for their inventive powers, and the French word for rock-work (*rocaille*) provided the internationally used expression 'rococo'. Decoratively, for domestic and even church furniture of all kinds, the rococo style was eagerly developed and patronized in Paris and elsewhere on the Continent, and was extensively employed in the fashionable grottoes that were built in England by some eccentric *dilettanti*. But in domestic designs the rock-work largely disappeared, though it was retained in the rough and shapeless elements to be found among the graceful and irregular S- and C-scrolls that are the chief ingredient of the style in its linear form. Theoretically the new style could be applied as well to three- as to two-dimensional designs and on the Continent this latter folly was pursued to some absurd results. As to silverware, in France, and in some isolated cases in England, full expression of fantasy was allowed in shape and decoration (cf. plates 32, 57b, etc.). Practical considerations, however, dictated that most silver vessels required for daily use could not depart far from tried shapes, and the new fashion was, on the whole, sparingly used in Britain.

Paul de Lamerie and Charles and Frederick Kandler were the boldest leaders of the style among English goldsmiths in the early thirties and produced some objects which, in spite of their marvellous virtuosity, appear unbalanced and impracticable to modern eyes. The spectacular appearance, inventive design, and superb workmanship of de Lamerie's gilt ewer and basin of 1741, which the Goldsmiths' Company commissioned and still possesses, are beyond dispute. This illustration of abstract and meaningless forms that are so far removed from their natural origin as to be wholly unconnected with it, attracted appropriately enough the intellects of the age of reason. This set also illustrates the occasional use throughout the period of motifs derived from classical mythology (cf. plate 32), though classical ornamental motifs appear incongruous. The demi-figure of a marine god forms the handle of the ewer, and the four relieved panels on the basin show *putti* holding the attributes of Hercules, Mercury, Minerva, and Vulcan respectively. On other pieces cast female figures or snakes naturalistically rendered were employed as handles or feet, and medallions containing classical busts are sometimes found.

The simple cut-card work of the last third of the seventeenth century developed into the complex strapwork employed even before 1700 by the Huguenots and finally under rococo influence assumed irregular foliate forms that encouraged the incorporation of flowers. About 1735 the application of cast sprays of naturalistic flowers (plate 44b) and leaves to much plate, and the embossing of them during the late fifties and sixties (plate 31), emphasize the fact that interest in the decorative use of botanical motifs is recurrent; in this context their use may be interpreted as a reaction against the abstraction of earlier rococo motifs.

Another characteristic which the Goldsmiths' ewer illustrates in an extreme form is the greater use of elabor-

Figure 38 – Perforations from a pounce box (1730)

ate castings in the high rococo period of the forties and fifties. Either a whole object, such as a candlestick (plate 57b), or its separate parts, feet, handles, and decorative panels were accurately cast and chased.

The covers of casters reflect in pierced work the same rococo asymmetry and in the many elaborately pierced cake-baskets (plates 54b and 55a) this technique reached its peak about 1735–50 (cf. fig. 38); in combination with casting and flat-chasing it resulted in some of the most exquisite pieces of domestic plate that have ever been produced.

A particularly French rococo form, applicable to caskets and tureens, was the shaped and 'bombé' bowl and cover (plate 44) which appeared about 1750. It is particularly well-suited to ceramic wares of a similar nature and is also found in furniture. From whatever angle it is viewed it seems to be composed of curves, but there is sufficient regularity in the design to give it an enduring attraction.

A feature of the last three decades of this period is the so-called 'dropped-bottom' (plate 31c), a waisted line given to the rounded bottoms of such containers as tea and coffee pots, castors, caddies, etc. During the fifties and sixties scrolls and floral motifs in the rococo style were embossed on milk jugs (plate 30c), tea pots, canisters (plates 31b and c), two-handled cups, and other vessels. To these are added *chinoiseries* which, as a result of the French passion for orientalia in the forms of lacquer or porcelain, led artists, such as Watteau and Gillot, to produce ornamental engraving of rococo *chinoiserie* of their own graceful but fanciful conception, which were applied to silver in a somewhat cruder form.

In spite of the ebullient impact of rococo ornament it must not be supposed either that the plainer traditional designs of the first years of the century were completely abandoned or that all the newer shapes were as heavily ornamented as the preceding paragraphs may imply. There are several plain two-handled cups which are hardly distinguishable from those made early in the century except by their marks or subsidiary scrolls on the cast handles.

Formal heraldic engraving was at its best during the first decades of this period when manipulative skill was at its height and designers particularly inventive. The coats themselves were generally accurately shown with their tinctures in oval or shaped shields, and surrounded by exquisitely delineated designs of scrolls, diaper panels, and human figures. Sometimes a traditional early-sixteenth-century design is found. Under the rococo influence, the shields lost their shape in a surround of scrolls, *rocaille*, and foliage of a less spectacular nature (cf. plate 49).

Inscriptions are in almost cursive italics with beautifully graduated thicknesses, interspersed with lines or words in Roman letters or entirely in Roman capitals. Whatever the form, the skill is of the highest. Only in exceptional cases did the engravers sign their names, and little is known about them. Occasionally fine examples of pictorial engraving are found. Perhaps the best of these is the punch bowl of 1726 by Paul de Lamerie (Ashmolean Museum) on one side of which is shown a procession of persons with a quay-side and ships in the background and on the other a group of men seated at a long table. The quality of this work is such that it has been attributed to William Hogarth, an unlikely assessment, because he had given up engraving on silver some years before. Another punch bowl (Hastings Corporation) made from the silver staves and mounts of the canopies supported over George II and Queen Caroline at their coronation in 1727, is engraved with figures of the King and Queen enthroned, possibly by the same hand (plate 23a). Several salvers were made from, and engraved with representations of, the Exchequer Seals or Great Seals of sovereigns and their consorts.

The great majority of domestic plate is of white metal, though the interiors of bowls, jugs, and salt cellars are often gilt; but even of important presentation and ceremonial plate, less than half is gilt. A few pieces of gold plate have survived, mostly as racing cups, and smaller objects such as snuff boxes and their mounts, watch cases, and other articles of personal use, which are not usually classified with plate.

PRINCIPAL ARTICLES OF DOMESTIC PLATE

Two-Handled Cups. Out of all the classes of vessels made during this half-century, more attention was paid to the design and finish of the many imposing two-handled cups and their covers than to other plate. That they had already almost completely superseded the standing cup which had been predominant during both the sixteenth and seventeenth centuries was shown in the previous chapter. Their weight and size alone indicate the importance which was attached to them, no less than do the original designs and ornaments conceived for them by such inventive gold-smiths as Paul de Lamerie, whose mark is found on many of the finest made between 1720 and 1750. Several pairs are known, and a set of twelve was made by Nicholas Clausen.

According to the shape of their bowls, they fall into two principal classes, the first continuing the earlier form (plate 14a), the second a new form brought in during the late thirties (plate 14b) presumably by the same gold-smith: both lasted until the seventies. Some developments to the first type can be noted. By 1720 a small subsidiary scroll was added into the lower part of the handles which, attached to a heavy moulding at the top, where a large leaf springs from the volute and forms the thumb-grip, taper gracefully away to the junction with the subsidiary C-scroll. A moulding usually encircles the body. The domed and moulded covers have large turned finials and the stem becomes increasingly tall and narrow, so that by the middle of the century the vessels had assumed a less bulky appearance. The bowls of many examples are plain; to others are applied straps of the Louis XIV and, later, of the rococo style, both applied and embossed.

The second type is comparatively infrequent and its ex-emplars have very varied but elaborate ornament. The tall bulged and waisted body extends in an inverted dome to the narrow stem. The handles may represent writhing serpents chased into unpleasant realism (plate 14b), as one by Paul de Lamerie (1737; Fishmongers' Company), or heavily ornamented scrolls springing from low down, loaded with grapes and terminating in goats' heads, on another of 1745, amid a profusion of rococo decora-tion, including lizards and squirrels, which is surmounted by the figure of the young Bacchus squeezing the juice from a bunch of grapes into his mouth. Later examples, with two handles of the more conventional kind, may be embossed with well-separated dependent sprays of flowers.

Cisterns. One of the most remarkable pieces of plate made in the eighteenth century deserves mention. In the spring of 1735 a Bill to authorize a lottery to raise one hundred thousand pounds towards the cost of a new Westminster Bridge was before the House. Henry Jerningham (died 1761) entered a petition proposing that a silver cistern, which remained on his hands, might be included. It 'had been acknowledged, by all persons of skill who had seen the same, to excel whatever had been attempted in the Kingdom'. After four years of application to the raising and adorning of the model and 'great hazards in the furnace' it had cost several thousand pounds in the workmanship alone, exclusive of the weight of silver, which

Figure 39 – Brandy warmer

amounted to 8,000 ounces. Five and a half feet long and three and a half feet in height, it was made by Charles Kandler after a sketch by George Vertue, the antiquary (1684–1756) and designs by Jerningham. The figures were modelled in wax by Michael Rysbrack. It was later acquired by Empress Catherine II and is presumably still in the Winter Palace, Leningrad.

Brandy Saucepans. Saucepans, often known as brandy warmers, are simple raised bowls, bulged or straight-sided, with everted lips, and a turned wooden baluster handle (fig. 39). Although an example is known from the Commonwealth, they mostly survive from the mid eighteenth century and later. They vary in weight from two to more than twenty ounces.

Punch Bowls. The bowl developed by being strengthened at the rim with a moulding above a slight shoulder, and it was raised up on a narrow pulley section about the moulded foot. Sometimes two drop-handles were added, as on the Treby punch bowl already mentioned. Most other examples, plain or engraved with arms, belong to corporate bodies; ornamental straps in the Louis XIV style are applied to some (plate 22b). Ladles were usually made to match, with long silver, whalebone, or wooden handles; their frequency suggests that their use was not confined to silver punch bowls.

Tankards and Mugs. The production of tankards seems gradually to have diminished and their capacity was generally limited to a quart or a pint, their height ranging from about ten to six inches. Colleges and other corporations seem to be the principal owners, a strongly conservative element in their shapes and ornaments indicating that they were copied from customary forms for presentation, or perhaps made to replace broken or worn vessels. The straight-sided variety (plate 19b) concurrently with that with the slightly curved side continued into the thirties; in both cases the handle was of double scrolls with a shield at its lower end, the cover pronouncedly domed. About the middle of the century the lip became everted, the body taller in proportion to its diameter and the cover more domed, so that the whole vessel acquired the shape of a baluster. At the same time the double-volute was replaced by a hoop, a new thumb-piece, sometimes containing vertical bars (plate 19d).

From about 1715 plain mugs with the tulip-shaped body began to replace the straight-sided variety; they have a smooth tapering scrolled handle and a small thumb-grip. In size they range from about three and a half to six inches, and contain half a pint or a pint (cf. fig. 34).

Salt Cellars. The earlier forms raised up from a single sheet of metal persisted into the sixties in various shapes, that with octagonal moulded sides and an oval depression being most usual (plate 42a). Of the two characteristic forms found in sets of as many as a dozen, the first, which lasts into the Adam period, has a shallow circular bowl on a low stem and a moulded foot of slightly less diameter than the bowl. Examples are both plain and ornamented with a band of chased vertical acanthus leaves round the foot, and with a calyx of foliate straps, often swirled round the bowl (plate 42b). The second, made through-out the period, consists of a cauldron-shaped bowl on three or four feet shaped as scrolls, or as lions' paws with a mask at the joint (plate 42c). The Corporation of the City of London owns a belated ceremonial salt with some features of the seventeenth-century kind made by Augus-tine Courtauld (1730); it consists of an ornamental cauldron on four dolphin feet with four scrolls above ending in female heads.

During the middle decades the popularity of the cockle shell as an ornamental motif led to its adaptation as the salt cellar itself, raised up on three scrolls or tiny spiral shells.

Mustard Pots. The separate mustard container, cor-responding to the separate salt, had already been made after the Restoration, as was shown above (p. 130), but only isolated examples preceded its common manufacture in the last quarter of the century. This is perhaps because mustard, like pepper and salt, was sprinkled dry and only gradually the custom of serving it as a paste created the need for a new type of vessel. An example of 1724, shaped like a barrel, with a notched and moulded cover, resembles a very small tankard. Another from the late forties has a glass container in a pierced frame on three feet, while others of about 1760 are raised on a stem and foot.

Spice Boxes. These consist generally of two compart-ments whose covers share two hinges, separated by a nut-meg grater set in the middle: the oval bulged box stands on four scrolled feet. Their shaped outlines clearly reflect French designs; and it is hard to assign an origin to some of those without marks.

Castors. The function of the castor limits the range of forms which it can be made to assume; it requires a removable perforated top and a body that is readily grasped yet not easily overturned. Castors thus continued to be made in the baluster form (plate 43b), to which some minor changes were made. They were constructed from several pieces, a raised surbase, moulded wires, cast finial, foot, and cover. The pear-shaped body was common, and the line of the medial moulding, which concealed a seam, was often emphasized by an arris, in some cases a right angle, between the concave curve of the long neck and the convex curve of the surbase; the tall slip-on cover was pierced with vertical patterns of shaped holes, or with all-over patterns of scrolls or crosses; the finial resembled an acorn or baluster. Castors like these were made throughout the period, and at the time when rococo influence was at its height, cast ornaments were applied or embossed. Generally, however, they were left with plain surfaces, sometimes relieved with horizontal mouldings or gadroonings, or with engraved arms, or crest. They were frequently made in sets of three, one being about eight inches high, a little larger than the remaining pair (of which one might be blind, that is, without perforations, though the outlines of these are sometimes indicated). A group of three was occasionally provided with a stand, two such having been made by Paul de Lamerie in 1735 (plate 43c).

During the forties the 'dropped bottom' began to appear on castors, an outline later matched by similar waisting on their covers, which were more boldly pierced, the pattern of the perforations being arranged in a spiral with parallel ridges, topped by a spiral finial.

A smaller and plainer castor, often referred to as a muffineer, was made throughout this period; its domed cover was hemispherical, sometimes without a finial, and with circular perforations.

Two or three rather small castors are sometimes found on cruet frames of the Warwick and other varieties.

Sauce Boats. The first sauce boats date from the early twenties and their shape does indeed somewhat resemble that of a boat (plate 46a). They stand on a moulded base with a protuberant lip at either end and opposed scrolled handles half-way along each side. This form is later elaborated, its upper rim shaped and moulded, and in the height of the rococo period profusely ornamented (plate 46b). During the fourth decade a different form appears; the base is replaced by three or four cast feet, masks, shells, claws, and *rocaille* being among the forms employed; the boat itself takes on an oval shape resembling a cauldron or the *bombé* shape corresponding to that of the tureen, with a high curved pouring lip opposed to a cast handle

(a)   (b)

Figure 40 – Two sauce boats

made up of several scrolls; the bowl is usually left plain, and the ornament is concentrated on the rim, feet, and handle (fig. 40b); sometimes, however, when made of less thick metal, it is embossed with rococo flowers all over, giving it a less robust appearance and making it more difficult to keep clean. Analogous is a third type made in the forties and fifties; a gracefully rounded bowl, often fluted like a shell, with a shaped rim is set on a short stem and a spreading rococo foot; opposite the lip is a cast handle of open or composite scrolls, sometimes in the form of an animal's or bird's head (fig. 40a).

In the fifties and sixties many sauce tureens were made as miniature replicas of the *bombé* tureens which they accompanied.

Tureens. The word is derived from the French *terrine*, an earthenware pot used to hold soup or stew. Some examples are known from Queen Anne's reign, and one of the earliest is that at Woburn Abbey, made in 1723 by Paul de Lamerie (plate 44a). Lavishly chased with Louis XIV ornament, it is oval in form, about eleven inches wide. During the forties tureens of an oblong *bombé* shape, supported on four mask and claw feet, with a moulded and domed cover, and a loop handle at either end, were introduced, and this remained the basic shape for the next twenty-five years (plate 44b). Vessels of a similar shape were also made of porcelain and earthenware in France and elsewhere, but, for lack of evidence which came first, they must be regarded as international and contemporary applications of several media to a new shape. Ornament, comprising cast *rocaille*, flowers, leaves, and masks, was lavishly applied. The covers were surmounted by loop handles, or finials of artichokes, flowers, fruit, or birds, etc. The outlines, from whichever angle they may be viewed, are graceful curves; even the mouth of the bowl, originally straight and horizontal, was sometimes curved as well so that no straight line can be seen (plate 44b).

Silver Plates and Dishes. Usually they resemble contemporary porcelain or earthenware shapes, a moulded border of five or more shaped lobes being common. The borders are sometimes gadrooned, and occasionally interspersed with shells. Plates were made in two sizes with a variety of dishes *en suite* to complete a service which may consist of several dozen pieces.

Centre Pieces and Épergnes. The earliest of these 'dumb waiters', made to embellish the centre of the dinner table, and at the same time to hold fruit or sweets within easy reach of the diners, is mentioned in a royal inventory of 1725; a gilt 'aparn containing one Table Basket and cover, one foote, four Salt boxes, four small Salts, four Branches, six Casters, four Sauceboats'. Another *épergne*, made by Paul de Lamerie in 1734, has eight waiters, six castors, four candle brackets, and two cruet frames. Smaller specimens, not uncommon in the thirties and forties, have a central salver covering a basket on a substantial four-footed frame, with four smaller salvers on scrolled arms. Though they generally comprise a large central dish surrounded by four smaller dishes, no design for these elaborate and elegant examples of mid-Georgian workmanship seems to have been used more than once.

Cruet Stands. These were frames of silver, with a substantial scrolled handle, to hold the small glass vessels usually with a silver lid, hinged or slip-on, and sometimes a handle, for vinegar and oil, as well as the set of three castors that were generally employed for pepper, sugar (largest), and mustard (blind). The earliest examples seem to date from just before the twenties, and thereafter a continuous series extends to the beginning of the present century.

Dish Rings. These circular rings, about three inches high and eight inches in diameter, were presumably designed to prevent heat-marks by supporting hot dishes above the table. Some seem to have been made in the reign of William and Mary, but the earliest specimens date from that of Queen Anne. Few of English manufacture remain, but in Dublin they were made in considerable quantities from 1745 onwards, particularly after 1760. The earliest type is shaped like a pulley-wheel, each rim strengthened with a moulding and of equal diameter, the sides being pierced with rococo ornament. Another theory, based on an analogy with ceramic wares, is that they were intended to be stood on a plate and to contain hot potatoes; whence derives their popular name 'potato rings'. But 'dish rings' was their consistent description at the Dublin Assay Office. A typical Dublin example of about 1770 from the Leeds Art Gallery is reproduced as plate 63a.

Dish Crosses. A device more ingenious than attractive seems to have served the same purpose as the dish ring from the fifties onwards by supporting dishes above the table top; a dish cross is obviously more suitable and adaptable for this purpose, because in addition to four arms which can be adjusted to fit dishes of different shapes or sizes, a small spirit lamp is generally fitted at their intersection.

- *Spoons.* The rat-tail continuing the stem along the back of the bowl began to be replaced by smaller ornaments, such as a droplet, or two or three droplets in diminishing size; and during the rococo period a shell, flower, or scroll, cast, or stamped in relief. At the same time the ridge along the centre of the stem disappeared, and the stem assumed a flattish section, ending in a curve in the opposite direction to that of the bowl; this is generally called the 'Old English' pattern (plate 61c) and was the basic form until the very many later innovations were introduced. This pattern was embellished with a feather-edge engraving or bright-cut (plate 61g), or a threaded edge (plate 61c) during the sixties and onwards; a less usual variant called the 'Onslow' pattern (plate 61g) ends in a curled and reeded volute which merges into the stem. It was named after Arthur Onslow (1691–1768) who was for thirty-three years Speaker of the House of Commons. Tea spoons, dessert spoons, table spoons, and long serving spoons are found in all these patterns, as well as ladles (plate 61g), and many canteens were made up of half-dozens of the various sizes. The tea spoon was the subject of many other varieties of ornament; sets may be found with swans, two-headed eagles, flowers, ships, short legends, etc.

Forks. Forks generally had three prongs, sometimes four, and their stems are similar to those of the spoons which they were probably made to match. The prongs became a little longer. The handles of the steel two-pronged fork continued to be made *en suite* with those of the steel knife, very commonly shaped like a cartridge or a pistol-grip, either smooth and plain, or very occasionally chased. A variety of other materials, porcelain or semi-precious stones, are found in conjunction with silver mounts. Fruit knives and forks were made in sets entirely of silver or silver-gilt, and, though usually smaller than the ordinary table size, followed the same designs.

Fish Slices. As with fruit, the unpleasant taste produced by contact of fish with steel led to the appearance at this time of the fish slice. Perhaps the first and probably the finest (Ashmolean Museum), being a work of 1740 by Paul de Lamerie, has a handle like that of a spoon and its blade consists of a flat oval disk pierced and engraved with scrolls and fishes which are the principal and very suitable motif. Its ornament closely resembles that of the pair of gilt *mazarines* of 1762 in the Royal collection; these are oval vessels with a pierced strainer for fish or vegetables.

Tea Kettles and Stands. The typical 'Queen Anne' tea kettle was superseded in the twenties by a lighter model, little more than a foot high. Its body, shaped like an Edam cheese, is not unlike that of the globular tea pot, and it has a single more slender swing-handle whose grip is generally shaped like a bow, sometimes bound with cane; occasionally it is of wood and turned as in earlier examples. An early Rococo extravaganza (before 1737) by Charles Kandler is shown in plate 32: each foot of its tripod is cast as a triton, its body is embossed with marine deities and their attendants, its spout is a demi-triton blowing a conch, its finial a boy, and the two arms of its swing-handle are writhing mermaids. It stands on a triangular salver, which, though almost certainly destined for a kettle, was not made for this one. In comparison with this strange fantasy, the normal kettles are comparatively plain, with perhaps some flat-chasing round the lid, pierced openwork on the stand, and arms engraved on the left side of the body. The later examples tend to be lighter and more fanciful in ornament, chased flowers, foliage, shells, scrolls, and even oriental and classical figures and masks being employed.

Tea Urns. By the mid sixties the tea urn, a larger vessel nearly two feet in height, had been introduced. The body, standing on a substantial base and stem, is bulged like an inverted gourd and has a necked upper part with a domed cover and finial: two handles on the shoulder and a spout with a tap at the bottom of the body complete it. They are very elaborately ornamented with all the floral and Chinese motifs of the later rococo style, and they combine the techniques of casting, piercing, and embossing in their manufacture.

Tea Pots. Although the pear-shaped tea pot (plate 26b) was still made during the twenties, the typical form of this and the following decades was the so-called 'bullet-shaped'

Figure 41 – Barrel-shaped tea pot

pot (plate 27a). It has a tapering, straightish spout, a looped wooden handle, carved with a protruding scroll for a thumb-grip, and a flattish lid which is often flush with the body, topped by a small knopped wooden or silver finial. Many Scottish examples have globular bodies, with long straight spouts, a short stem and spreading foot, and a handle set high on the body (fig. 35).

An interesting instance of a silversmith (John Wirgman) following a ceramic design can be noticed in connexion with a tea pot of 1748 (Victoria and Albert Museum). Its crab-stock spout and handles, embossed vine-leaf tracery and finial in the form of a fox *couchant* are similar to those made of stoneware or porcelain, particularly in Staffordshire, from about 1740 to 1765.

During the fifties the drop-bottom began to be applied to the tea pot, producing a rather less attractive and top-heavy form raised on a stem and moulded foot. Ornament, other than engraved arms or flat-chased borders, is seldom found until well into the fifties when embossed rococo flowers and scrolls may be found. The spout is generally cast in an ornamental curve, and the handle has a double scroll.

Another variety first noted in the early twenties, also principally made in Scotland, is rather incongruously like a barrel, a form widely copied in ceramic wares (fig. 41).

Coffee Pots. The straight-sided variety lasted until the mid thirties, at first with a domed cover and later with a flatter moulded cover. Generally the handle is opposed to the spout; the height ranges from nine to twelve inches. Late examples of the sixties are often taller and more capacious, eighteen inches not being exceptional. The handle is almost invariably shaped as a double scroll of lime or fruit-wood, occasionally of ivory or of silver insulated with ivory.

The pear-shaped body, already noted on castors and tankards, was adapted to the coffee pot and became gradually more bulged and more waisted until the late sixties, when the dropped bottom was incorporated. The lids and ornament likewise became more flamboyant.

Until the late forties the pots were usually plain or flat-chased in contemporary style, and engraved with armorials: some pear-shaped examples by the Kandlers, fluted and elaborately flat-chased, rank among the most elegant and highly finished vessels of the mid thirties (plate 29). In the late forties they are embossed with rococo scrolls and foliage, later with sprays of flowers.

Jugs. The earliest pear-shaped jugs (plate 30b) date from the first years of the century; the form lasts into the sixties. They are characterized by a pointed and everted spout with a scrolled handle, occasionally set at right angles to it. On many larger jugs the spout was ornamented and a small C-scroll was inserted into the lower part of the handle. Small cream jugs, about three inches in height, retain almost universally the S-scrolled form of handle and are without decoration, except engraved arms. A small variety with a side-handle and lid was made until the mid thirties (plate 30a).

During the thirties the helmet-shaped ewer served as the model for a much smaller form of jug, sometimes set on three feet instead of a stem and base; the metal employed was later reduced in thickness and strengthened with embossing.

About the middle of the century the pear-shaped body is set on three cast hoof-feet; the neck became narrower, turning forward into the broad curved spout with a shaped edge, and considerably everted all round; it has a scrolled wire handle of two or three members. Jugs of this form are common and were often embossed and their interiors gilded (plate 30c).

During the sixties the dropped bottom set on a high moulded circular foot was adapted to the milk jug.

Another variety which is paralleled in ceramic forms of the time appears in the sixties; its barrel-shaped body, with slight neck, small lip, and moulded foot, being at once practical and attractive. A rather curious form of milk jug which enjoyed a short vogue is modelled as a hollow standing cow whose tail is curled to serve as a handle; it is filled through a hole on the back, of which the cover is ornamented with a circlet of flowers and a fly, and emptied through the mouth. It was made principally by John Schuppe (working 1753 to 1773) who was presumably an immigrant from the Netherlands where such cows were earlier made.

Tea Canisters. Canisters seem to have been produced with a greater variety of ornament and in more shapes than any other vessels. Simple, well-proportioned boxes with vertical sides on rectilinear plans, with horizontal mouldings and armorial engraving were common during the twenties (fig. 42). This form was adapted to the more sophisticated outlines and ornament introduced in the thirties, by rounding the shoulders and by heavily embossing their surfaces with rococo or Chinese ornament until the mid sixties (plate 31b). The transition into the *bombé* form typical of rococo ornament, likewise developed from flat-chasing to *chinoiseries, rocaille,* and flowers in low relief.

Though the rectangular plan is perhaps more common, circular canisters were a later development, made in con-

Figure 42 – Canister for tea

siderable variety (plates 31a, c). In the early fifties a form midway between that of a castor and an 'Adam' vase was developed, with a slip-on cover and two handles on which special spoons were to be hung.

Sugar Bowls. The plain hemispherical sugar bowl, which probably derived from Chinese porcelain tea bowls, with or without a saucer cover, continued until the fifties (plate 52a). The purpose of this cover is not certain, for in the painting in the Victoria and Albert Museum (see p. 175) it is shown leaning against its bowl unused, and certainly it had disappeared by the middle of the century. Perhaps it was used to hold spoons, a function that is performed by an oval fluted dish in the painting. A few are ornamented and the dropped-bottom was applied to the bowl and its cover (plate 31c). Dublin examples are of taller proportion and sometimes octagonal. A single example made at Aberdeen is an enlarged version of the tripod salt.

Baskets. Typical of the twenties and thirties is the oval basket, with a flat bottom heavily flat-chased about a space reserved for the engraved arms; the side is pierced, often with interlacing reeded straps; at each end is a cabled handle (plate 54a). During the early thirties these two handles were replaced on an otherwise identical basket by a single swing handle, and the oval basket with a swing handle became the standard form until the end of the century. In the later thirties panels pierced alternately with scrolls and diaper pattern gave a pleasing and lively appearance (plate 55a). Sometimes the sides are embossed but not pierced and the loop handle is fixed. At the end of that decade the plain moulding round the base was elaborated into a shaped and pierced skirting with scrolls to raise it on low feet, and every device of pierced and cast rococo was lavished on the many fine examples surviving from the middle decades (plate 54b). After about 1740 the body was frequently raised from one piece to which was applied four cast feet.

A novel and attractive form of basket made in the late forties is a large cockle shell on three dolphin feet with a heavy handle ending in a female term (plate 55a).

Salvers and Trays. The circular charger or tray, which has already been mentioned (p. 183), was made until the end of the twenties; its diameter ranges from twelve to as many as thirty inches. Some of them are gilt and many are engraved with armorials in the best manner (plate 48b, etc.), with finely conceived and original ornament about them. Up to the late thirties, many salvers were made with raised rims of six, eight, and ten curved sections. But most characteristic of the twenties were the square, or rectangular, salvers on four feet with the corners of the moulded rims shaped in two principal outlines (plates 48b and figs. 43b and c). During the thirties these forms were replaced by the almost circular salvers on four feet, with a moulded piecrust border made up of sections repeated six or eight times, in which the shaped moulded rim was combined with rococo shells and gadrooning. Until the 'Adam' period this remained the standard variety, with or without engraved arms and flat-chased rococo ornament (plate 49b).

During the rococo period a number of less common designs were made. One is triangular with heavy rococo ornament (cf. the tray supporting the kettle and stand,

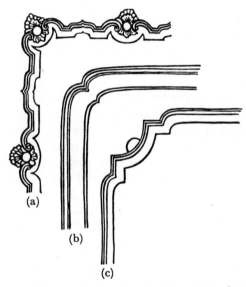

(a)

(b)

(c)

Figure 43 – Three varieties of corners for rectangular salvers, of the mid 18th century

plate 32). Piecrust borders were also given to square salvers and larger rectangular trays with bowed or serpentine sides. An exceptional pair is in low relief with *rocaille* borders on whose edge are three cherubs in clouds from which descends lightning.

Candlesticks. Little need be said about the ordinary candlesticks, made in pairs or in larger sets of even numbers, which retained the plain baluster form of the 'Queen Anne' style until the thirties. Even before 1720 the hexagonal or octagonal bases as well as the stem became shaped and ornamented (plate 57a), and some are raised on three or four feet. Cast and chased guilloche patterns in low relief were used and some examples were cast with rococo ornaments (plate 57b). An exceptionally ambitious pair of three-branched candelabra made in 1738 by Frederick Kandler may be described; the stand is made up of two nude figures, male and female, perhaps representing Adam and Eve, cast and chased in the round, seated on a rococo hump. The heavy ornament is very extravagant but of superb quality, including diverse masks, shells, swirled fluting, floral and foliate motifs. The more ornamental candlesticks tend to become taller, ranging from about six to as much as ten inches, and those with branches often reach sixteen inches.

Tapersticks. Most tapersticks follow in miniature the shapes of the candlesticks. In the fifties was introduced, perhaps by William Cafe, a taperstick in the form of a harlequin on a round base supporting in each hand a socket with a fluted grease pan (Victoria and Albert Museum); this might appear to have analogies with medieval latten figures supporting a socket or pricket in each hand. A large variety of mechanical coiled taper stands also exist which are variants in precious metal of the more common brass examples.

Chambersticks still continued to consist of the socket of an ordinary candlestick mounted with a low neck on a small dish, with or without feet; they have a scrolled handle and perhaps a conical extinguisher.

Wall Sconces. A few isolated wall sconces from the twenties and thirties are known, but very few were made after the accession of Queen Anne. In the royal inventories of 1725 there were ninety at Windsor, seventy-one at St James's, twenty-four at Kensington, twenty at Hampton Court and four in the Jewel Office, but they were perhaps even at that date no longer used.

Chandeliers. Of the three late chandeliers now surviving, two by Paul de Lamerie of 1734 are in the Kremlin and the third and latest, of 1752, with seventeen branches spreading from a body decorated with dolphins and seaweed, belongs to the Fishmongers' Company.

Standishes. Pounce or 'sand' (the powder of gum sandarach) was sprinkled over writing paper to make it less absorbent or on parchment to make it take the ink. The nibs of quill-pens quickly became clogged with the ink then used, so that a container of small lead shot was necessary in which to clean them. A wafer or sealing wax, which required a taperstick, was used to seal letters.

The standish therefore consisted basically of a footed tray holding a sandbox with perforations through which the sand could be sprinkled (fig. 38), and a matching inkpot lined with horn or glass, with a single round hole in the top. When only these two pots occur, the ink container, with a large central hole over it, is surrounded by shot reached by three or four small holes about the centre. If three separate containers were used, one contained ink, one the pounce, and the third shot. Often the inkpot and sandbox flank a small bell with a baluster handle, or a taperstick. The containers are usually bulged, with moulding or gadrooning on the upper and lower edges (plate 62a); with straight-sided trays, the pots are generally plain and cylindrical. Rectangular trays, with a deep trough parallel to almost the whole length of one side and a flattened baluster handle at right-angles lasted into the fifties. They have a bracket foot at each corner and a moulded or gadrooned rim. A common type about 1730 has a shaped rim ornamented with cast scrolls and shells, while oblong, octagonal, oval, rectangular, or shaped trays with a plain moulded edge or varyingly ornamented edges are not uncommon. In the late forties and fifties two oblong shallow depressions for the pens are to be found.

Toilet Sets. One of the finest and most complete toilet sets extant from the reign of George I is that now exhi-

bited in the Ashmolean Museum. It was made in 1724 by
Paul de Lamerie for George Treby, M.P., and consists of no
less than twenty-six pieces, including a mirror framed
in silver, two large and one small rectangular caskets, two
large and two small circular caskets, two whisks and two
clothes-brushes, a ewer (plate 37), four salvers (plate 48b),
two candlesticks, two pomade pots, two canisters, a pair of
snuffers and pan, and two glass jars. It is remarkable that
groups of like objects such as the rectangular caskets are
en suite, but there is no close relationship between other
groups within the set. It has a certain further interest
because the account still remains and shows the costs of
the metal, fashioning, and engraving respectively as well
as giving contemporary evidence about the exact purpose
which each item fulfilled.

	£	s.	d.
Delivred a fyne sett of dresing plate, fynely carved all over and chased, weighing together 637 oz 18 dwt, at 6s 2d per oz	196	13	10
Fashion 5s per oz	159	10	0
Engraving of all ye armes, &c	6	6	0
For ye glase and wooden frame	5	5	0
For ye 2 glasses for whater	0	16	0
For lyning of ye two comme [comb] boxes, ye 2 draughts, and that of ye juelle tronk . . .	2	2	0
For ye locke to ye juelle tronke	1	1	0
For ye tronk for all ye dresing plate . . .	5	5	0
For 4 brushes to clean ye cloth and commes . .	0	15	0
	£377	13	10

Comparable sets were made during this decade by
David Willaume, Isaac Liger, and John White.

Sir W. Williams-Wynn owns a pale gilt set made in
1768 by Thomas Heming, goldsmith to George II, which
reflects pure French rococo designs and ornament.

Soap Boxes. There are a small number of these spherical boxes on a moulded or gadrooned base; their covers
are hinged horizontally across the centre. These adjuncts

to the dressing-room seem to be of French origin and are about four inches in diameter.

Clocks and Watches. The ornamental spandrels and metal fittings on bracket clocks were usually of brass and sometimes of silver. During the eighteenth century watch cases were commonly made of gold and silver. They are generally classed as jewellery rather than plate, and their makers' marks, incuse initials, have not been reproduced by Sir Charles Jackson. Moreover, their quality is often very high. The pair-case, that is the inner case containing the movement and hinged to the glass cover over the dial, and the outer case of two solid covers hinged together, were generally assayed and hall-marked in the middle of the eighteenth century. The inner case is plain or engraved, pierced to allow the sound of the bell to escape, and the outer case is embossed and pierced with medallion heads, figures, and rococo ornament.

Miscellaneous. Embossed oval arm badges continued to be worn by, e.g., the crews of barges or the inmates of almshouses. They generally bear armorials, inscriptions, or symbols connected with the institution served. A large badge formerly worn by one of the crew of the Admiralty barge is ten inches in height, embossed in the centre with an anchor and about it a trophy of nautical equipment, and fish in rococo ornament (Victoria and Albert Museum). Many others, usually of inferior quality, are preserved elsewhere.

Some corporations had beadle's staff-heads, cast in the shape of emblems, such as the lyre of the Musicians' Company above a shield embossed on both sides with their arms; a later rococo example of 1755 by Samuel Courtauld is embossed with panels containing the City Arms and scenes symbolizing the manufacture of cloth, and surmounted by the arms and crest of the Clothworkers' Company complete with supporters.

CHAPTER EIGHT

1770–1800: The Neo-Classical Revival and the 'Adam' Style

THE improvement of manufacturing techniques and the cumulative results of new inventions had important effects on the methods of the silversmiths and on their status. Moreover, the position of London as the leading centre of plate manufacture was challenged and considerably reduced by competition from Sheffield and Birmingham.

About 1742 Thomas Boulsover, a Sheffield cutler (working 1740–88), discovered that if a sheet of silver be fused on to a thicker one of copper and the compound billet rolled, both metals, expanding equally, become a thin sheet of copper coated with a layer of silver. He sold buttons of this new compound which were much cheaper than the comparable ones of sterling silver and which yet seemed to be of the finer metal. This idea was exploited by Joseph Hancock and about 1755 applied to the manufacture of such domestic articles as candlesticks, coffee pots, and saucepans. Matthew Boulton (1728–1809), an established and enterprising manufacturer of metal goods at Birmingham, visited Sheffield to master this technique and began production of this new 'Sheffield plate' at his Soho factory in 1762. He obtained a monopoly of its manufacture there and retained the position of being the largest single manufacturer of Sheffield plate, although in about 1770 others began to imitate him. The quality of his products was exceptionally high, as can be judged from the examples in the Greenberg Collection in the City Museum and Art Gallery at Birmingham and elsewhere.

The rolling-mill had been used for more than half a

century with increasing frequency for the production of sheets of silver evenly rolled to any gauge, especially to the very thin gauges. During the sixties machinery was developed which could repeat with precision any number of times the same operations of stamping, embossing, or piercing that before had required the exertions of several craftsmen for many times as long. A stamping machine, patented in London in 1769 and soon improved, enabled simple sections to be shaped and repetitive patterns to be pierced with speed and accuracy. In 1779 a machine for making beaded wires was patented. Fly-presses were quickly put into use by the leading manufacturers, though many objects pierced during the last quarter of the century show such irregularities in the sizes of the apertures that it must be assumed that they were done by hand with drills and files in the traditional way.

Harder steels and more efficient mills increased the speed of production and reduced the thickness of the silver, so that some articles, especially candlesticks, needed interior strengthening with resin, pitch, or other filling, and to be weighted in their feet to give them stability.

While water-power was generally used to turn these machines, Boulton, with his partner Fothergill, introduced the steam engine into their factory in the late seventies. Indeed, it was at about this time that Boulton and others began to reproduce shaped parts in quantity for sale to smaller firms and individual makers for assembly – the first signs of the mass production that was in the following century to be overwhelmingly important.

These rapid improvements and the increasing use of mechanical techniques were followed by three results. In the first place, domestic plate cost less and therefore could be bought as a normal thing by proportionately less wealthy people than before; although the population was increasing, plate was being produced more than proportionately as quickly. Secondly, mechanical manufacturing methods required that many of the smaller wares should be of simple structure, with straight sides and lines of ornament that could be easily repeated. Thirdly, the flood of machine-made plate and plated wares, from Sheffield and Birmingham in particular, challenged the more conservative techniques of the London goldsmiths, whose virtual monopoly began to cease. Nevertheless, it was only the less imposing plate that could be produced in the factory, articles such as salt cellars, castors, candlesticks, spoons and forks, small jugs, and tea pots; any commissioned article or service was still made by hand in the traditional ways; the superiority in design and finish of these latter make the machine-made products look the uninspired and unsubstantial articles that they are because of, rather than in spite of, the huge variety in their designs and the regular nature of their ornament. It seems that less was expected from the manufacturers, craftsmen, designers, and machine minders because less could be demanded of them. The widespread possession of small domestic plate, at least of spoons and forks, was becoming normal throughout the upper-middle class which came to rely more and more on the stock-in-trade of a retailer, whose interest lies rather in selling what he has in his shop than in the potentials of the goldsmith who probably prefers to have a limited amount of work locked up in stock and to make whatever his client might want to order.

As a result of the Parliamentary Committee's enquiry of 1773, the energy of Matthew Boulton, and a petition presented to Parliament, *An Act for appointing Wardens and Assay Masters for assaying wrought plate in the towns of Sheffield and Birmingham* was passed in that year. The silversmiths and plate-workers in and about Birmingham and Sheffield were found to be 'under great difficulties and hardships in the exercise of their trades, for want of assayers in convenient places to assay and touch their wrought plate'. The incorporation of these two companies, known as 'The Guardians of the Standard of Wrought Plate', was justified by the great distances of these two rapidly developing centres from assay offices; Birmingham is rather more than a hundred miles from London, its principal market, and more than sixty miles from Chester, while Sheffield is situated at about the latter distance from both Chester and York. Regulations similar to those in force elsewhere were imposed, but the Act contains interesting information about the organization of the Companies, which was probably common to all others at that time, and had been from a much earlier date. Each company was to select four wardens annually and to have a permanent Assay Master and such assistants as were necessary; the former was to enter into a bond to the Master of the Mint for five hundred pounds with two guarantors. Each company had an office to which wrought plate was brought for examination by two wardens and the assayer:

to see if it all be of one sort of silver, and forward enough in the workmanship, and whether all the pieces be affixed together, and whether it be marked with the maker's or owner's mark or be not charged with unnecessary solder; and that if they shall find any such plate liable to either of the objections aforesaid, that then they shall return the same without making any assay thereof; but if they shall find such plate free from all the objections aforesaid that then there shall be drawn, scraped or cut off, in the presence of two of the wardens and assayer, so much from each piece, in proportion to the weight thereof, as will not exceed in the whole the rate of eight grains for every pound weight; and the drawings, scrapings or cuttings off from each piece shall immediately after be divided into moieties in the presence of the said wardens and assayer; and a moiety of the drawings, scrapings or cuttings off from each piece be delivered to the assayer for him to make his assays, and the other moiety shall be locked up with three different locks in a box to be provided for that purpose ... and the respective keys thereof shall be kept by two of the wardens and assayer of such respective company. ...

The same Act also forbade the stamping of any letters upon any manufactured article of metal plated, or covered with, or looking like, silver. This prohibition provoked doubts whether manufacturers of such articles might strike their name on their wares without incurring the penalty, and they were

deterred from striking their names upon plated goods, whereby a proper distinction betwixt plated goods, of the different manufacturers [was] prevented, and all emulation in that branch of business [was] destroyed, to the certain and manifest prejudice of the said manufactory.

Therefore the surname of the maker or the name of the firm in plain and legible characters, struck with one punch only, and also a mark, figure, or device easily distinguishable from those used by the assay offices, was granted to them subject to the approval of and registration by the Guardians. Some marks on plated goods, e.g. that of Boulton and Fothergill, might easily be mistaken for marks of sterling silver, consisting, as they do, of small punches containing the *Crown* and initials of the firm, very similar in form to those used by an assay office or silversmiths.

By another Act of the year 1784 a duty was imposed of eight shillings on every ounce of gold plate and sixpence on every ounce of silver plate made in the country, to be acknowledged by stamping the mark of the *Sovereign's Head* (fig. 44): such small wares as were already exempted from marking continued so. By this additional mark, used until its removal in 1890, the total number of punched marks was brought up to at least five, and on London-made Britannia plate, and on sterling plate made at Chester, Newcastle, and York, to six.

Figure 44
Sovereign's Head
(introduced 1784)

In 1784 two additional standards of gold plate of twenty and eighteen carats were added to that of twenty-two carats in Ireland to promote goldsmiths' work because

various manufacturers of Gold require gold of different degrees of hardness and purity, and it is expedient that the different standards of gold should be ascertained, and the manufacturers thereof be particularly distinguished.

In 1790 the provisions of the Acts of 1738 and 1784 about the exemption of small articles of silver were amended and clarified. Chains, necklace beads, lockets, any filigree work, shirt buckles or brooches, stamped medals, and anything weighing less than 5 dwt, except the necks, collars, and tops for castors, cruets, or glasses, etc., were exempted.

In 1798 the eighteen carat gold standard was introduced into England, to be marked with a *Crown* and the figure 18, instead of the *Lion passant*.

A survey of the number of men working in the precious metals, excluding makers of watch cases, buckles, and buttons, and other small workers, was made in the Parliamentary return of 1773. Of the 307 names listed, most with addresses in London, but a few as far away as Banbury, Bath (3), Chichester, Oxford (2), Sheffield, and Worcester, one hundred and fifty-six are described as 'goldsmiths', ninety-six as 'plateworkers', twenty-seven as 'spoon-makers', twenty-four as 'haft and hilt-makers', and two as 'candlestick makers' (James Gould, cf. plate 57a, and Jonathan Horsley).

Makers' marks are seldom other than Roman capitals in square or oval punches, and are often difficult to assign where the letters are the same. The number of partnerships requiring the use of two or three sets of initials is as many as a fifth of the whole number recorded by Jackson for this period.

Among the more prominent makers, Hester Bateman, who entered her mark in 1774 from Bunhill Row, has a reputation that derives from a large production of sound articles rather than any remarkable talent for design. She was presumably the capable head of a family concern which with others of her name, Jonathan, Peter, Anne, and two Williams lasted into the nineteenth century.

Among the spoon-makers are Thomas Chawner, Daniel Smith, and Robert Sharp (1763–96; Aldermanbury and Bartholomew Close); John Crouch and Thomas Hannam (1766–93; Giltspur Street); George Heming and William

Chawner (1773–81; New Bond Street); Charles Aldridge and Henry Green (1713–82; Aldersgate Street and St Martin's-le-Grand, plate 55b); John Wakelin and William Taylor (1786–96; Panton Street). Among other well-known makers the following deserve mention:. Henry Chawner, Burrage Davenport, William Eley, John Emes, William Fearn, Andrew Fogleberg, Robert Hennell, and John Schofield.

Occasionally objects bear a maker's mark and are yet inscribed as though they were made by a different firm, such as the cup and cover of 1772 (Corporation of the City of London) which is stamped with the maker's mark of John Romer but is inscribed 'PORTAL AND GEARING FECIT LUDGATE HILL'. Such inscriptions by retailers continued into the nineteenth century (cf. plate 63b) and illustrate their growing importance.

STYLE AND ORNAMENT*

Very quickly and completely the taste for rococo ornament disappeared; one could almost date the change to 1770, but some forerunners of the neo-classical designs date from the end of the previous decade and some few articles of rococo form or ornament come from as late as the last quarter of the century, particularly from Dublin and the provincial towns.

It will have been noticed that isolated classical motifs had persisted on the ornament of some English plate ever since the Middle Ages, but not even in the late Tudor period was the influence so marked and pervasive as it was during the half-century between 1770 and 1820. It was realized that the study of antiquity from objects was necessary to supplement knowledge obtained from books, and several groups were formed to pursue this purpose. The Society of Dilettanti was founded in London in 1732 to promote and encourage the excavation and examina-

* See plates 15a, 19d, 25a, 27b, 30d, 42d, 42c, 45a, 50b, 55b, 57c, 57d, 62b, 63a.

tion of Greek antiquities. Exploration of the ancient sites of Herculaneum, begun in 1711, and of Pompeii, was renewed in 1738. English travellers and artists visited these places and brought home sculpture, pottery, and other remains, which all became the subject of careful study and served to modify the conception of classical art as interpreted by the antiquaries of the Renaissance. Numerous illustrated works described the finds and the buildings; Giovanni Battista Piranesi, *Le Antiquità Romane* (1748); Comte de Caylus, *Recueil d'Antiquités égyptiennes, étrusques, etc.* (1752–67); Robert Wood, *Ruins of Palmyra* (1753); J. D. le Roy, *Les ruines des plus beaux monuments de la Grèce* (1758); G. B. Piranesi, *Della Magnificenza ed Architettura de' Romani* (1761); James Stuart and Nicholas Revitt, *Antiquities of Athens* (1762–1815); Robert Wood, *Ruins of Baalbec* (Heliopolis) (1757); Johann Joachim Wincklemann's *Monumenti Antichi* (1767), and other works.

The interest was international: in England the most influential figure was that of Robert Adam (1728–92), who was an antiquary as well as an architect and designer. He travelled in Italy (1754–8) and shortly after his return was appointed architect to George III. Some of his designs for silversmiths are preserved in the Soane Museum, e.g. a prize cup for the Richmond Races (the cup itself now belonging to the Marquess of Zetland (1770)), a candlestick and a cup for the Duke of Roxburgh (1775), and two tureens and a dish cover for the Duke of Northumberland (1779).

The first signs of the change seem to have come in architecture, then in interior decoration, after which plate was required to harmonize with the new interiors and furniture by Adam, Hepplewhite, Sheraton, and their followers.

New vessels were shaped to contrast sweeping regular and graduated curves with vertical and horizontal straight lines; sometimes these curves diverge only slightly from regular arcs or are perhaps based on volutes (plate 15a): in profile view concave curves are often separated from convex curves by a sharp shoulder (plate 30d). The calm repose of regularity and symmetry was the aim of every plan and elevation. The elegant lightness of Greek designs, if only imagined, was before the designer's eyes, so that he might make his products look as though poised,

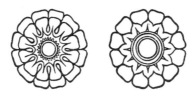

Figure 45 – *Paterae*

weightless, in perfect balance. Lightness in appearance was matched by lightness in actual weight, for thinner gauges of metal were much employed and even demanded by multiple production techniques.

Relief ornament was generally embossed or applied; delicate shallow fluting, vertical (plate 30d) or spiral, pal-

Figure 46 – Horizontal mouldings: (a) scrolling foliage, (b) Greek key pattern, (c) bay leaf garland

mettes and acanthus leaves (plate 25a), *paterae* (fig. 45), rams' heads (plate 25a), key patterns (fig. 46b), running floral scrolls (fig. 46a), bound bay-laurel wreaths (fig. 46c), swags of foliage or cloth draped over oval medallions, or tied up with ribbon bows. The most common mouldings are regular beading (plate 55b), astragals, and reeding (cf. plates 15a and 45a). Horizontal or vertical tablets in moulded borders served as a ground for inscriptions, embossed heads or figures in relief, e.g. race-horses in a close finish. Conventional engraving of patterns other than of armorials (plate 45a) or inscriptions was seldom used, for it was superseded by bright-cut engraving, a new technique whereby shallow curved grooves were cut with sides of varying steepness, the curving facets producing a brighter and more sparkling effect than the earlier deep and narrow incisions.

Coats of arms were placed in shields of four curves corresponding to the basic shape of the style (plate 45a) and surrounded with slender graceful palmettes or with drapes tied up with bows (plate 50b), in ovals surrounded by chains of diminishing husks. The style of lettering was usually a 'classic' copperplate with graduated thicknesses of great delicacy and precision, quite remote from the broader hands of the later seventeenth century.

Gold was seldom used and gilding was uncommon, though the interiors of sugar bowls, goblets, and other drinking vessels were often parcel-gilt. In some instances the covers or liners for silver dishes, tureens, etc., were made of Sheffield plate, especially in the nineteenth century, presumably to combine the appearance of massiveness with economy.

PRINCIPAL ARTICLES OF DOMESTIC PLATE

Two-Handled Cups and Covers. These became objects for decoration and award rather than for use as they had been during the previous hundred years. They were largely produced in the most typical of the neo-classical shapes (plate 15a), that is to say a deep bowl tapering almost to a point at its junction with the trumpet stem, which stands on a moulded circular base, itself sometimes raised on a low square or four-membered plinth. The cover is usually a simple scotia moulding with another scotia on a dome above surmounted by fruit, acorn, or vase finial.

Many of the handles are cast foliate S-scrolls, sometimes of irregular designs associated with the rococo period, sometimes not unlike those of the late seventeenth century. More generally, however, they are of a lightly tapering loop, reeded or beaded, rising from the lowest point of the bowl to above the level of the arris and then returning sharply in to the shoulder. The bowls are almost invariably embossed with an ornamental surbase of acanthus leaves of flutes, and further decorated, sometimes very lavishly, with heavy combinations of motifs from the neo-classical repertoire – acanthus leaves or husks, palmate leaves or honeysuckle flowers, bay-laurel wreaths or vine leaves; reeded, beaded, or guilloche moulding, straight, tapering, or spiral flutes; key and wave patterns; *paterae*, ribbons, and medallions of masks, heads, or figures; friezes of racing horses, and many more.

A second group of cups is distinguished by an egg-shaped bowl, such as is also found in Wedgwood's black basalt ware and wood. A particularly attractive small gilt example of 1772 by John Arnell is in the Victoria and Albert Museum; its principal decorative features are the vertical stripes, alternately plain and matted in imitation of veneers, and the curved horns on the head of the two satyrs' masks. A very tall and elaborate example of the same year belongs to the Corporation of London. Each of the massive handles represents a satyr clutching a bunch of grapes in one hand and with the other supporting the end of a bay laurel wreath which winds round the shoulders of the cup and loops beneath the handles. On the sides are large embossed panels, one an animated scene representing the Lord Mayor's procession and the other a composition of allegorical figures.

Tankards and Mugs. A combination of circumstances seems to have led to the decline in importance of these vessels – a greater consumption of wines and spirits being the most obvious. The straight-sided tankards of the Restoration and early Georgian period were reproduced but with small variations in the thumb-piece, mouldings, or proportions which distinguish them; many are examples of the eclecticism that is so noticeable a feature of the nineteenth century. Some, of barrel or drum form, reproduce in their ornament the staves and hoops in the manner noted in connexion with Elizabethan tankards (p. 99). Mugs resemble in particular those of the early eighteenth century (fig. 34) or continue the rococo styles.

Another small vessel, the fox-head stirrup cup, is perhaps based on the Greek *rhyton* of terracotta which represents a cow's head or that of a boar, sheep, or human, and has obvious associations with hunting. A fox-head rhyton from the Mycenean civilization (*c.* 1200 B.C.) is known. The form lasted into the nineteenth century, when greyhounds' and other heads were adopted to the same purpose.

Wine Coolers. Made singly, or in sets of two or four, the principal type designed to hold a single bottle is based on the Greek red-figured kalyx-krater of the fifth and fourth centuries B.C., with ring or loop handles, and vine branch ornament. Another kind, derived from a dairy bucket, imitates the wooden wine cooler with polished mahogany staves, brass hoops, and loop handles. They stand from seven to ten inches in height (plate 25a).

Coasters. A small circular device with plain or pierced silver or plated sides on wooden bases mounted on baize, to slide decanters and bottles along the table to prevent scratches and stains, are found from the sixties onwards often in sets of up to half a dozen (cf. plate 63b). The ornament generally relates closely to that on salt cellars or dish rings: sometimes ring-handles are added.

Wine Labels and Bottle Tickets. They are commonly rectangular, oval, or crescent-shaped, engraved or pierced with the name of a wine or sauce within a beaded or gadrooned border; they hang round the neck of a bottle or decanter by a loop of chain attached at either end. Very many shapes are found with various ornaments and inscriptions. They form a popular field for the specialist collector (see Bibliography).

Tea Services. Hitherto the tea service had been scarcely known as a group of vessels designed to match, and the necessary items, though maybe agreeing in style, seem to have been assembled, purchased, or at least designed individually. In the later Adam period tea services consisting of a tea pot, a sugar bowl, and a milk jug, with the addition of a hot-water jug and sometimes a tray, were made in large quantities in the thinner gauges of metal that allowed a wide sale.

Tea Pots. The most typical of tea pots had vertical sides on oval, octangular, circular, or shaped plans (plate 27b); from near the base rose a straight tapering spout with a slipped lip at the level of the shoulder: the handle with a thumb-grip, generally of ebony, is looped, sometimes with a straight horizontal top. The egg-shaped vase was adapted to the tea pot, its vertical stripes, or flutes, imitating the alternate veneers of wooden vases of like shape. In the nineties the curved side rising from a narrow foot, curved spout, and curved lid of one or two concave stages became popular.

Tea Kettles. Although the tea kettle had retained its basic form for two generations, the disadvantage of pivoting the whole receptacle led to new and ungainly types, holding up to three pints, with sloping sides, a wide cane-covered handle, a flat lid, and a long horizontal spout operated by a tap: the body is supported on a frame of four curved and reeded legs, with a lamp between them. These are half-way to the urn.

Tea Urns. Based on the vase form and similarly ornamented, these have a spout and tap in front, the end sometimes cast and chased as animal, bird, or dolphin. A second type, repeated many times with variations by Paul Storr, resembles a soup tureen, with two handles on each side and a longish horizontal spout, the handle of the tap being in the form of an anthemion (fig. 48), on a square four-footed pedestal. Monumental in appearance, they are as much as fifteen inches in height and 180 ounces in weight.

Jugs. Jugs follow the contemporary forms, with a tall
scotia neck, a broad curved lip and loop handle of wood,
covered in basket work, or in the form of entwined snakes.
They are set on a trumpet stem or three cast legs on a
three-armed base. There is some confusion about the purpose of such vessels, which may be used for a variety of
purposes. Many have lamps and stands, fitting them as
hot-water jugs or chocolate pots.

Milk and Cream Jugs. Rococo shapes and ornament
lasted on the variety with dropped bottom and double-
or treble-scrolled handle, which was made of very thin
plate, sometimes embossed and strengthened by applied
mouldings. The prevailing elevations though in a weaker
form were adapted to the jug, one type in particular, a
small version of the tall jugs, being very pleasing (plate
30d). Their lightness and disproportionately narrow base
make them easily overturned. Perhaps for this reason a
lower and broader type, analogous in design to the tea
pot, was introduced in the nineties, of oval, often lobed,
plan and slightly curved sides, with a loop handle and
narrow curved lip. Occasional examples of glass set in
pierced silver frames are found.

Tea Caddies. A common type during the seventies was
based on the Adam vase, though the proportions were
sometimes rather distorted, embossed with ornament, and
sometimes ring-handles were added. A second severer
variety is a box with vertical sides and a flat top, of square,
rectangular, or oval plan. They are often bright-cut with
neo-classical ornament in horizontal or vertical bands with
imitated Chinese characters, or with coats-of-arms. Some
are fitted with a lock, others have a tall cover and finial.
On slightly later caddies the sides were a little bulged and
tapered to the base, with horizontal mouldings at the top
and base.

Coffee Pots. After the late rococo designs had been dis-
carded in the seventies, coffee pots seem either to have
been included in a tea and coffee set, or to have been
made separately with the elevation of the vase, on a

shaped or oval plan, a recurved and tapered spout and a long loop handle. Although they lack a lamp, it may be supposed that such jugs were used for hot water as well.

Sugar Bowls. Glass liners, of blue or other colours, were inserted in pierced frames for holding sugar, without the reason (to prevent tarnishing) that had applied in the case of salt cellars, probably because silver with pierced designs was found to be very pretty against such a background. Sugar and cream pails were made en suite, the latter being a little larger.

The principal pattern consisted of a bucket-shaped glass liner supported in a pierced frame itself modelled like an ornamental bucket with a swing handle. These were sometimes made as cream pails, and are equally serviceable for sugar, cream, or jam; but the fact that they are often found in cases with two tea caddies indicates that they were originally for holding sugar. Other varieties are based on the boat-shaped tureen with a central swing-handle, the Adam vase, and the cauldron salt with three feet.

Baskets. The oval form of basket with swing-handle hitherto current was developed with more graceful lines in a very much thinner metal and to it was applied neo-classical ornament. Baskets are either built up of ornamental wires or of pierced sections, or raised up from a single sheet and pierced afterwards. The handles were often of plaited wire or open guilloche pattern or in the late eighties and through the nineties of a reeded loop tapering slightly towards the hinges, at which time a more pointed plan, almost approaching a vesica, is found, and the basket becomes rather boat-shaped with the upswept ends prevalent in that decade (plate 55b). Another variety consists in an oval cut-glass liner set in a pierced frame on four feet or raised on a low plinth, with solid drop ring-handles suspended from a lion's or ram's mask at either end.

Trays. In their most usual form, trays were oval with a moulded, or pierced, edge with a reeded or gadrooned rim, on four feet. Their flat surface is frequently engraved with bright-cut swags of husks or flowers, or with armorials in the centre. Late examples in particular have a loop handle at each end (plate 50b).

Salvers. Taking the prevailing circular, or oval, forms, they have, like trays, moulded or pierced borders; the centres engraved with armorials. They are sometimes made in matching sets of different diameters, the largest serving as a tray.

Candlesticks and Candelabra. The acceptance of neo-classical patterns produced two principal forms of candlestick. Firstly the pillar with a Corinthian, composite, or ornamental capital, its base usually raised upon a square pedestal embossed with suspended wreaths, draperies, or some other appropriate motif recalling a classical altar (plate 57c). Secondly on a square base with a concave moulding, the tall, slender, four-sided pedestal surmounted by an urn; a less elaborate variant has a tapering stem with a bell-shaped socket on a circular foot (plate 57d). Embossed from this metal and weighted within the foot with some heavy composition, they usually stand about eleven to thirteen inches in height. Other forms of stem are shaped as balusters or trumpets. The branches, two or three, fit into the socket, which is capped by a finial in the form of an ornamental cup, or an urn, or by another candle socket, and almost invariably curve round in the opposite direction to that from which they spring. These branches bring the height up to twenty or more inches. Another variety of branch which does not recurve, gives the appearance of being attached to the central pillar by small arched members that fit into sockets at either end.

Inkstands. The words 'standish' was in this period replaced by 'inkstand' to describe a tray holding cut flint-glass bottles with silver mounts (plate 62b); three bottles (for ink, sand, and lead shot), or sometimes four, are found on a tray, of which the sides are often pierced; oval and boat-shaped examples are found, sometimes with swing-handles; the least substantial stands are no more than silver wires soldered together.

Dinner Services. From the last quarter of the century many complete dinner services of considerable size have survived. Two soup tureens and four or more sauce tureens of the same design each with its own stand are not unusually found together. Both soup and sauce tureens, the former being about twice as high and of much greater capacity than the latter, follow for the most part the same two shapes. The earlier pattern (plate 45a) has an oval bowl with a loop handle at each end on a spreading stem and broad base; its cover like those of many vases is formed of a single scotia surmounted by a dome and finial; common ornaments round the body are swags of husks or bay wreaths, looped over *paterae.* The later pattern gives a lighter effect; the rim of the tureen itself curves up in a sweep to the handles, to which shape the lower edges of the cover have to conform, curving up at each end with a domed centre, and a foliate or vase-shaped finial. The edges are frequently gadrooned, reeded, or beaded: shallow radiating flutes or gadroons are embossed on the covers and surbases. A less common form of handle is a solid ring suspended from a mask at each end.

Entrée Dishes. These low oval or octagonal dishes are generally made in sets of two, four, or more, their length being about eleven inches. Some examples have a handle at each end. They have an unattached domed lid with a loop handle and are seldom ornamented with more than a moulded edge, and engraved arms, or crest on the cover. Some examples are raised up on a frame to hold a spirit lamp beneath.

Épergnes. Providing a useful centre piece for the dinner table, their baskets and dishes assume most of the elements and ornaments of the period. Yet they are remarkable for lacking anything of the neo-classical unity of design, for which fault the inclusion of the earlier type of branches with their recurving and scrolled members is largely responsible. More harmoniously designed *épergnes* have an oval tray with a pierced gallery standing on four or six feet, above each of which a pillar continues upwards to support pierced dishes all containing glass liners, while in the centre of the tray a spreading pedestal supports a large oval dish of similar pattern.

Dish Rings. They are shaped like a pulley wheel, three or four inches in height, but the upper rim is generally a little smaller in diameter, about seven or eight inches, than the lower; along both are soldered square wires for rigidity, which later are omitted, and the same purpose achieved by bending back the edge. Their pierced ornament, particularly in the seventies, is often most original, consisting in sporting or *genre* scenes, designs of animals, birds, flowers, of fruit on elaborately designed openwork grounds (plate 63a): during the last two decades the increasing use of fly-presses in factory production brought more repetitive and regular designs, vertical pierced pales being most characteristic: bright-cut engraving heightens the effect of lightness.

Salt Cellars. Cauldron salt cellars like those made during the middle decades of the century were still produced, the tripod and the hoof motifs not clashing with the general conception of classical art. On the other hand new forms were introduced, notably many designed with four feet and a vertical side to contain a glass liner, usually blue, sometimes red. The new facilities for piercing and embossing by machinery and the lightness of the metal employed allowed quick cheap production and limitless combinations of ornament. The most common salt cellars of oval plan on flat bases with straight sides, supported on four feet, are of many designs with classical analogies. In the seventies and eighties the upper edge with a plain or beaded moulding was generally horizontal, straight, or slightly shaped (plate 42d): in the nineties upcurved ends were common (plate 42e). The ornament was generally of vertical repetitive piercings with solid oval panels at the centre of each side; some are unpierced, others have bands of very small piercings, plain or with bright-cut engraving; the edges are usually strengthened with beading, reeding, or other light mouldings.

Mustard Pots. Their individual patterns are as numerous as those of salt cellars. Generally oval or circular, with straight vertical sides engraved, pierced or plain scrolled handles, small thumb-pieces on the domed or flat covers, they are about two or three inches in height on a moulded base and show many resemblances to contemporary salts and, on a smaller scale, to tankards. They often have glass liners and spoons, which were supplied with them.

Castors. The retention of the baluster forms throughout the Adam period is remarkable. Some new shapes were introduced analogous to the two-handled vase and the Elizabethan castor.

Flat Plate. To the old English pattern of spoon and fork was given various ornaments, the reeded edge (plate 61c), a feathered edge, during the last two decades bright-cut, threaded edge or thread and shell, and most the fiddle pattern (plate 61e) which has had such a long vogue since, with threaded edge, which developed through the thread and shell pattern to the heavy King's pattern (plate 61f).

Among the many other articles of plate made during the last thirty years of the century may be enumerated egg cruets, toasted-cheese dishes, beehive honey pots, butter dishes, asparagus servers, fish slices, and skewers.

CHAPTER NINE

1800–37: The Regency and the Beginnings of Romanticism

THE nineteenth century opened during the French Wars, with violent alternations of victory and setback in the spheres of politics, diplomacy, and war. The reign of the ageing George III ended under the restricted regency for nine years of his extravagant and unpopular son, who succeeded him in 1820. George IV was nevertheless a patron of wealth, taste, and imagination and, as both Prince of Wales and King, should perhaps be singled out as the director of contemporary fashions that are grouped under the heading 'Regency'. It is too superficial to use the phrase 'Regency style' to cover any particular and isolated series of motifs, because the designers of this generation drew eclectically on motifs from the Far and Near East, from ancient Egypt, Greece, and Imperial Rome, and from Gothic architecture. The construction within so few years of such diverse buildings as Brighton Pavilion, the British Museum, Eaton Hall ('Cathedral Gothic'), and the Egyptian Library at Plymouth could not fail to be reflected in the mixture of motifs used in furnishings. The conjunction in plate no less than in architecture of motifs from widely separated sources is constantly found. Moreover, Great Britain was established at the Congress of Vienna (1815) as the most powerful country in the world; and London was the greatest city, and still rapidly expanding. It is therefore to be expected that some monumental pieces of plate should have been made at this period, and several occasions for their presentation were afforded by the exploits of the Duke of Wellington and others. At the same time advances in mechanical techniques allowed great quantities of simple inexpensive plate to be produced for an ever-growing market of successful merchants and professional people. Between the extremes of the machine-made fork (plate 61e) and the large pair of gilt candelabra at Apsley House (plate 58) lies a huge and somewhat neglected expanse of silver wares for so many purposes and of so many designs, on paper and executed, that a thorough and systematic exposition would be tedious, were it indeed feasible. But certain general observations will perhaps help in the recognition of some of the more dominant characteristics of 'Regency' plate.

While the Greeks employed simple ornaments and pure forms the Romans were inclined to overwhelm the beholder by the weight of ornament on works already on a monumental scale. The Greco-Roman style of Adam was almost abandoned in favour of the heavier elaborations of late Imperial Roman forms, sometimes combined with additional motifs from Egypt, mostly based on the sphinx and royal masks with their characteristic headdresses. The latter were more prominent in France than England, because Napoleon had taken French archaeologists to Egypt; some of the material they had collected was captured by the English.

A pioneer in outmoding the Adam style was Charles Heathcote Tatham (1772–1842), who in 1799 published *Ancient Ornamental Architecture at Rome and in Italy,* and in 1806 *Designs for Ornamental Plate.* He complains in the latter work that 'instead of *Massiveness,* the principal characteristic of good Plate, light and insignificant forms have prevailed, to the utter exclusion of all good Ornament whatever'. His insistence on great attention to finish, especially to chasing, seems to have been heeded widely by the manufacturers. Nevertheless, the lightness of metal, the tall slender forms, and the general absence of ornament on plate made during the last three decades of the previous century may seem today to compare more than favourably with the heavier weight of metal. the low forms and the heavy sculpted ornament that characterize the 'Regency' period.

The most acute and powerful personality among the goldsmiths of this generation was Philip Rundell (1743–1827) who quickly dominated his partners at the sign of the 'Golden Salmon' on Ludgate Hill. About 1780 John Bridge, their principal maker, joined the partnership. They profited enormously from trade in jewels and valuables brought to England by refugees from the French Revolution. From 1805 Rundell, Bridge, and Rundell, having already attracted the patronage of George III, the Prince of Wales, and the Duke of York, prospered until the business was bought in 1839 by Francis Lambert (d. 1841) and transferred to Coventry Street. About 1806–8 they were continuously employing a thousand hands, an exceptional number for such an enterprise at any time, and received more orders than they could fulfil. Very large quantities of plate marked by the firm survive today, ranging from cutlery to the most massive pieces of the period; it is not therefore surprising that they were obliged to pass on the manufacture of some of their commissions to other firms, for example to the partners Digby Scott and Benjamin Smith (who entered their mark in 1802) or to Paul Storr (working 1792–1821). More than any other of the many highly skilled plate-workers of the period Storr stands out as a personality and executant of the highest merit. An important early work (1797) is the font, weighing 245 ounces, made for the christening of the eldest son of the fourth Duke of Portland: it consists in a high-shouldered bowl with ornamental bands supported on four winged cherubim, on a base thirteen inches square, with six sculpted figures; one, standing, represents Faith, and two seated figures represent Hope and Charity, with three children.

During the nineteenth century all the London hall-marks were made in various sizes, from one quarter to one sixteenth of an inch in height. It will be noticed (fig. 47) that the smaller ones are grouped together in regular alignment, their punches having been set in a frame so that they could be stamped together at one blow. This feature is particularly useful for quick recognition of copies made in the nineteenth and twentieth centuries after traditional designs. The *makers' mark,* separately punched, is usually the initials of the Christian name and surname, sometimes of two or three partners together, in roman, italic, or gothic letters in simple outlines. The crowns denoting royal patronage on the marks of Philip Rundell and John Bridge are almost the only emblems found.

Changing partnerships controlled considerable workshops and large staffs of highly skilled workmen who stamped small incuse signs or initials on plate bearing their employers' punch (cf. the hall-marks on the fork of 1837 (plate 61f) and the workman's letter T and two crescents (fig. 47)).

Figure 47
Hall-marks
(London, 1815;
William Eley
and
William Fearn)
(Note that the
Leopard's Head
was not
punched)

Besides sub-contracting to other firms, Rundells were able to employ designers and to commission outstanding artists for their more important orders. Among the latter were Francis Chantrey (1781–1841) the sculptor, John Flaxman (1756–1834) the painter and book-illustrator, the younger Charles Catton (1756–1819), the Italian Benedetto Pistrucci (1784–1855) the medallist and gem engraver who came to London in 1815, and William Theed (1764–1817) who, after studying at the Royal Academy Schools and in Rome, worked on his return for Wedgwood, and from 1803 for Rundells; in 1814 he showed two models at the Royal Academy, one for a Bacchanalian group commissioned by the Prince Regent. Several interesting but undated designs by Boileau for more ordinary work are in the Victoria and Albert Museum.

Garrard's is another well-known firm remarkable for a

continuity that can be traced under various names from George Wickes, a plateworker who entered his mark in 1721, until its merger in 1952 with the Goldsmiths' and Silversmiths' Company of Regent Street. It succeeded Rundells as the royal goldsmiths, an appointment which it still holds. Other substantial makers are Hennells, the Batemans, the Barnards, William Fountain, John Emes, William Burwash, and John Crouch, to name only a few.

The application of power-driven machinery to the manufacture of plate was developed, and successful enquiries into electrical phenomena showed that electric currents too could be used for depositing metal. Volta published a successful experiment in 1805 and the 'Galvanic Goblet' (Paul Storr after Flaxman, 1814) in the Royal collection seems to be the first isolated example of applied electro-gilding. It was not until Arthur Smee published his results in 1840 that these possibilities could be taken up commercially, a field in which Messrs Elkington were pioneers.

STYLE AND ORNAMENT*

The predominant influence of classical sculpture, architecture, and literature can be exemplified by reference to a few important pieces not illustrated here. At Windsor Castle is preserved one of the four silver versions of the round *Shield of Achilles* commissioned in 1818, designed by Flaxman, and, though William Pitts claimed to have executed all the chasing, bearing the mark of Philip Rundell (1821). Three feet in diameter and weighing six hundred and sixty ounces, they have a continuous frieze in low relief round the border, and a chariot drawn by four horses (*quadriga*) in high relief on the boss.

Flaxman also designed two candelabra (1809–10) in the Royal Collection; one represents the Three Graces gathering the Apples of the Hesperides and the other Mercury

* See plates 15b, 23b, 25b, 42f, 45b, 47, 52b, 53, 58, 59, 61c, 61e, 61f, 63b.

presenting Bacchus to the Nymphs; also preserved there are his large cup, bearing Storr's mark for 1812, its frieze in low relief illustrating the first Idyll of Theocritus, his four ice-pails (J. Bridge, 1807), which together weigh two thousand and eighty-eight ounces, and the same maker's vase with scenes of the Gold and Silver Ages (1826). Another imposing cup from Flaxman's design and modelled by his pupil E. H. Bailey was presented to the actor John Kemble (1757–1823).

The organizers of Lloyd's Patriotic Fund – being very closely concerned with the outcome of the Napoleonic Wars especially in so far as the sea-routes were concerned – made many presentations of vases, valued at three hundred pounds each, after the Battle of Trafalgar (1805) to the admirals and some of the captains who had taken part in the action. This series was made by Scott and Smith after designs by John Flaxman about 1805–6.

Perhaps the most remarkable of all the presentations made to the Duke of Wellington is the pair of huge gilt candelabra (plate 58) nearly five feet in height; they were commissioned by the Merchants and Bankers of the City of London from Green, Ward and Green, and were made by Benjamin Smith in 1816–17. A later part of the same set is the Wellington Shield, about 1822, designed by Thomas Stothard in the manner of the Achilles Shield; forty inches in diameter, its central medallion in high relief representing Wellington and his officers is surrounded by twelve panels embossed with battle scenes, based on those of the Elgin marbles. Some of the drawings reveal that these designers were men with little experience of the techniques of the goldsmith. The stem and branches of a candelabrum designed by Catton, but probably not executed, is decorated with a fruiting vine-bush with tendrils and branches in a profusion that poses the greatest technical difficulties. Generally speaking, however, the superior drawing of such designers was put to most advantageous use by the modellers of figure compositions, either in the round or in relief. That the techniques of casting and embossing achieved a higher standard of naturalistic design and modelling at the beginning of the nineteenth century than at any time since the Italian Renaissance, may be borne out by the examples on plates 15b and 25b.

Turning to the more generally manufactured articles of domestic plate, a most striking feature is the absence of any style capable of simple explanation and illustration.

Figure 48 – Anthemion (palmette, honeysuckle)

Perhaps the anthemion (fig. 48) is the most characteristic single decorative motif, being used on the largest vessels as well as on cutlery. Decorative motifs of various ancient and modern origins were reproduced with meticulous finish. Most domestic plate of the first fifteen years of the century was moderately plain and its ornament was drawn from moulding, repetitive stamped patterns, horizontal bands of chased scrolling foliage, or key-pattern designs.

The loop handles of cups and other vessels are often flat at the top with angles instead of being rounded (fig. 49), and in some cases with a key-pattern volute.

In some instances the Adam style lingered on with little modification. Its pure curved forms are often obscured by undulations in the horizontal lines that were formerly straight, by being given square, octagonal, or shaped plans, or by having sharper curves. But many new shapes were introduced, the straight vertical sides of many vessels were bowed

Figure 49 – Handle with flat top

while retaining a square or octagonal plan; the peaked top forming a sort of flange round the forward curve of a tea pot lid came in about 1800. Hot-water jugs were set on classical tripod legs with a spirit lamp between. Rococo ornament was reintroduced into the designers' repertoire; C-scrolls, *rocaille*, and flowers, generally flat-chased or applied, but amorphous and heavy by comparison with the imaginative asymmetry and grace of the mid eighteenth century. Yet a few extremely delicate examples do exist, full of spirit and invention, including *chinoiseries* in the rococo manner. At this period many earlier vessels, tea pots, jugs, spoons, or tankards began to be sent to a silversmith for embossing in the rococo style. Very many vessels were given a low vase shape derived from the Greek lamp; if a higher vessel was required a tall concave neck might be added above (fig. 51).

Even before the reign of William IV (1830–7) the Romantic movement began to affect the ornament on plate with an eclectic mixture of inventions. Many fanciful new ornaments or combinations of ornament modified classical or eighteenth-century motifs with contemporary ideas. The Weymouth Regatta Cup (Victoria and Albert Museum) is essentially a kalyx-krater, whose handles are cast as a garland of flowers; round the body are no less than ten different types of foliate ornament including lotus and acanthus leaves, roses, and grapes, cast and chased in horizontal bands, together with a view of Weymouth from outside the harbour; on the cover the figure of a sailor stands by an anchor.

PRINCIPAL ARTICLES OF DOMESTIC PLATE

Cups and Vases. The original purpose of such vessels, namely, to be drinking cups, was now lost. They were almost always made for presentation, and are therefore largely ornamental. They differ very considerably one from another in size, outline, and ornament, according to the purpose of the commission and the taste of the selectors.

The sharp light outlines of the Adam period have been replaced by something less graceful and more heavily decorated with embossed, applied, or engraved ornament; this includes all kinds of classical motifs, such as anthemion, key (plate 15b) and wave patterns (plate 25a), gadrooning, formal water-plant or acanthus leaves (plate 53), bay-wreaths (fig. 46c), naturalistic vine branches and sprigs of oak (plate 45b), scrolling foliage (fig. 46a), and, later, more particularized motifs such as human and other figures (plate 58), vistas, and landscapes. In some cases the same form of ornament was strictly repeated on cover,

Figure 50 – Tea pot

body, and base in horizontal bands; in others the motifs were mixed. The handles present a variety of forms, including the graceful Adam loop with an arched or straight top, often decorated with guilloche bands and *paterae*, many varieties of snakes, horizontal loop handles with heavy cast joints, and the volute handle, an innovation to English plate derived from the Attic volute-krater.

Common finials are some sort of fruit or seed in an open calyx, feathers, animals, and many other devices appropriate to a particular commission. The Brighton Cup (plate 15b) made by John Emes (1805) for Rundell, Bridge and Rundell, has been selected to represent, as far as any single example can, some of the more common features of these vessels.

Tea Services. The falling prices and greater imports of tea and sugar, resulting from the stronger hold on India, are reflected in the numbers of tea services made during the period. The tea service comprised a tea pot, a milk jug, a sugar bowl, and a hot-water jug to match; sometimes the jug is mounted on a tripod stand with a spirit burner below: occasionally a kettle on a stand was added and sometimes tea and coffee sets were combined. Imitations of earlier Georgian patterns are not unknown. Tea

Figure 51 – Jug

pots and other items were made for sale separately. For use in hot countries, the sugar bowl and milk jug were given lids like the tea pot and jug.

Tea Pots. The great variations in size, shapes, proportions, and ornament prevent any concise description. In plan they may be square, polygonal, oval, or circular; in elevation the side generally curves upwards and outwards to an angular shoulder above which the incurved neck is surmounted by a domed cover. The spouts of flattish D-section taper towards the open end in an ogival curve (fig. 50). The handles, of ivory, of wood, or of silver with inserted insulators, are often of rectangular section with a flat top and a thumb-piece, or curved of an oval section. The covers, with button, vase, or plant finials, are flat, domed, or moulded. Some follow Adam designs save for the spout and the slightly bowed sides. One notable shape has a peaked front (fig. 50). Low moulded bases, low stems, and three feet are found; others with four ball feet are common. Ornament, sometimes absent altogether, includes embossed or applied gadrooning, bands of running nebulée lines, imitation rococo embossing, repetitive branch patterns derived from Wedgwood borders. They commonly hold about two pints.

Milk Jugs. These follow the many shapes and ornaments of tea pots and are rather low, lacking the tall stems

Figure 52 – Salt cellar

of the Adam period. Their spouts are broad and their handles narrow.

Sugar Basins. Their bodies are rather larger than, but match those of the milk jugs, the two opposed handles being of the same design as the single handle on the jugs. One remarkable and popular pattern of sugar vase, unconnected with any tea service, but rather for use on the dinner table, is shown in plate 53. See also p. 250.

Hot-Water Jugs. These are sometimes mistaken for coffee pots but may equally well be used for either purpose. Some resemble the tea pot in plan but they are proportionately taller; others resemble the tea pot closely only up to the shoulder above which an elongated scotia neck rises, ending in a broad curved and everted lip, with

a shaped mouth or with a cover like that of the tea pot
(fig. 51). Their pedestals, if any, are based on classical
tripod forms with paw feet, sometimes on three-armed
bases; the burners are shaped like the bodies of classical
lamps.

Salt Cellars. Very many varieties of salt cellars are
found; they seldom weigh more than a few ounces. They
are generally circular or oval in section, occasionally
angular, and they stand either on low moulded bases with
a waisted stem, or on three or four cast feet. The former
have a shallow or almost hemispherical bowl, with a
moulded or gadrooned border, sometimes very like those
of the mid eighteenth century (plate 42f). Others are
based on the Adam tureen, and may have looped or
scrolled handles (fig. 52). Those on feet are either late
versions of the cauldron salt (plate 42c), or miniature
bombé tureens (plate 45b) or small versions of baskets,
sometimes with a fixed handle (cf. plate 54).

Castors. For the most part castors are little more than
copies or variations of earlier patterns, those of the rococo
period being especially imitated. In the collection of H.M.
the Queen is a copy (1824) by Robert Garrard of a castor
very like those in Paul de Lamerie's set of 1735 (plate 43c).

Candelabra and Candlesticks. The introduction of Sheffield plate and weighted bases in the last third of the
eighteenth century allowed candlesticks to be on a more
grandiose scale, at a low cost and for the use of a small
amount of silver; often they survive in pairs or in sets of
up to a dozen. Candlesticks of this nature vary in height
from about nine inches to candelabra of more than two
feet and, in the exceptional case of the huge gilt pair at
Apsley House (plate 58), to nearly five feet. Silver candlesticks are found with branches of Sheffield plate which
were either made for them at the same time or added
later. Sheffield plate candelabra may be found matching
with a set of smaller silver candlesticks by the same maker.
This increased scale of production required a more digni-
fied design than that of the small cast baluster forms of

1680–1770 or even Regency copies of them, such as the single gilt example of 1814 by Paul Storr made for Rundell's, perhaps to replace one lost from a set belonging to the Duke of Cumberland (Victoria and Albert Museum). A good example of the massive, heavily ornamented candelabra, in the style characteristic of Paul Storr, is reproduced on plate 59.

The most usual design had a tapering shaft, rising from a domed and moulded circular foot to a knopped shoulder, with a narrow neck surmounted by a vase-shaped socket, often with gadrooning and bay-laurel leaf ornament. The two, three, or four branches are each shaped in an identical complex curve, rather like tendrils, and are sometimes ornamented with a double foliate knop, reeding, or ribbons: their sockets, each with a grease pan below, resemble those on the parent candlestick: sometimes there is an additional socket in the centre directly above the stem, which replaces the more general ornamental vase or other figure. Other stems are based on the square classical pedestal, ornamented with masks, swags, and draperies, or on ornamental columns. Partly draped female supporting figures, standing on waisted and ornamental plinths, follow an earlier tradition.

Inkstands. The commonest form of inkstand is made up of a rectangular tray with border of reeding or heavy ornament supported on four ornamental feet: some examples are floridly pierced and cast in the rococo manner. Two oblong depressions flank a raised pedestal on which are generally fitted three receptacles, the inkwell and the sandbox flanking the wafer box: on the cover of the last is often fitted a small low taperstick, usually with a conical extinguisher attached by a chain, and a ring finger grip. These three containers, square or circular, are generally of cut glass, but sometimes the central vessel or all three are entirely of silver. An elaboration of this pattern has two inkwells and two sand-boxes of glass, with a wafer box in the centre and taperstick mounted on four foliate scrolls. Another variety of inkstand on an oblong octangular tray has three identical covered cups with chased acanthus ornament and rayed cover with a rosette of leaves and a bud-finial, which resembles the sugar vase in plate 53. A few small inkstands resemble circular plinths about five inches in diameter with a covered inkwell in the centre and holes for quills around it and simple moulding or gadrooned edges. The inventiveness of the designers showed a mechanical turn in some spherical ink caskets, on ball feet with hinged or revolving lids, covering the several compartments inside.

Dinner Services. Complete silver dinner services were sometimes commissioned, and would include, for example, a pair of soup tureens with ladles, four sauce tureens with ladles, which were replicas, but half the height, of the soup tureens, four *entrée* dishes, and a dozen or two each of large and small plates.

Tureens. At the turn of the century the Adam forms persisted, but in the first decade there began to appear a rounded oblong bowl constricted just below the rim above bulged sides and moulded covers: the stem and base were replaced by four substantial cast feet and the vertical loop handles by foliate horizontal loop handles, springing from human or animal masks. Paul Storr made several massive and imposing tureens almost in the *bombé* rococo style with fluted sides, heavy cast feet, a loop handle at each end, and a single symmetrical pierced handle on the cover, all with heavy and profuse foliate repetitive ornament leaving large plain areas (cf. plate 45b): a pair of these, on matching stands, weighs almost seven hundred ounces: the weight of a single tureen and cover varies from fifty to two hundred ounces.

For the most part sauce tureens are miniature replicas of soup tureens or *entrée* dishes in the same service, or simplified versions sometimes in better proportions. A tureen of 1819, in the florid style characteristic of Paul Storr, is in the Victoria and Albert Museum (plate 45b). There are nevertheless some independent varieties, among them vessels of considerable distinction. At Apsley House is a parcel-gilt tureen made by John Edward (1806), part of the Deccan Service, which consists in an unusual conjunction of motifs, Indian and classical, that yet combine appositely to produce an imposing vessel. On a low circular plinth, surrounded by a concave moulding chased with a continuous wreath of bay leaves, stand four elephants, facing outward and supporting on their backs a low circular bowl, entwined serpent handles, chased with a band of interlacing victor's wreaths, and a surbase of leaves and *paterae*: in the centre of the almost flat cover, on a raised rayed plinth, sits an Indian woman beneath an umbrella. The whole design, only eight inches in height, would lose nothing were it twice or even three times as large.

Entrée Dishes. The word *entrée* (a prepared dish coming at dinner between the fish and the joint) was appropriated to the covered vessels that could be used for keeping vegetables, *purées*, or any other dish hot. The dishes themselves are of two principal types, usually low and rectangular with curved corners, though oval and lobed plans are not uncommon. One has a slightly smaller cover that fits within the rim of the base, and a detachable loop handle, so that cover and base can both be used as dishes if necessary: and those with a tall domed lid usually surmounted by a large cast finial-handle, representing flowers, a coronet, a crest, or simply a loop. Sometimes these last are supported so that they rest in a shallow hot-water container *en suite* sometimes plated, or sometimes a later addition, which stands on four cast legs and has a loop handle at each end: the surbase is often gadrooned.

A stack of up to ten or more oval meat dishes, graduated in size, sometimes accompanied the service. The largest, for the joint, about two feet long, has depressed runnels leading down to a well to collect the gravy: the others are usually smaller by two border widths, singly, in pairs or in fours. Sometimes they have domed covers, of silver or more often of Sheffield plate, with a loop handle on top. The borders are oval or shaped, usually gadrooned with shells and scrolls at symmetrical intervals, or of bound reeding and flowers.

Plates were often made in dozens, the border ornaments on the shaped and moulded edge of five, six, or eight segments corresponding with those of the dishes. They are of two distinct sizes, for the main dish and dessert, which vary in diameter from eleven to eight inches. Some are accompanied by circular covers like those on the dishes, presumably for the occasions when food was taken individually on trays to the bedroom or study.‑

Centre Pieces. These are, strictly speaking, ornamental objects with no other purpose than to be admired on the centre of a dining table, and are derived in many cases from the Roman type of tripod altar. An example by Scott and Smith (1806) consists of a shallow dish supported by three female winged demi-figures, back to back, tapering to a horse's leg on a triangular plinth. These figures are connected by *thyrsi* with *paterae* at their intersections, and from above each spring two candle branches.

Two magnificent parcel-gilt centre pieces, both made by Paul Storr, are at Apsley House. The earlier one (1810), thirty-three inches in height, commemorates the battles of Roliça and Vimiera two years before. It consists of a square plinth with cut corners, and large mouldings of bay-laurel, acanthus, and ovolo: at each corner stand three piled rifles and a banner: on the plinth stands a shallow circular two-handled cup on a spreading foot surmounted by a figure of Victory holding aloft a wreath. The second, made in the following year (plate 47) and presented by the General Officers, is shorter by a foot, and consists of a similar cup with a wreath finial supported by three draped and winged figures carrying victors' wreaths, on a circular base guarded by three lions *couchant*. Two other centre pieces recall Storr's example of 1805; their central feature is a fruit basket supported by three cast draped female figures each holding a wand in either hand, that crosses those on either side, and standing at the angle of a tripod plinth; these plinths are raised, the one by dolphins, the other by bearded masks, with rich swags suspended between them.

The *épergne*, although a form of centre piece for the table, belongs to a different category. Like all specially commissioned works of high quality, its exemplars vary very much. An example (1816) by Paul Storr on an ornamental tripod base supports a large central bowl, the lower part imitating basket work, the upper part chased with a running vine branch edged with turned-over vine leaves. From the stem below spring three detachable foliate branches which diverge into two treble loops supporting small dishes: each dish carries a bowl of cut glass. Other examples are of lighter construction, with four or eight dishes. Another suite, undated, of three pieces that would be considered a centre piece were it not provided with glass fruit dishes, probably designed by Antoine Vechte for Elkingtons, consists of a large and elaborate central bowl supported by four female figures; to each end is added, almost as an afterthought, a peninsular pedestal on which a child is seated holding up a horn that carries a dish; the set is completed by a pair of stands with kneeling figures holding aloft a dish between them.

Cruet Frames. It has been estimated that, between 1788 and 1815, a single firm produced more than five hundred different patterns of cruet frames. Basically they consist of a variety of cut glass bottles for cayenne, harvey, anchovy, soy, tarragon, and other sauces set in racks on a stand, from the centre of which rises a shaft ending in a loop handle. Pepper pots, mustard pots, salt cellars and their spoons, as well as bottle labels, may be included.

Wine Coolers. Designed to hold one or two bottles and enough ice to pack round them, these vessels are very much smaller than the massive cisterns like those on plate 24. They are shaped like a bulged tub with two handles and ornamented with gadroons, palms, and vine branches. Generally based on the shape of the Greek kalyx-krater (plate 25b) of red figured earthenware, they were often ornamented in relief with suitable subjects recalling their classical origin and their purpose. A set of six, formerly in the possession of the Earls Howe, have various ornaments; running grape branch and acanthus leaves, leaf-and-dart, and egg-and-dart, with a frieze of Bacchanalian subjects in low relief. Others vary considerably in their treatment; the Weymouth Regatta Cup (1827) in the Victoria and Albert Museum was described on page 239 above, while others are fringed with large vine leaves and clusters of grapes, and engraved with elaborate coats-of-arms, or ornamented with mythological scenes.

Punch Bowls. A pair of punch bowls (plate 23b) made by Paul Storr (1814) belongs to the Corporation of Dover. Two shields, one engraved with St Martin dividing his cloak, are applied to the body, which has a double dropped bottom characteristic of the rococo period. The accompanying ladle with its exotic shell and bowed handle ending in acanthus leaves show the mixed motifs.

Trays. The design of the oval tray, on four shell feet, with a moulded and gadrooned border, gradually became more elaborate with the application of chased anthemion, foliate, and shell ornaments, and they look heavier than in fact they are. Already by 1815 the rectangular type with heavy shaped cast and chased ornamental borders and awkward handles, and a profusion of flat-chased ornament over the central surface, had made its appearance. Though they are often described as tea trays, it is unusual for them to be found *en suite* with a tea service.

Salvers. There was so little room for invention in the design of salvers that, aside from the rectangular pattern with rounded corners, a shape typical of so many other vessels of the period, other designs repeat those of the early and middle part of the eighteenth century: they were sometimes made singly, more usually in pairs; but sets of four and six are known.

Wine Coasters. Circular wooden base on baize, with silver sides, usually pierced and embossed with vine branch ornament, and rimmed with gadrooning. Some examples to hold two bottles were shaped like the figure eight or like a boat, while more fanciful models were raised on wheels like little carts.

Sugar Vases. Among the many varieties of vases is one based on the Greek volute-krater, with egg-and-dart and key patterns flanked with beading, and gadrooning; it has two handles forming broad volutes with masks facing inwards over the rim (plate 52b).

A very beautiful design, associated with the marks of Benjamin Smith, is known in several examples from the first two decades; it consists of a bulged circular vase with two horizontally looped handles on a slight narrow stem and spreading foot on a circular four-footed stand; it has a moulded cover and a bud-finial. It is principally remarkable for the ornaments chased in low relief over all the outer surface, a continuous broad band of fine scrolling foliage flanked by a narrow leaf pattern with acanthus leaves alternating with pendant husks above and a gadrooned surbase below (plate 53).

Sauce Boats. A strange pair of 1824, which calls to mind some bizarre designs of the German High Renaissance, consists of a bowl shaped as a nautilus-shell, with a scalloped lip, supported by a bearded demi-figure, and a handle representing a winged figure, half man, half hippocamp, sipping from a conch shell; it is attached to the back of a tortoise by eagles' legs. An improvement on the covered sauce boat, named after its reputed inventor the Duke of Argyll, is heated by an iron fitted into the central socket inside a spouted vessel not unlike a tea pot.

Tea Urns. Paul Storr's pattern, of which several versions exist, has a low container, with two horizontal loop handles springing from lions' masks, a projecting spout with an anthemion tap, on a narrow stem with circular base, supported on a square pedestal with four cast volute and lion's paw feet: the upper part has gadrooned moulding and a bud-finial. It contains a compartment for the insertion of a hot iron. A contemporary variant on four ball feet is heated by a lamp fixed between its four curved legs below the deep hemispherical body; drop-handles hang from a lion's mask and the low domed cover is surmounted by·a fruit finial.

Tea Caddies. As during the preceding century, a great diversity of designs were used. An oval box with a cylindrical cover is embossed with a scene on a tea plantation and combines ornaments of the early Georgian and Adam periods with embossed *chinoiseries.* Embossed figure scenes also ornament the four bulged sides of a tea caddy (1821) in the Victoria and Albert Museum, whose cover recalls the rococo style with its twisted foliage and flowers in cast openwork: one panel represents *The Prodigal Son,* probably derived from a Netherlandish engraving.

Lamp. Based on classical and renaissance bronze lamps, a cast gilt example of 1806 (Victoria and Albert Museum) has a low circular container on a low foot, with a handle of entwined serpents opposite a covered spout, with a cast imitation flame: it has gadrooning, beading, and anthemion ornament.

Flat Plate. Two new patterns were introduced, the massive King's pattern (plate 61f) and the lighter Queen's pattern, both of which are based on the fiddle pattern (plate 61e), with scrolled and threaded edges and the head ornamented on both sides with anthemion and shells in relief.

It has been hinted in the introduction that so many objects were made of silver in more modern times that it would be tedious to describe their special features in any detail. It must suffice to say that during the early years of the nineteenth century there were few utensils used in the house that were not made in silver. Among them may be mentioned vegetable and muffin dishes, toast racks, table bells, goblets, mugs, and bowls.

During the eighteenth century small ornamental figures in porcelain and bronze were made to decorate the living-rooms by many now well-known potters and factories. In the nineteenth century the quality of these became much debased because of mechanical methods of production, and moreover such ornaments were made in precious metals, particularly figures and models. The artistic convention that had persisted since the renaissance of sculpting, though seldom of painting, kings and outstanding figures as Roman emperors or classical heroes nude or semi-nude, changed, and they were clothed more appropriately in contemporary garments in the naturalist spirit of the age. Two examples may be cited: the figure of George III by Paul Storr (1812) and an equestrian figure of Queen Victoria by the royal goldsmith Robert Garrard (1840). More imposing and in keeping with the minute attention to detail common to many designers of the Gothic revival is the exact model in silver-gilt of Eton College Chapel on a platform three feet long, ordered by William IV to present to the Provost and Fellows of the College, which was made in 1834 for Rundells by John Thompson; at each end is an inscribed circular plaque and on one side the royal Arms of Henry VI, the founder, and on the other those of the Hanoverian king in relief with the supporters modelled in the round.

1837–1962: Victorian and Modern Plate

ARTIFICIAL control of international trade has extended the description 'antique' to objects made a century before the present, and so to those made in the early years of the long reign of Queen Victoria (1837–1901). No detailed descriptions of plate made since her accession are attempted here, partly from lack of previous studies, partly by reason of its great diversity and quantity, and partly because it is doubtful according to present standards of taste whether more than a little of it deserves much study. Such plate is usually labelled 'Victorian' or 'Modern', especially in sale catalogues, without indication of its date or makers. Recent exhibitions of nineteenth-century decorative arts have been more concerned with the products of artist-craftsmen than with the numerically far larger group of products from factories and smaller workshops.

The tremendous increase during the nineteenth century of the quantities of gold and silver refined into metallic form and in circulation all over the world was noted above (p. 47). This trend has changed the viewpoint from which these metals are regarded. Formerly scarce and expensive, they are now cheap and plentiful by comparison with metals of the platinum group, and their capacity to satisfy human vanity has thereby been lessened. Besides, the greatly increased cost of fashioning them in relation to their intrinsic value (cf. pp. 130 and 211) and the heavy tax (temporary it is hoped) on newly manufactured articles have reduced the market for modern plate and conversely increased that for antique plate. Serviceable items from the early nineteenth century can often be bought for little more than their bullion value, but cost per ounce rises steeply as the date of manufacture becomes earlier until more than £150 per ounce is reached for exceptional pieces from the sixteenth and seventeenth centuries. Articles of exceptional rarity command a price which is unconnected with their weight, but depends on such factors as artistic value, historical importance, antiquarian or associational interest, uniqueness, the state of the market at the time, and the actual competition for the acquisition of a particular item.

In 1845 Sir Henry Cole won the prize which was offered by the Society of Arts for the design of a tea service; he contended that public taste would be promoted if established sculptors or painters could be induced to design objects that could be manufactured industrially for widespread markets. His contention extended to modern times the much earlier practice whereby plate was commissioned from designs drawn by artist-craftsmen or the actual objects were made from such designs and then submitted to the purchaser's approval. One of the results of the strong movement that Cole and others began was the Great Exhibition of 1851, on the executive committee of which he served. This stimulating venture was a commercial success, national prestige became involved, and similar exhibitions were staged in other capitals, Dublin (1853), Paris (1855), London (1862), Paris (1867), etc., which during the present century developed into trade fairs, organized annually by groups of manufacturers. For the goldsmith, attention was centred on the submission of competition pieces for the hoped-for award of a prize, and this led to technical virtuosity.

The practical result of Sir Henry Cole's first success was Summerley's Art Manufactures (1847-51), for which the sculptor John Bell (1811-95), the painter John Linnell (1792-1882), and the painter and lexicographer Richard Redgrave (1804-88) were among the designers. Two of Redgrave's designs for embossed christening cups are preserved in the Victoria and Albert Museum; such things were manufactured on a large scale by Hunt and Roskell from 1848 to 1865. Two more distinguished artists, A. W. N. Pugin (1812–52) and Alfred Stevens (1817–75), produced many designs, the former in the Gothic style for Rundells, and John Hardman and Co. Church plate in the medieval tradition, with enamels, jewels, pastes, gilding, and correct ornamental motifs, is so perfectly and minutely finished that it suffers from a dry and severe inhumanity by comparison with the vigorous and broadly treated examples it is intended to imitate. Yet most competition plate, while ensuring that the standard of the best craftsmanship remained high, was artificial and ostentatious, being designed for the enhancement of the reputations of nations, companies, and individuals, rather than for practical domestic purposes. Indeed eminent foreign workers, for example L.-M. Ladeuil (1820–88) and Antoine Vechte (1799–1868) and Rafaello Monti were brought to England to work for such firms as Elkingtons and Hancocks.

Increasing dissemination of the results of archaeological studies and the improvement in global communications introduced fresh influences from classical antiquity and from the Orient. As each new source was made known, it was quickly available to the designers. The hoards of Roman plate discovered at Bernay (1830), Hildesheim (1868), Chaourse (1883), and Boscoreale (1895), as well as from other early civilizations round the Mediterranean offered metalwork for copy and adaptation. Moreover, the growing interest in Chinese and Japanese culture, particularly in the ceramics of the former and the woodcuts of the latter, caused as much excitement among artists during the last half of the nineteenth as more primitive art forms have during the first half of the present century.

A reaction against factories was championed by William Morris (1834–96) who made a strong but little-supported effort to encourage an ideal return to the methods of the Middle Ages with the aid of many Pre-Raphaelite painters, and founded a firm which has now dropped all other activities except the manufacture of stained glass. Although they produced no plate, their convictions caused a number of artist-craftsmen to follow their example by setting up small independent workshops and manufacturing plate of original design. It was a strange mixture of

Figure 53 – Cup in Art Nouveau style (about 1903)

Japanese and medieval that evoked the Art Nouveau style which lasted from about 1890 till 1910 and in which these artist-craftsmen excelled, using embossing and casting (fig. 53), stones set *en cabochon*, enamels and mother-of-pearl to obtain their effects. Among them were Charles Robert Ashbee (1863–1942), W. A. S. Benson (1854–1924), and Omar Ramsden (1873–1939).

The activities of the artist-craftsmen were too divergent to have more than a superficial effect on the manufacture of plate intended for the retail trade. Rather were the firms content to enlarge their sales by spreading into new fields in which machine-produced or easily made hand-wrought plate could provide a quick turnover. The retail system has prevented easy contacts between designer, workman, and purchaser, because the latter is more or less compelled to choose from stock and the retailer to take what the manufacturers' salesmen offer. The categories of plate become more diverse and the price range in each category very broad, from articles in electro-plated nickel silver, through Sheffield plate, thin and light modern productions, to copies after or in the style of earlier patterns, reproductions of various antique pieces, and modern hand-wrought plate of the finest quality (plate 64).

To a craftsman silver and gold are most satisfying metals to work with; to the machine-minder they give no more satisfaction than aluminium or brass. The organizations of the craftsmen's guilds have been relentlessly submerged by production systems, by capital investments, by the use of machines to replace men. In four generations of unforeseeably swift development, the rise in the costs of labour in proportion to those of the precious metals compels a trend towards quantitative rather than qualitative standards. The present economic pressure on the middle classes, even on the upper-middle classes, has prevented them from continuing to employ personal servants, without whom it is inconvenient to use plate to the extent thought fitting during the Victorian and Edwardian periods. Many people prefer to sell their plate, or to keep it locked away, than to use it tarnished, or to clean it themselves. The rich, and the members of corporations, municipal, city, or college, are again, as they were in the later Middle Ages, the privileged minority who can enjoy the pleasure of eating and drinking from plate. The reputation of the British silversmiths has been maintained throughout this time until today. But this prestige will dwindle unless the craftsmen are exempted from working under the penalty of a crippling taxation, except in a small percentage of instances where, for originality of design, the tax is lifted. This scheme makes for inventiveness but not for the solid and steady development of traditions in design and ornament that each generation of apprentices has had behind it in the past. The craftsmen, their tools and their materials are ready in abundance, but, in spite of publicity by the Goldsmiths' Company in the form of brochures, exhibitions, commemoration hall-marks (figs. 54a and b), and tax concessions, the market is ebbing and must be revived.

Figure 54 – (a) Jubilee hall-mark (1935), (b) Coronation hall-mark (1953)

APPENDIX

Tables of Date Letters punched at British Assay Offices

THE following information is necessarily condensed and most problems that arise in connexion with hall-marks can be solved by reference to Frederick Bradbury's invaluable pocket *Guide to Marks of Origin*, obtainable at most silversmiths, or to Sir C. J. Jackson's much larger and more comprehensive *English Goldsmiths and their Marks* (2nd ed. or reprint). No maker's marks are illustrated here, nor those for gold when they differ (see page 217), nor for plate of Britannia standard made after 1719.

The nine principal assay offices follow that of London, by far the most important, in alphabetical order, and some of the more controversial and less common early cycles have been omitted. The importance of the Act of 1697 will be observed in the breaks in many sequences at or shortly after that date (see p. 161). They are:

Birmingham (1773 to date)   Glasgow (1819 to date)
Chester (1701–1962)   Newcastle (1721–1883)
Dublin (1720 to date)   Sheffield (1773 to date)
Edinburgh (1681 to date)   York (1559–1886)
Exeter (1701–1883)

Norwich was an important centre with an erratic system of date letters operating from the sixteenth into the beginning of the eighteenth century. There were also many smaller provincial offices which had no regular system of assay. In the West of England were Barnstaple (14th–17th century), Bristol (18th c.), Plymouth and Taunton (17th c.). In Eastern England, Hull (16th–18th c.), King's Lynn (17th c.), and Lincoln (15th–18th c.) have been credited with town marks; in the north there was an office at Leeds (17th c.).

More numerous but of little importance were the Scottish offices at Aberdeen, Arbroath, Banff, Canongate, Dundee, Elgin, Greenock, Inverness, Montrose, Perth, Tain, and Wick. Some of their punches spell the name of the town.

In Ireland there were offices at Cork, Galway, Kilkenny, Limerick, and Youghal.

LONDON

The mark of the *Leopard's Head* was introduced in 1300 (see above p. 64), and the *maker's mark* in 1363 (p. 66).

A letter, changed annually to mark the year of manufacture, was first incorporated within the mark of the *Leopard's Head* from 1463 to 1478. Thereafter a separate *date letter* has always been punched. Thus from 1478 to 1544 three marks were used (viz., *Leopard's Head, maker's mark,* and *date letter*). In 1544 the *Lion passant* was added, making a total of four thenceforward, except for (i) the temporary or optional changes made by the Acts of 1696 and 1719 respectively, and (ii) from 1784 until 1890, when a fifth mark, the *Sovereign's Head,* was punched (p. 217).

In each of the two tables on page 264, the twenty letters of the reduced alphabet used at Goldsmith's Hall are columnated on the left and against them in the following columns are placed the years which the letters signify. It should perhaps be repeated that the letter was changed on 19 May in the period covered by the upper table and 29 May in that by the lower; thus one letter served from, e.g., 19 May 1550 until 18 May 1551; in these tables (and in similar cases in the succeeding pages) only the prior of the two calendar years involved is placed against the appropriate letter.

In the upper table, which embraces the eleven cycles from the introduction of the separate *date letter* until the break in sequence in 1696-7, and the cycle following this break, only the marks from 1558 onwards are included. The lower table of thirteen and a half cycles brings the series up to date. In both tables the regularity of the London cycles has allowed two lines to be ruled across the tables at ten-year intervals to aid reference. The letter *A* of each alphabet with the *Leopard's Head* are shown: no *makers' marks* are shown, and information about them should be sought in Sir C. J. Jackson's *English Goldsmiths and their Marks,* 2nd ed., 1921 (or the 1949 ed.).

TABLES OF DATE LETTERS

1. The *Lion passant* introduced about 1545.

2. The *A* of the first sequence lasted only from 27 March till 29 May 1697.

3. After 1 June 1720 the marks of the old standard were resumed, as in the third column, while those of the new standard were used concurrently, with the same date letter, on such plate as was made of the higher standard required (p. 167).

4. The *Sovereign's Head* mark was added on 1 December 1784 (see p. 217) to show the payment of tax and continued until 30 April 1890.

5. The *Leopard's Head* is no longer crowned after 1821.

6. The *Sovereign's Head* mark was not used after 1890.

7. *Jubilee* mark, cf. fig. 54a, p. 258.

8. *Coronation* mark, cf. plate 64 and fig. 54b, p. 258.

A	1478	1498	1518	1538	1558	1578	1598	1618	1638	1658	1678
B	1479	1499	1519	1539	1559	1579	1599	1619	1639	1659	1679
C	1480	1500	1520	1540	1560	1580	1600	1620	1640	1660	1680
D	1481	1501	1521	1541	1561	1581	1601	1621	1641	1661	1681
E	1482	1502	1522	1542	1562	1582	1602	1622	1642	1662	1682
F	1483	1503	1523	1543	1563	1583	1603	1623	1643	1663	1683
G	1484	1504	1524	1544	1564	1584	1604	1624	1644	1664	1684
H	1485	1505	1525	1545[1]	1565	1585	1605	1625	1645	1665	1685
I	1486	1506	1526	1546	1566	1586	1606	1626	1646	1666	1686
K	1487	1507	1527	1547	1567	1587	1607	1627	1647	1667	1687
L	1488	1508	1528	1548	1568	1588	1608	1628	1648	1668	1688
M	1489	1509	1529	1549	1569	1589	1609	1629	1649	1669	1689
N	1490	1510	1530	1550	1570	1590	1610	1630	1650	1670	1690
O	1491	1511	1531	1551	1571	1591	1611	1631	1651	1671	1691
P	1492	1512	1532	1552	1572	1592	1612	1632	1652	1672	1692
Q	1493	1513	1533	1553	1573	1593	1613	1633	1653	1673	1693
R	1494	1514	1534	1554	1574	1594	1614	1634	1654	1674	1694
S	1495	1515	1535	1555	1575	1595	1615	1635	1655	1675	1695
T	1496	1516	1536	1556	1576	1596	1616	1636	1656	1676	1696
U	1497	1517	1537	1557	1577	1597	1617	1637	1657	1677	——

A	1697[2]	1716	1736	1756	1776	1796	1816	1836	1856	1876	1896	1916	1936	1956
B	1697	1717	1737	1757	1777	1797	1817	1837	1857	1877	1897	1917	1937	1957
C	1698	1718	1738	1758	1778	1798	1818	1838	1858	1878	1898	1918	1938	1958
D	1699	1719	1739	1759	1779	1799	1819	1839	1859	1879	1899	1919	1939	1959
E	1700	1720[3]	1740	1760	1780	1800	1820	1840	1860	1880	1900	1920	1940	etc.
F	1701	1721	1741	1761	1781	1801	1821[5]	1841	1861	1881	1901	1921	1941	
G	1702	1722	1742	1762	1782	1802	1822	1842	1862	1882	1902	1922	1942	
H	1703	1723	1743	1763	1783	1803	1823	1843	1863	1883	1903	1923	1943	
I	1704	1724	1744	1764	1784[4]	1804	1824	1844	1864	1884	1904	1924	1944	
K	1705	1725	1745	1765	1785	1805	1825	1845	1865	1885	1905	1925	1945	
L	1706	1726	1746	1766	1786	1806	1826	1846	1866	1886	1906	1926	1946	
M	1707	1727	1747	1767	1787	1807	1827	1847	1867	1887	1907	1927	1947	
N	1708	1728	1748	1768	1788	1808	1828	1848	1868	1888	1908	1928	1948	
O	1709	1729	1749	1769	1789	1809	1829	1849	1869	1889	1909	1929	1949	
P	1710	1730	1750	1770	1790	1810	1830	1850	1870	1890[6]	1910	1930	1950	
Q	1711	1731	1751	1771	1791	1811	1831	1851	1871	1891	1911	1931	1951	
R	1712	1732	1752	1772	1792	1812	1832	1852	1872	1892	1912	1932	1952	
S	1713	1733	1753	1773	1793	1813	1833	1853	1873	1893	1913	1933	1953[8]	
T	1714	1734	1754	1774	1794	1814	1834	1854	1874	1894	1914	1934	1954	
U	1715	1735	1755	1775	1795	1815	1835	1855	1875	1895	1915	1935[7]	1955	

BIRMINGHAM

The Assay Office was established at Birmingham in 1773, with the *Anchor* as its distinguishing punch. When the duty was doubled in 1797, the *King's Head* was duplicated for a short time (†). The sequences are of twenty-five, omitting *J* or *I*, or twenty-six letters.

A	1773	1798	1824	1849	1875	1900	1925	1950
B	1774	1799	1825	1850	1876	1901	1926	1951
C	1775	1800	1826	1851	1877	1902	1927	1952
D	1776	1801	1827	1852	1878	1903	1928	1953[8]
E	1777	1802	1828	1853	1879	1904	1929	1954
F	1778	1803	1829	1854	1880	1905	1930	1955
G	1779	1804	1830	1855	1881	1906	1931	1956
H	1780	1805	1831	1856	1882	1907	1932	1957
I	1781	1806	1832	1857	1883	1908	——	——
J	——	1807	——	1858	——	——	1933	1958
K	1782	1808	1833	1859	1884	1909	1934	1959
L	1783	1809	1834	1860	1885	1910	1935[7]	etc.
M	1784[4]	1810	1835	1861	1886	1911	1936	
N	1785	1811	1836	1862	1887	1912	1937	
O	1786	1812	1837	1863	1888	1913	1938	
P	1787	1813	1838	1864	1889	1914	1939	
Q	1788	1814	1839	1865	1890[6]	1915	1940	
R	1789	1815	1840	1866	1891	1916	1941	
S	1790	1816	1841	1867	1892	1917	1942	
T	1791	1817	1842	1868	1893	1918	1943	
U	1792	1818	1843	1869	1894	1919	1944	
V	1793	1819	1844	1870	1895	1920	1945	
W	1794	1820	1845	1871	1896	1921	1946	
X	1795	1821	1846	1872	1897	1922	1947	
Y	1796	1822	1847	1873	1898	1923	1948	
Z	1797†	1823	1848	1874	1899	1924	1949	

CHESTER

There seems to have been a succession of moneyers at Chester from Saxon times and of goldsmiths from the thirteenth century. The omission of any mention of Chester in early Acts has been explained on the ground that both the city and county were under the Earl of Chester and not under the Crown until the time of Henry VIII. There were *makers' marks,* but no regular assay office marks until 1686; a sequence of date letters began in 1701 (see p. 163) with cycles of irregular lengths. The assay office closed in 1962.

A	1701	1726	1751	1776	1797	1818	1839	1864	1884	1901	1926	1951
B	1702	1727	1752	1777	1798	1819	1840	1865	1885	1902	1927	1952
C	1703	1728	1753	1778	1799	1820	1841	1866	1886	1903	1928	1953[3]
D	1704	1729	1754	1779	1800	1821–2	1842	1867	1887	1904	1929	1954
E	1705	1730	1755	1780	1801	1823	1843	1868	1888	1905	1930	1955
F	1706	1731	1756	1781	1802	1824	1844	1869	1889	1906	1931	1956
G	1707	1732	1757	1782	1803	1825	1845	1870	1890[6]	1907	1932	1957
H	1708	1733	1758	1783	1804	1826	1846	1871	1891	1908	1933	1958
I	1709	1734	1759	1784[4]	1805	1827	1847	1872	1892	1909	1934	——
J	——	——	——	——	——	——	——	——	——	——	——	1959
K	1710	1735	1760	1785	1806	1828	1848	1873	1893	1910	1935[7]	etc.
L	1711	1736	1761	1786	1807	1829	1849	1874	1894	1911	1936	
M	1712	1737	1762	1787	1808	1830	1850	1875	1895	1912	1937	
N	1713	1738	1763	1788	1809	1831	1851	1876	1896	1913	1938	
O	1714	1739	1764	1789	1810	1832	1852	1877	1897	1914	1939	
P	1715	1740	1765	1790	1811	1833	1853	1878	1898	1915	1940	
Q	1716	1741	1766	1791	1812	1834	1854	1879	1899	1916	1941	
R	1717	1742	1767	1792	1813	1835	1855	1880	1900	1917	1942	
S	1718	1743	1768	1793	1814	1836	1856	1881	——	1918	1943	
T	1719	1744	1769	1794	1815	1837	1857	1882	——	1919	1944	
U	1720	1745	1770	1795	1816	1838	1858	1883	——	1920	1945	
V	1721	1746	1771	1796	1817	——	1859	——	——	1921	1946	
W	1722	1747	1772	——	——	——	1860	——	——	1922	1947	
X	1723	1748	1773	——	——	——	1861	——	——	1923	1948	
Y	1724	1749	1774	——	——	——	1862	——	——	1924	1949	
Z	1725	1750	(1775)	——	——	——	1863	——	——	1925	1950	

DUBLIN

Goldsmiths were working in Dublin at least as early as the thirteenth century. In 1605 the City Council required that each maker strike his mark, and that three others, *Lion, Harp,* and *Castle,* be stamped, and in 1637 the goldsmiths were granted a charter. Three cycles of date letters are found from 1638 into the eighteenth century, but so little plate survives that the table below does not begin until 1720; the figure of *Hibernia* was added in 1731(†); the duty stamp of the *King's Head* was not punched till 1807(*).

	A	B	C	D	E	F	G	H	I	J
A	1720	1747	1773	1797	1821	1846	1871	1896	1916	1942
B	1721	1748	1774	1798	1822	1847	1872	1897	1917	1943
C	1722	1749	1775	1799	1823	1848	1873	1898	1918	1944
D	1723	1750	1776	1800	1824	1849	1874	1899	1919	1945
E	1724	1751	1777	1801	1825	1850	1875	1900	1920	1946
F	1725	1752	1778	1802	1826	1851	1876	1901	1921	1947
G	1726	1753	1779	1803	1827	1852	1877	1902	1922	1948
H	1727	1754	1780	1804	1828	1853	1878	1903	1923	1949
I	1728	1757	1781	1805	1829	——	1879	1904	1924	1950
J	——	——	——	——		1854				1951
K	1729	1758	1782	1806	1830	1855	1880	1905	1925	1952
L	1730–1†	1759	1783	1807*	1831	1856	1881	1906	1926	1953
M	1732	1760	1784	1808	1832	1857	1882	1907	1927	1954
N	1733	1761	1785	1809	1833	1858	1883	1908	1928	1955
O	1734	1762	1786	1810	1834	1859	1884	1909	1929	1956
P	1735	1763	1787	1811	1835	1860	1885	1910	1930–1	1957
Q	1736	1764	1788	1812	1836	1861	1886	1911	1932	1958
R	1737	1765	1789	1813	1837	1862	1887	1912	1933	1959
S	1738	1766	1790	1814	1838	1863	1888	1913	1934	etc.
T	1739	1767	1791	1815	1839	1864	1889	1914	1935	
U	1740	1768	1792	1816	1840	1865	1890^s	1915	1936	
V	——	——	——	——	1841	1866	1891	——	1937	
W	1741–2	1769	1793	1817	1842	1867	1892	——	1938	
X	1743–4	1770	1794	1818	1843	1868	1893	——	1939	
Y	1745	1771	1795	1819	1844	1869	1894	——	1940	
Z	1746	1772	1796	1820	1845	1870	1895	——	1941	

EDINBURGH

The goldsmiths of Edinburgh were associated with the other hammermen there and their records date from 1525. In 1457 a deacon and other officers were appointed by statute and the *deacon's mark* and the *maker's mark* had to be stamped. The town mark, a *Triple-towered Castle*, was added in 1485. In 1681 a variable *date letter*, changed in September, was adopted and the *Deacon's mark* was replaced by the *Assay-master's mark*; in 1759 this last was replaced by the *Thistle*.

A	1681	1705	1730	1755	1780	1806	1832	1857	1882	1906	1931	1956
B	1682	1706	1731	1756	1781	1807	1833	1858	1883	1907	1932	1957
C	1683	1707	1732	1757	1782	1808	1834	1859	1884	1908	1933	1958,
D	1684	1708	1733	1758	1783	1809	1835	1860	1885	1909	1934	1959
E	1685	1709	1734	1759	1784⁴	1810	1836	1861	1886	1910	1935⁷	etc.
F	1686	1710	1735	1760	1785	1811	1837	1862	1887	1911	1936	
G	1687	1711	1736	1761	1786–7	1812	1838	1863	1888	1912	1937	
H	1688	1712	1737	1762	1788	1813	1839	1864	1889	1913	1938	
I	1689	1713	1738	1763	1789⎫	1814	1840	1865	1890⁶	1914	1939	
J	—	—	—	—	1789⎭	1815	—					
K	1690	1714	1739	1764	1790	1816	1841	1866	1891	1915	1940	
L	1691	1715	1740	1765	1791	1817	1842	1867	1892	1916	1941	
M	1692	1716	1741	1766	1792	1818	1843	1868	1893	1917	1942	
N	1693	1717	1742	1767	1793	1819	1844	1869	1894	1918	1943	
O	1694	1718	1743	1768	1794	1820	1845	1870	1895	1919	1944	
P	1695	1719	1744	1769	1795	1821	1846	1871	1896	1920	1945	
Q	1696	1720	1745	1770	1796	1822	1847	1872	1897	1921	1946	
R	1697	1721	1746	1771	1797	1823	1848	1873	1898	1922	1947	
S	1698	1722	1747	1772	1798	1824	1849	1874	1899	1923	1948	
T	1699	1723	1748	1773	1799	1825	1850	1875	1900	1924	1949	
U	—	1724	1749	1774	1800	1826	1851	1876	1901	1925	1950	
V	1700	1725	1750	1775	1801	1827	1852	1877	1901	1926	1951	
W	1701	1726	1751	—	1802	1828	1853	1878	1902	1927	1952	
X	1702	1727	1752	1776	1803	1829	1854	1879	1903	1928	1953⁸	
Y	1703	1728	1753	1777	1804	1830	1855	1880	1904	1929	1954	
Z	1704	1729	1754	1778	1805	1831	1856	1881	1905	1930	1955	

1779

 EXETER

Goldsmiths were working at Exeter from the fourteenth century onwards and much plate, bearing the town mark, e.g. 𝕏 or ⊛, remains from the sixteenth and seventeenth centuries. It was not until the Act of 1701 (see p. 163) that eleven of the small number of goldsmiths working there established a sequence of date letters. The amount of plate produced there declined in the nineteenth century and little was assayed after 1850. The office was closed in 1883. The *Leopard's Head* was not used after 1777(*).

A	1701	1725	1749	1773	1797	1817	1837	1857	1877
B	1702	1726	1750	1774	1798	1818	1838	1858	1878
C	1703	1727	1751	1775	1799	1819	1839	1859	1879
D	1704	1728	1752	1776	1800	1820	1840	1860	1880
E	1705	1729	1753	1777*	1801	1821	1841	1861	1881
F	1706	1730	1754	1778	1802	1822	1842	1862	1882
G	1707	1731	1755	1779	1803	1823	1843	1863	
H	1708	1732	1756	1780	1804	1824	1844	1864	
I	1709	1733	1757	1781–2	1805	1825	1845	1865	
K	1710	1734	1758	1783	1806	1826	1846	1866	
L	1711	1735	1759	1784⁴	1807	1827	1847	1867	
M	1712	1736	1760	1785	1808	1828	1848	1868	
N	1713	1737	1761	1786	1809	1829	1849	1869	
O	1714	1738	1762	1787	1810	1830	1850	1870	
P	1715	1739	1763	1788	1811	1831	1851	1871	
Q	1716	1740	1764	1789	1812	1832	1852	1872	
R	1717	1741	1765	1790	1813	1833	1853	1873	
S	1718	1742	1766	1791	1814	1834	1854	1874	
T	1719	1743	1767	1792	1815	1835	1855	1875	
U	—	1744	1768	1793	1816	1836	1856	1876	
V	1720	—	—	—	—	—	—	—	
W	1721	1745	1769	1794	—	—	—	—	
X	1722	1746	1770	1795	—	—	—	—	
Y	1723	1747	1771	1796	—	—	—	—	
Z	1724	1748	1772	—	—	—	—	—	

GLASGOW

The Glasgow goldsmiths were incorporated with other metal-workers there as early as 1536, and a minute-book covering the period 1616–1717 survives. Although a cycle of date letters has been tentatively traced from 1681 to 1705, when the *Fish, Tree, and Bell* mark (from the burgh arms) was used, it was not until as late as the Act of 1819 that the Glasgow Goldsmiths' Company was constituted a body corporate and the *Lion Rampant* mark (from the Royal Standard of Scotland) was introduced. A regular sequence of date letters began in that year and the sixth cycle is now in progress.

A	1819[4]	1845	1871	1897	1923	1949
B	1820	1846	1872	1898	1924	1950
C	1821	1847	1873	1899	1925	1951
D	1822	1848	1874	1900	1926	1952
E	1823	1849	1875	1901	1927	1953[5]
F	1824	1850	1876	1902	1928	1954
G	1825	1851	1877	1903	1929	1955
H	1826	1852	1878	1904	1930	1956
I	1827	1853	1879	1905	1931	1957
J	1828	1854	1880	1906	1932	——
K	1829	1855	1881	1907	1933	——
L	1830	1856	1882	1908	1934	1958
M	1831	1857	1883	1909	1935[7]	1959
N	1832	1858	1884	1910	1936	etc.
O	1833	1859	1885	1911	1937	
P	1834	1860	1886	1912	1938	
Q	1835	1861	1887	1913	1939	
R	1836	1862	1888	1914	1940	
S	1837	1863	1889	1915	1941	
T	1838	1864	1890[6]	1916	1942	
U	1839	1865	1891	1917	1943	
V	1840	1866	1892	1918	1944	
W	1841	1867	1893	1919	1945	
X	1842	1868	1894	1920	1946	
Y	1843	1869	1895	1921	1947	
Z	1844	1870	1896	1922	1948	

NEWCASTLE

Goldsmiths were working at Newcastle at least from the middle of the thirteenth century, although no extant plate made there seems to date from before the middle of the seventeenth century, when the mark of the *Three Castles* stood alone with that of the maker. The Newcastle Assay Office was re-established in 1702, with an erratic cycle in gothic capitals, and closed in 1884.

A	1721	1740	1759	1791	1815	1839	1864
B	1722	1741	1760–8	1792	1816	1840	1865
C	1723	1742	1769	1793	1817	1841	1866
D	1724	1743	1770	1794	1818	1842	1867
E	1725	1744	1771	1795	1819	1843	1868
F	1726	1745	1772	1796	1820	1844	1869
G	1727	1746	1773	1797	1821	1845	1870
H	1728	1747	1774	1798	1822	1846	1871
I	1729	1748	1775	1799	1823	1847	1872
J	—	—	—	—	—	1848	—
K	1730	1749	1776	1800	1824	1849	1873
L	1731	1750	1777	1801	1825	1850	1874
M	1732	1751	1778	1802	1826	1851	1875
N	1733	1752	1779	1803	1827	1852	1876
O	1734	1753	1780	1804	1828	1853	1877
P	1735	1754	1781	1805	1829	1854	1878
Q	1736	1755	1782	1806	1830	1855	1879
R	1737	1756	1783	1807	1831	1856	1880
S	1738	1757	1784[a]	1808	1832	1857	1881
T	1739	(1758)	1785	1809	1833	1858	1882
U	—	—	1786	1810	1834	1859	1883
W	—	—	1787	1811	1835	1860	
X	—	—	1788	1812	1836	1861	
Y	—	—	1789	1813	1837	1862	
Z	—	—	1790	1814	1838	1863	

SHEFFIELD

The assay office was instituted at the same time as that at Birmingham, with the *Crown* as its town mark. The first two cycles are complicated because the letters are jumbled and not in sequence.

A	1779	1806	1824	1844	1868	1893	1918	1943
B	1783	1805	1825	1845	1869	1894	1919	1944
C	1780	1811	1826	1846	1870	1895	1920	1945
D	1781	1812	1827	1847	1871	1896	1921	1946
E	1773	1799	1828	1848	1872	1897	1922	1947
F	1774	1803	1829	1849	1873	1898	1923	1948
G	1782	1804	1830	1850	1874	1899	1924	1949
H	1777	1801	1831	1851	1875	1900	1925	1950
I	1784	1818	——	1852	——	1901	1926	1951
J	——	——	——	——	1876	——	——	——
K	1786	1809	1832	1853	1877	1902	1927	1952
L	1790	1810	1833	1854	1878	1903	1928	1953
M	1789–94	1802	1834	1855	1879	1904	1929	1954
N	1775	1800	——	1856	1880	1905	1930	1955
O	1793	1815	——	1857	1881	1906	1931	1956
P	1791	1808	1835	1858	1882	1907	1932	1957
Q	1795	1820	1836	——	1883	1908	1933	1958
R	1776	1813	1837	1859	1884	1909	1934	1959
S	1778	1807	1838	1860	1885	1910	1935[7]	etc.
T	1787	1816	1839	1861	1886	1911	1936	
U	1792	1823	1840	1862	1887	1912	1937	
V	1798	1819	1841	1863	1888	1913	1938	
W	1788	1814	——	1864	1889	1914	1939	
X	1797	1817	1842	1865	1890[6]	1915	1940	
Y	1785	1821	——	1866	1891	1916	1941	
Z	1796	1822	1843	1867	1892	1917	1942	

YORK

Being the second city in the land during the Middle Ages, York had a mark as early as 1411 and a cycle of date-letters is thought to have begun in 1559, with the town mark – *'the halfe leopard head and half flowre-de-luyce'*; the former half may have been a half *rose* crowned from 1632–98, but there seems to be no record of a change until the re-establishment of the office in 1701 (see p. 163), when the *Cross charged with five Lions passant* (from the city arms) was introduced, with the *Leopard's Head erased* and *Britannia,* and a new but short-lived cycle. In 1717 the office closed, wares being marked at Newcastle until it was reopened about 1780. After an interval of seventy-three years another incomplete cycle has been noted, followed by two cycles, each of twenty-five letters, omitting J, and part of a third which brought the series to an end when the office was closed in 1857.

A	(1559)	1583	1607	1631	1657	1682	1700	(1776)	1787	1812	1837
B	(1560)	1584	1608	1632	1658	1683	1701	(1777)	1788	1813	1838
C	(1561)	(1585)	1609	1633	1659	1684	1702	1778	1789	1814	1839
D	(1562)	(1586)	1610	1634	1660	1685	1703	1779	1790	1815	1840
E	(1563)	1587	1611	1635	1661	1686	(1704)	1780	1791	1816	1841
F	1564	(1588)	1612	1636	1662	1687	1705	1781	1792	1817	1842
G	1565	(1589)	1613	1637	1663	1688	1706	1782	1793	1818	1843
H	1566	1590	1614	1638	1664	1689	——	1783	1794	1819	1844
I	(1567)	(1591)	1615	1639	1665	1690	——		1795	1820	1845
J	——	——	——	(1640)	——	——	——	1784	——	——	——
K	1568	1592	1616	1641	1666	1691	——	1785	1796	1821	1846
L	1569	1593	1617	1642	1667	1692	——	1786	1797	1822	1847
M	1570	1594	1618	1643	1668	1693	——	——	1798	1823	1848
N	(1571)	1595	1619	1644	1669	1694	——	——	1799	1824	1849
O	1572	1596	1620	1645	1670	1695	——	——	1800	1825	1850
P	1573	1597	1621	1646	1671	1696	——	——	1801	1826	1851
Q	1574	1598	1622	1647	1672	1697	——	——	1802	1827	1852
R	1575	1599	1623	1648	1673	1698	——	——	1803	1828	1853
S	1576	(1600)	1624	1649	1674	1699	——	——	1804	1829	1854
T	1577	1601	1625	1650	1675	——	——	——	1805	1830	1855
U	——	——	1626	1651	1676	——	——	——	1806	1831	——
V	(1578)	(1602)	——	1652	1677	——	——	——	1807	1832	1856
W	(1579)	(1603)	1627	1653	1678	——	——	——	1808	1833	
X	(1580)	1604	(1628)	1654	1679	——	——	——	1809	1834	
Y	(1581)	(1605)	1629	1655	1680	——	——	——	1810	1835	
Z	1582	(1606)	1630	1656	1681	——	——	——	1811	1836	

Glossary

ACANTHUS. Plant with fleshy prickly leaves, used in stylized form as enrichment on Corinthian capitals and derivatively as a frieze on plate, particularly about 1670–90 (plates 11, 17a) and during the classical revival about 1770–1825 (plate 15a).

ALLOY (earlier 'allay'). (*a*) A base metal mixed with a precious metal to harden it, improve its working qualities, modify its colour, etc. (*b*) Combination of different metals fused together, e.g. brass, bronze, etc.

ANTHEMION (Greek = flower). Stylized motif based on the honeysuckle or branch of date palm (palmette), widely used in classical architecture (see p. 238, fig. 48).

ARABESQUE. Fanciful stylized line ornament of scrolling and intertwining foliage and figures, usually symmetrical, derived from Roman murals (cf. GROTESQUE).

ARGENTIFEROUS. Yielding silver (Latin *argentum* = silver; whence its symbols Ag and Æ used by chemists, etc., and numismatists, respectively).

ARRIS. Sharp edge at the join of two plane or curved surfaces, much emphasized during the classical revival (Chapter 8).

ASTRAGAL. Small continuous half-round moulding, often enriched with beading, etc.; smaller version of the torus, and reverse of the scotia.

AURIFEROUS. Yielding gold (Latin *aurum* = gold; whence its symbols Au and Ä used by chemists, etc., and numismatists, respectively).

BALUSTER. Small pillar or column of fanciful outline, translated into metalwork especially for stems of wine cups, standing cups, communion cups, candlesticks, etc.

BAY-LEAF GARLAND. Worn as crown by heroes or poets of classical tradition and used in stylized form to enrich torus mouldings, etc., especially in later seventeenth century and neo-classical revival (see p. 221, fig. 46c).

BEAD AND REEL. Enrichment of astragal, of alternate beads and reels, copied from classical architecture.

BILLET. (*a*) Thumb-piece on tankard, flagon, ewer, etc. (*b*) Gothic moulding of short cylinders or squares at regular intervals (see p. 92, fig. 19a).

BOLECTION. Moulding, usually of S-section, to cover joint of two parallel planes.

BOSS UP. Beat sheet of metal from the back into roughly its final shape.

BRITANNIA METAL. Leadless alloy of tin and regulus of antimony, in appearance resembling silver or polished pewter, used from about 1790 into the nineteenth century.

BRITANNIA STANDARD. New standard of silver alloy slightly finer (95·8%) than sterling (92·5%), compulsory from 1697 to 1719, and optional thereafter; distinguished by punch with figure of Britannia (see p. 162).

BURNISHER. Tool with very hard, polished working surface, of agate, dog's tooth, etc., for burnishing gold and silver.

CABLE. Moulding like twisted rope, derived from Norman architecture, cast, embossed, or made of twisted wires.

CARAT. Measure of purity of gold; pure gold is 24 carats, an alloy half gold and half other metal is 12 carats; see p. 283.

CARTOUCHE. Originally scroll ornament like Ionic volute, now tablet, usually oval, with scrolled or ornate frame, containing inscription on pictorial ornament.

CAVETTO. Quarter-round concave moulding.

CHALICE. Wine cup used at Mass; 'communion cup' denotes vessel used in English reformed churches.

CHAMPLEVÉ. Enamelling done by cutting out troughs from the metal to be decorated, into which the frit is melted; the surface is ground flush and polished (plate 1).

CHASE. To model surface of metal with hammer and punches.

CLOISONNÉ. Enamelling done by melting the frit into fields defined by wire soldered to the surface to be decorated; principally an oriental technique, but much used in early Middle Ages (fig. 6).

CREST, CRESTING. Medieval ornament, usually foliate and regular, along top of horizontal members (fig. 13b, inverted; plate 1).

CROCKET. Medieval ornament, like cresting, along the steep sloping surfaces of pinnacles, finials, etc. (plates 2, 3).

CYMA RECTA. Moulding with section of two contrary curves, the upper concave.

GLOSSARY

CYMA REVERSA. Moulding with section of two contrary curves, the lower concave.

DAMASCENE. To inlay metal, usually steel, with gold and silver beaten into undercut grooves (from Damascus, where the technique was much practised).

DIAPER WORK. Surface ornament of regular network of squares, lozenges, etc. (fig. 16, plate 54a).

ECHINUS. Quarter-round moulding, often enriched with egg and dart.

EGG AND DART, EGG AND TONGUE. Ornament used, strictly speaking, for astragal and echinus mouldings (fig. 19c).

ELECTRO-PLATE. Wares, usually copper, coated with silver by electrolysis.

ENGRAVE. To cut lines with a scorper, or graver, into metal, etc. (plates 4b, 17c, 51b, etc., and fig. 3).

FESTOON. Garland of fruit or flowers, etc., suspended at each side, sometimes in the middle as well; used on plate principally in sixteenth century and in the neo-classical revival.

FILLET. Narrow flat band, often between two mouldings.

FLUTING. Half-round parallel channels, vertical, oblique, or curved, derived from classical architecture, and usually embossed on plate (plates 13b and 57d).

FRET. Repetitive pattern made up of straight lines intersecting at right angles, derived from classical Greek architecture and much used in the classical revival; also called key pattern and meander (fig. 46b).

FROSTED SILVER. Film of pure silver left on surface after copper-silver alloy has been heated and dipped in hot dilute sulphuric acid.

GADROONING. Inverted fluting (see above), usually applied to edging (plates 13b and 24b).

GROTESQUE. Decoration, often in relief, with human and animal forms fantastically interwoven with foliage, scrolls, etc., derived from Roman murals, where bizarre, exaggerated or distorted forms prevail; e.g. auricular style, p. 118, and fig. 25.

INGOT. Block of metal cast into shape and weight convenient for bulk handing and processing.

KEY PATTERN. See FRET.

KNOP. Bulbous projection on shaft, pillar, or stem of cup, chalice, etc. (plate 1 and fig. 21).

277

KRATER. Greek vessel, of vase shapes, with two handles.

LATTEN. Base yellow alloy, like or the same as brass.

MANNHEIM GOLD. Pinchbeck alloy of copper, zinc, and tin.

MATTING. Tiny dots punched with a matt tool, or small circles punched closely over a surface to give a broken texture in contrast with a polished one.

MEANDER. See FRET.

MORESQUE (Arabesque moresque). Line ornament, usually of stylized scrolling and intertwining foliage, derived from Near Eastern art (fig. 18).

NIELLO. Fusible black alloy of sulphur, lead, silver, and copper, used to fill engraved ornament to heighten the contrast with silver; suggested one of earliest printing techniques.

OGEE. Moulding, etc., made up of a concave and a convex curve; cf. CYMA RECTA and CYMA REVERSA above.

OVOLO. Half-round or curved convex moulding derived from classical architecture and much used on Tudor plate with egg and dart enrichment.

PATERA. Circular classical ornament, based on the saucer used in sacrificial libations, much used on English plate 1770 to 1830, fig. 45.

PATINA. Oxide produced naturally or artificially on surface of metal.

PEWTER. Alloy of tin and lead in varying proportions, sometimes with other additions, for making vessels cheaply to resemble silver.

PICKLE. Solution of acid or acids in water, used to remove the films of oxides or sulphides from surface of metal.

PLANISH. To give smooth face or level surface to sheet of metal by beating it on an anvil with a broad-faced polished hammer.

PLATE. (a) (Spanish plata = silver). Utensils and vessels of silver for table and other domestic purposes; used alone it generally refers, as here, to wares of solid silver, or to silver-gilt, or gold; 'silver plate' is often used to distinguish it from Sheffield plate, electro-plate, pewter plate, etc. (b) Shallow, usually circular, vessel generally ceramic, for eating from.

PLIQUE À JOUR. Translucent enamel without a metal backing and strengthened by strips of metal within its thickness, somewhat in the manner of stained glass windows.

POUNCE. (*a*) Fine powder used in earlier times to prevent ink from spreading on unsized paper. (*b*) To produce a powdered effect on surface of metal, like matted work.

REEDING. Ornament of thin contiguous parallel mouldings, stylized from long reed leaves, and much used in later seventeenth century.

SCORPER. Small chisel for engraving; blades of various shapes.

SCOTIA. Half-round concave moulding originally between two torus mouldings to give deep shadowed line (Greek = darkness); reverse of astragal.

SHEFFIELD PLATE. (*a*) Generally, wares made of sheets of copper sandwiched by rolling between films of silver (see p. 213). (*b*) Loosely, silver wares made at Sheffield, as Norwich plate, Exeter plate, etc.

SPANDREL. Triangular area between the curve of arch and corner made by horizontal line from its apex and vertical line from its springing, or between two adjacent arches.

SPINDLE AND BEAD. Enrichment of scotia moulding.

SPRINGING. Level at which arch curves from its vertical supports.

SWAG. Festoon of cloth (see above).

TORUS. Large half-round convex moulding (Latin = swelling).

TREFOIL. Three leaves (French *trois feuilles*); cf. quatrefoil, cinquefoil, etc.

VERMEIL (French = silver-gilt).

VOLUTE. Scroll, especially that in Ionic capital (Latin *voluta* = scroll).

WATER-LEAF. Stylized motif taken from large broad unribbed tapering or rounded leaf, much used on plate 1770–1830.

How to Clean Plate

SILVER. Things used continually need little more than washing in hot soap and water or a detergent, rinsing thoroughly and drying with a soft cloth or chamois-leather. Salt corrodes silver badly and silver salt cellars should be emptied after use and, with their spoons, be well washed; glass liners often conceal the salt that has slipped between the liner and its casing; gilt salts are safe until the gilding becomes worn. Bad corrosion is best dealt with by a silversmith, but jewellers' rouge is effective in less severe cases. Ornament should be cleaned with ammonia and french chalk, lightly brushed in the crevices if there are intricate surfaces, and lightly rubbed with a soft cloth. Certain new liquid cleaners have been marketed and are safe if the directions are strictly followed and the silver well rinsed and dried; they combine the advantages of quickness and avoidance of abrasion. Most piped and natural water contains chlorine, which discolours silver; silver should never be left wet. Stored silver should be wrapped in acid-free tissue paper or kept in baize bags.

SILVER-GILT. Paul de Lamerie's instructions cannot be bettered. 'Clean it now and then with only warm water and soap with a spunge, and then washe it with cleane water, and dry it very well with a soft Linnen Cloth, and keep it in a dry place for the damp will spoil it.' Never use any abrasive or brush.

GOLD. Wash in a weak solution of liquid ammonia or other detergent and polish with a soft cloth. Gold is much softer than silver and needs very gentle handling.

Tables of Weight

THE *Tower Pound* (or Saxon Moneyers' pound) of 5,400 grains Troy was abolished in 1527 and replaced by the slightly heavier *Troy Pound* which had already been in use for more than a century. The *Mark*, of 3,600 grains, was the equivalent of two-thirds of a Tower Pound. The *Troy Pound* was abolished by the Weights and Measures Act of 1878, except for weighing precious metals and stones, and its place was taken by the older *Avoirdupois Pound* for ordinary commercial use. A decimal subdivision of the ounce is legal, but in practice goods are weighed only in ounces and pennyweights, however heavy they may be.

TOWER WEIGHT

[1 lb Troy]	1½ marks	20s.	240 dwt	5,400 grains Troy
	1 mark	13⅓s.	160 dwt	3,600 grains Troy
		1s.	12 dwt	270 grains Troy
			1 dwt	22½ grains Troy

TROY WEIGHT

[1 lb Troy]	12 oz Troy	240 dwt Troy	5,760 grains Troy
	1 oz Troy	20 dwt Troy	480 grains Troy
		1 dwt Troy	24 grains Troy

AVOIRDUPOIS WEIGHT

1 lb Av	16 oz Av	256 drams Av	7,000 grains Troy
	1 oz Av	16 drams Av	437.5 grains Troy
		1 dram Av	27.3 grains Troy

CARAT WEIGHT FOR GOLD

1 oz Troy	24 carats (gold)	96 carat grains
	1 carat (gold)	4 carat grains

lb=pound; oz=ounce; dwt=pennyweight; s.=shilling

Select Bibliography

THE bibliography is confined to works about English, American, and Dominion plate in English, and with only a few exceptions to printed books.

Numerous articles, long and short, of varying interest but usually well illustrated, on a wide variety of specialized topics, for example, small collections, individual makers, interesting pieces of plate, the development of particular types, etc., can be found in many periodicals, international and local, and especially in *Antiques, Apollo, Archaeologia, Burlington Magazine, Connoisseur, Country Life,* etc.

SYNOPSIS

I. PLATE OF THE BRITISH ISLES

A. General Historical Studies.
B. Special Topics.
C. Hall-marks.
D. Biographies and Biographical Sources.
E. Metallurgy and Manufacturing Techniques.
F. Catalogues of Public Collections.
G. Picture Books of Public Collections.
H. Catalogues of Private Collections.
I. Catalogues of Corporate Collections.
J. Catalogues of Important Exhibitions.
K. Monographs on Church Plate.

II. PLATE OF THE UNITED STATES OF AMERICA

A. Historical Studies.
B. Catalogues of Collections and Exhibitions.
C. List of Principal Public Collections.

III. PLATE OF CANADA

IV. PLATE OF THE UNION OF SOUTH AFRICA

In each section the books are in an alphiabetical arrangement based either on the surnames of authors or owners of collections, or on place-names, but in I. *J.* and II. *B.* the order is chronological. Unless otherwise stated, the place of publication is London.

SELECT BIBLIOGRAPHY

I. PLATE OF THE BRITISH ISLES

A. General Historical Studies

Board of Trade. *Working Party Reports: Jewellery and silverware*, 1946, v, 105 pp.

Chaffers, W. *Gilda aurifabrorum: a history of London goldsmiths and plateworkers and their marks stamped on plate*, 1883 (ed. 1899, viii, 267 pp.).

Cripps, W. J. *Old English plate, ecclesiastical, decorative and domestic: its makers and marks*, 1878 (11th ed., 1926, xxvi, 540 pp., 122 figs.).

Finlay, I. *Scottish Gold and Silver Work*, 1958, 178 pp., 96 plates.

Hayward, J. F. *Huguenot Silver in England, 1688–1727*, 1959, xx, 89 pp., 97 plates.

Jackson, C. J. *An illustrated history of English plate, ecclesiastical and secular*, 2 vols., 1911, xxxviii, 1085 pp., 77 plates, 1507 figs.

Jones, E. A. *Old silver of Europe and America*, 1928, xi, 376 pp., 96 plates.

Okie, H. P. *Old silver and old Sheffield plate*, 1952, 420 pp., 12 plates.

Oman, C. C. *English domestic silver*, 1934 (4th ed., 1959, xii, 240 pp., 135 illustrations).

Prideaux, W. S. *Memorials of the Goldsmiths' Company, 1335–1815*, 2 vols., 1896–7; I, xxviii, 388 pp.; II, viii, 404 pp.

Watts, W. W. *Old English silver*, 1924, xxx, 149 pp. 134 plates.

Wyler, S. B. *The book of old silver: English, American, foreign*, New York (9th ed., n.d. [1947], x, 447 pp., 46 plates).

FABER MONOGRAPHS ON SILVER

General Editor: A. G. Grimwade.

Hayward, J. F. *Huguenot Silver in England, 1688–1727*, 1959, xx, 89 pp., 96 plates.

B. Special Topics

GOLD PLATE

Jones, E. A. *Old English gold plate*, 1907, xxiii, 35 pp., 37 plates.

PRICES

Caldicott, J. W. *The values of old English silver and Sheffield plate*, 1906, 293 pp., 87 plates. (N.B. An invaluable record of past prices, but entirely misleading as a guide to current prices.)

SHEFFIELD PLATE

Bradbury, F. *History of old Sheffield plate*, 1912, 539 pp., profusely illustrated.

Veitch, H. N. *Sheffield plate*, 1908, 359 pp., 75 plates.

Wyllie, B. *Sheffield plate*, 1908, 116 pp., 121 plates.

SELECT BIBLIOGRAPHY

SNUFF BOXES

Hill, H. D. *Antique gold boxes, their lore and their lure,* New York, 1953, xiii, 223 pp., illustrated.

Norton, R. and M. *A history of gold snuff boxes,* 1938, viii, 115 pp., 43 plates.

SPOONS

Gask, N. *Old silver spoons of England,* 1926, xviii, 189 pp., 33 plates.

How, G. E. P. and J. P. *English and Scottish silver spoons,* p.p., 3 vols., 1952– ; I, xix, 366 pp.; II, vii, 402 pp.; profusely illustrated.

Rupert, C. G. *Apostle spoons: their evolution from earlier types, and the emblems used by the silversmiths for the Apostles,* Oxford, 1929, 36 pp., 23 plates.

WINE-LABELS

Dent, H. C. *Wine, spirit and sauce labels of the 18th and 19th centuries,* Norwich, 1933, 9 pp., 6 plates.

Penzer, N. M. *The book of the wine-label,* 1947, 144 pp., 28 plates.

C. Hall-marks

Board of Trade. *Report of Departmental Committee on Hallmarking,* 1959, v, 137 pp.

Bradbury, F. *Guide to marks of origin on British and Irish silver plate from mid 16th century to the year 1959,* Sheffield (10th ed.), 1959, 93 pp.

Castro, J. P. de. *The law and practice of marking gold and silver wares,* 1926 (2nd ed., 1935, xxxviii, 372, t pp., 34 plates).

Jackson, C. J. *English goldsmiths and their marks,* 1905 (2nd ed., enlarged, 1921, xvi, 747 pp.; reprinted 1949).

D. Biographies and Biographical Sources

Dickinson, H. W. *Matthew Boulton,* Cambridge, 1937, xiv, 218 pp., 15 plates.

Evans, Joan. *Huguenot goldsmiths in England and Ireland,* 1933, 59 pp., 6 figs.

Evans, Joan. *Huguenot goldsmiths of London,* 1936, 5 pp. (both reprinted from the Proceedings of the Huguenot Society, XIV and XV).

Garrard's. *Garrard's, 1721–1911, crown jewellers and goldsmiths during six reigns and in three centuries,* 1912, 182 pp., 43 plates.

Heal, A. *The London goldsmiths, 1200–1800: a record of the names and addresses of the craftsmen, their shop-signs and trade-cards,* Cambridge, 1935, 279 pp., 80 plates.

Jones, E. A. *Silver wrought by the Courtauld family,* Oxford, 1940, xii, 128 pp., 64 plates.

Penzer, N. M. *Paul Storr, the last of the goldsmiths*, 1954, 292 pp.,
81 plates.
Phillips, P. A. S. *Paul de Lamerie: citizen and goldsmith of London,
1688–1751*, 1935, xvii, 115 pp., 164 plates.

E. Metallurgy and Manufacturing Techniques

Abbey, S. *The goldsmith's and silversmith's handbook: a practical
manual for all workers in gold, silver, platinum and palladium*
(based on handbooks by G.' E. Gee), 1952, xi, 105 pp., 57 figs.
Cellini, B. *The treatises of Benvenuto Cellini on goldsmithing and
sculpture* (translated by C. R. Ashbee), 1898, 164 pp.
Cuzner, B. *A silversmiths' manual: treating of the designing and
making of the simpler pieces of domestic silverware*, 1935, 224 pp.,
133 figs.
Eissler, M. *The metallurgy of silver*, 1891, 362 pp.
Eissler, M. *The metallurgy of gold*, 1900, 528 pp.
Evans, Joan. *Pattern: a study of ornament in Western Europe, 1180–
1900*, 2 vols., 1931; I, xxxvi, 179 pp., 252 figs.; II, 249 pp., figs.
253–455.
Forbes, R. J. *Metallurgy in antiquity*, Leiden, 1950, 489 pp., 98 figs.
Gee, G. E. *The goldsmith's handbook*, 1881 (ed. 1936, 285 pp.).
Gee, G. E. *The silversmith's handbook*, 1885 (ed. 1907, 221 pp.). *See
also above*, Abbey, S.
Goldsmiths, Worshipful Company of. *The scientific and technical
factors of production of gold and silverwork*, 1936, v, 89 pp.
Maryon, H. *Metalwork and enamelling: a practical treatise on gold-
and silver-smiths' work and their allied crafts*, 1912 (3rd ed., 1954,
xvi, 331 pp., 382 figs.).
Rose, T. K. *The metallurgy of gold*, 1898 (ed. 1915, 601 pp.).
Selwyn, A. *The retail silversmith's handbook*, 1954, vii, 239 pp., 89
figs.
Wilson, H. *Silverwork and jewellery: a textbook*, 1903 (ed. 1948,
496 pp., 255 figs., 16 plates).

F. Catalogues of Public Collections

BATH, HOLBURNE OF MENSTRIE MUSEUM
Anonymous. *Catalogue. Part II: Silver*, p.p., 1929, 32 pp., 16 plates.
LONDON, BRITISH MUSEUM
Read, H., and Tonnochy, A. B. *Catalogue of the silver plate . . .
bequeathed . . . by Sir Augustus Wollaston Franks . . .*, 1928,
xxxviii, 58 pp., 62 plates, figs.
LONDON, TOWER OF
Jones, E. A. *Old royal plate in the Tower of London*, Oxford.
1908, xxxv, 79 pp., 22 plates, 6 figs.

SELECT BIBLIOGRAPHY

LONDON, VICTORIA AND ALBERT MUSEUM
Watts, W. W., and Mitchell, H. P. *Catalogue of English silver-smiths' work (with Scottish and Irish): civil and domestic*, 1920, 75 pp., 65 plates.
Watts, W. W. *Catalogue of chalices and other communion vessels*, 1922, vi, 78 pp., 28 plates.

MOSCOW, KREMLIN
Jones, E. A. *Old English plate of the Emperor of Russia*, p.p., 1909, lvi, 115 pp., 49 plates.

G. Picture Books of Public Collections

BIRMINGHAM, CITY MUSEUM AND ART GALLERY
Rowe, R. (ed.). *Silver in the City Museum and Art Gallery, Birmingham*, n.d., 20 pp., 12 plates.

GLASGOW, GLASGOW ART GALLERY
H., A. (ed.). *The Burrell collection: silver*, n.d., 36 pp., 39 plates.

LONDON, VICTORIA AND ALBERT MUSEUM
English medieval silver (Small picture book, about 30 plates, No. 27), 1952.
Tudor domestic silver (No. 6), 1948.
Early Stuart silver (No. 24), 1950.
Charles II domestic silver (No. 17), 1949.
Queen Anne domestic silver (No. 25), 1951.
Mid-Georgian domestic silver (No. 28), 1952.
Adam silver (No. 35), 1953.
Regency domestic silver (No. 33), 1952.
Royal plate from Buckingham Palace and Windsor Castle (No. 37), 1954.
Sheffield plate (No. 39), 1955.
Irish silver (No. 46), 1959.

OXFORD, ASHMOLEAN MUSEUM
British Plate, 29 plates, 1961.

H. Catalogues of Private Collections

H.M. THE QUEEN
Grimwade, A. G. *The Queen's silver*, 1953, vii, 120 pp., 64 plates.
Jones, E. A. *The gold and silver of Windsor Castle*, 1911, 241 pp., 103 plates.

BENETT-STANFORD
How, G. E. P. *Catalogue of entire collection left by the late H. D. Ellis, Esq., . . . the property of Lieut.-Col. J. Benett-Stanford* (Sotheby Sale, 13–14 November 1935), 1935, xi, 205 pp., 33 plates, 200 figs.

FARRER
Jones, E. A. *Catalogue of the collection of old plate of William Francis Farrer*, 1924, xxxii, 191 pp., 94 plates.

SELECT BIBLIOGRAPHY

LEE OF FAREHAM

Watts, W. W. *Works of art in silver and other metals belonging to Viscount Lee of Fareham*, p.p., 1936, xxii pp., 118 plates (section I, British silver).

PORTLAND

Jones, E. A. *Catalogue of plate belonging to the Duke of Portland at Welbeck Abbey*, 1935, 183 pp., 21 plates.

I. Catalogues of Corporate Collections

Jewitt, Ll., and Hope, W. H. St J. *The Corporation plate and insignia of office of the cities and corporate towns of England and Wales*, 2 vols., 1895; I, cxxxv, 367 pp.; II, xiii, 631 pp.; about 400 engravings.

ABINGDON

Preston, A. E. (ed. Agnes Baker). *The Abingdon Corporation plate*, 1958, xii, 84 pp., 27 plates.

CAMBRIDGE

Jones, E. A. *The old plate of the Cambridge colleges*, Cambridge, 1910, xxxvi, 125 pp., 120 plates.

Jones, E. A. *Catalogue of the plate of Clare College, Cambridge*, Cambridge, 1939, xxxvii, 87 pp., 27 plates.

ETON

Jones, E. A., and Others. *The plate of Eton College*, 1938, xxi, 71 pp., 32 plates.

LONDON, LIVERY COMPANIES, ETC.

ARMOURERS AND BRASIERS

Ellis, H. D. *Description of some of the ancient silver plate belonging to the Worshipful Company of Armourers and Brasiers*, 1892, 24 pp., 16 plates: Supplementary description . . ., 1910, plates xvii–xxx.

DRAPERS

Greenwood, M. A. *Ancient plate of the Drapers' Company, with some account of its origin, history, and vicissitudes*, Oxford, 1930, viii, 127 pp., 34 plates.

GOLDSMITHS

Carrington, J. B., and Hughes, G. R. *The plate of the Worshipful Company of Goldsmiths*, 1926, vi, 158 pp., 83 plates.

MERCERS

Anonymous. *Mercers' Company plate*, p.p., 1941, 85 pp., 19 plates.

MERCHANT TAYLORS

Fry, F. M., and Tewson, R. S. *Illustrated catalogue of the silver plate of the Worshipful Company of Merchant Taylors*, p.p., 1929, xiii, 163 pp., 47 plates.

MIDDLE TEMPLE

Williamson, J. B. *Catalogue of silver plate, the property of the Honourable Society of the Middle Temple*, 1930, 145 pp., illustrated.

290

SELECT BIBLIOGRAPHY

OXFORD
Moffatt, H. C. *Old Oxford plate*, 1906, xv, 209 pp., 96 plates.
CHRIST CHURCH
Jones, E. A. *Catalogue of the plate of Christ Church, Oxford*, Oxford, 1939, xxi, 52 pp., 18 plates.
MAGDALEN
Jones, E. A. *Catalogue of the plate of Magdalen College, Oxford*, Oxford, 1940, xxi, 103 pp., 7 plates.
MERTON
Jones, E. A. *Catalogue of the plate of Merton College, Oxford*, Oxford, 1938, xix, 58 pp., 12 plates.
ORIEL
Jones, E. A. *Catalogue of the plate of Oriel College, Oxford*, Oxford, 1944, xxviii, 102 pp., 20 plates.
QUEEN'S
Jones, E. A. *Catalogue of the plate of the Queen's College, Oxford*, Oxford, 1938, xvii, 87 pp., 18 plates.

J. Catalogues of Important Exhibitions

1895, CAMBRIDGE, FITZWILLIAM MUSEUM
Foster, J. E., and Atkinson, T. D. *An illustrated catalogue of the loan collection of plate exhibited at the Fitzwilliam Museum, Cambridge*, 1896, 131 pp., 16 plates, 15 figs.
1901, LONDON, BURLINGTON FINE ARTS CLUB
Gardner, J. S. (ed.). *Exhibition of a collection of goldsmiths' work of European origin*, 1901, vii pp., 120 plates, 185 pp.
1902, LONDON, ST JAMES'S COURT
Gardner, J. S. *Old silver work, chiefly English, from the sixteenth to the eighteenth centuries: a catalogue of the unique loan collection exhibited in 1902 at St James's Court, London*, 1903, 198 pp., 121 plates.
1928, OXFORD, ASHMOLEAN MUSEUM
Watts, W. W. *Catalogue of a loan exhibition of silver plate belonging to the colleges of the University of Oxford*, Oxford, 1928, xii, 80 pp., 73 figs.
1929, LONDON, 25 PARK LANE
Catalogue of a loan exhibition of old English plate (in aid of the Royal Northern Hospital), 1929, [112] pp., 81 plates.
1929, LONDON, SEAFORD HOUSE
Hughes, G. R., and Others (eds.). *Queen Charlotte's loan exhibition of old silver*, 1929, xxxviii, 82 pp., 81 plates.
1931, CAMBRIDGE, FITZWILLIAM MUSEUM
Catalogue of an exhibition of silver belonging to the university and colleges of Cambridge, Cambridge, 1931, viii, 37 pp.
1938, LONDON, GOLDSMITHS' HALL
Exhibition of modern silverwork, 1938, 64 pp., illustrated.

1951, CAMBRIDGE, FITZWILLIAM MUSEUM
Silver plate belonging to the University, the colleges, and the City of Cambridge, Cambridge, 1951, 21 pp.

1951, LONDON, GOLDSMITHS' HALL
British silverwork, including ceremonial plate by contemporary craftsmen, 1951, 20 pp., 14 plates.

1951, LONDON, GOLDSMITHS' HALL
Historic plate of the City of London, 2 vols., 1951; I, 86 pp.; II, 77 plates.

1952, LONDON, GOLDSMITHS' HALL
Oman, C. C., Hayward, J. F., and Grimwade, A. G. (eds.). *Catalogue of corporation plate of England and Wales,* 2 vols., 1952; I, 62 pp.; II, 46 plates.

1954, LONDON, VICTORIA AND ALBERT MUSEUM
Oman, C. C., and Hayward, J. F. (eds.). *Exhibition of Royal plate from Buckingham Palace and Windsor Castle,* 1954, 51 pp. (see above, p. 289, G).

1955, LONDON, CHRISTIE, MANSON AND WOODS
Grimwade, A. G. *Silver treasures from English churches: an exhibition of ecclesiastical plate of domestic origin,* 1955, 52 pp., 24 plates.

K. Monographs on Church Plate

GENERAL
Hope, W. H. St J., and Fallowe, T. M. 'English medieval chalices and patens', *Archaeological Journal,* XLIII (1886), pp. 137–61, 364–402, illustrated.

Jones, E. A. *The old silver sacramental vessels of foreign protestant churches in England,* 1908, xxx, 48 pp., 22 plates.

Oman, C. C. *English Church Plate, 597–1830,* 1957, xxx, 326 pp., 200 plates.

BANGOR
Jones, E. A. *The church plate of the diocese of Bangor,* 1906, xlvi, 160 pp., 34 plates.

BERKSHIRE
Walker, J. W. and M. I. *The church plate of Berkshire,* p.p., 1927, xlv, 384 pp., 37 plates.

BRECONSHIRE
Evans, J. T. *The church plate of Breconshire,* Stow-on-the-Wold, 1912, xviii, 160 pp., 15 plates.

CARDIGANSHIRE
Evans, J. T. *The church plate of Cardiganshire,* Stow-on-the-Wold, 1914, xxiv, 163 pp., 20 plates.

CARLISLE
Ferguson, R. S. *Old church plate in the diocese of Carlisle,* Carlisle, 1882, 326 pp., 29 plates, 17 figs.

SELECT BIBLIOGRAPHY

CARMARTHENSHIRE

Evans, J. T. *The church plate of Carmarthenshire,* 1907, xxxii, 148 pp., 14 plates.

CHESTER

Ball, T. S. *Church plate of the city of Chester,* Manchester, 1907, xvi, 158 pp., 12 plates.

CORK, CLOYNE AND ROSS

Webster, C. A. *The church plate of the diocese of Cork, Cloyne and Ross,* Cork, 1909, xv, 168 pp., numerous plates.

DORSETSHIRE

Nightingale, J. E. *The church plate of the county of Dorset,* Salisbury, 1889, 216 pp., 16 illustrations.

ESSEX

Pressey, W. J. (ed.). *The church plate of the county of Essex,* Colchester, 1926, x, 335 pp., 27 plates.

GLOUCESTERSHIRE

Evans, J. T. *The church plate of Gloucestershire,* p.p., 1906, xxiv, 264 pp., 21 plates, 2 figs.

GOWERLAND

Evans, J. T. *The church plate of Gowerland with an exhaustive summary of the church plate in the diocese of St Davids,* Stow-on-the-Wold, 1921, x, 146 pp., 39 plates.

HAMPSHIRE

Braithwaite, P. R. P. *The church plate of Hampshire,* 1909, xxxi, 375 pp., 67 plates.

HEREFORDSHIRE

Stanhope, B. S., and Moffatt, H. C. *The church plate of the county of Hereford,* 1903, 244 pp., 26 plates.

LEICESTERSHIRE

Trollope, A. *An inventory of the church plate of Leicestershire,* 2 vols., 1890; I, xxvi, 430 pp.; II, pp. 431–628, 30 plates.

LLANDAFF

Halliday, G. E. *Llandaff church plate,* 1901, x, 106 pp., 59 figs.

LONDON

Freshfield, E. *The communion plate of the churches in the city of London,* 1894, xxxviii, 152 pp., 10 large and numerous smaller plates.

Freshfield, E. *The communion plate of the parish churches in the county of London,* 1895, xxxiii, 111 pp., 11 large and numerous smaller plates.

MAN

Jones, E. A. *The old church plate of the Isle of Man,* 1907, xxxii, 33 pp., 20 plates.

MIDDLESEX

Freshfield, E. *The communion plate of the parish churches in the county of Middlesex,* 1897, xix, 83 pp., 15 plates.

SELECT BIBLIOGRAPHY

NORTHAMPTONSHIRE

Markham, C. A. *The church plate of the county of Northampton*, 1894, xxvii, 368 pp., 28 illustrations.

OXFORDSHIRE

Evans, J. T. *The church plate of Oxfordshire*, Oxford, 1928, xxxiii, 223 pp., 31 plates.

PEMBROKESHIRE

Evans, J. T. *The church plate of Pembrokeshire*, 1905, xxxii, 147 pp., 10 plates.

RADNORSHIRE

Evans, J. T., *The church plate of Radnorshire*, Stow-on-the-Wold, 1910, xxiv, 156 pp., 6 plates.

RUTLAND

Hope, R. C. 'An inventory of the church plate of Rutland', *The Reliquary*, N.S., 1 (1887), pp. 32–43, 97–105, and 129–38, illustrated.

SCOTLAND

Burns, T. *Old Scottish communion plate*, Edinburgh, 1892, 651 pp., 56 plates, 105 figs.

SOMERSETSHIRE

Bates, E. H., and Others. 'An inventory of church plate in Somerset', *Somersetshire Archaeological Society's Proceedings*, XLIII–XLIX, LIX (1897–1903, 1914).

STAFFORDSHIRE

Jeavons, S. A. *Church plate in the Archdeaconry of Stafford*, 1957.

SUFFOLK

Hopper, E. C., and Others. 'Church plate in Suffolk', *Proceedings Suffolk Institute of Archaeology*, IX (1897), pp. 1–76, 145–230, 279–306, illustrated.

SURREY

Cooper, T. S. 'The Church plate of Surrey', *Surrey Archaeological Collections*, X–XVI (1891–1901).

SUSSEX

Couchman, J. E. *Sussex church plate*, 1913.

WILTSHIRE

Nightingale, J. E. *The church plate of the county of Wilts*, Salisbury, 1891, 256 pp., 22 plates.

WINDSOR CASTLE

Jones, E. A. *The plate of St George's Chapel, Windsor Castle*, 1939, viii, 37 pp., 12 plates.

WORCESTERSHIRE

Lea, W. *Church plate in the archdeaconry of Worcester*, 1884, 80 pp., 5 plates.

YORKSHIRE

Fallow, T. M., and McCall, H. B. *Yorkshire church plate*, 2 vols., 1912, 1915.

II. PLATE OF THE UNITED STATES OF AMERICA

A. Historical Studies

Avery, C. L. *Early American silver*, New York, 1930, xliv, 378 pp., 63 plates.

Bigelow, F. H. *Historic silver of the colonies and its makers*, New York, 1917, xxiv, 476 pp., 325 figs.

Brix, M. *List of Philadelphia silversmiths and allied artificers from 1682–1850*, Philadelphia, p.p., 1920, vii, 125 pp.

Buck, J. H. *Old plate: its makers and marks*, New York, 1903, 327 pp., with numerous illustrations.

Burton, E. M. *South Carolina silversmiths, 1690–1860*, Charleston, S.C., 1942, xvii, 311 pp., illustrated.

Clarke, H. F. *John Coney, silversmith, 1655–1722*, Boston, Mass., 1932, xv, 92 pp., 31 plates.

Currier, E. M. *Marks of early American silversmiths, with notes on silver spoon types and list of New York City silversmiths, 1815–41*, Portland, Me., 1938, xv, 184 pp., 2 plates.

Curtis, G. M. *Early silver of Connecticut and its makers*, Meriden, Conn., 1913, 115 pp., illustrated.

Cutten, G. B. *The silversmiths of North Carolina*, Raleigh, 1948, v, 93 pp., illustrated.

Cutten, G. B. *The silversmiths of Virginia, together with watchmakers and jewelers, from 1694–1850*, Richmond, Va., 1952, xxiv, 259 pp., illustrated.

Ensko, S. G. C. *American silversmiths and their marks, 1650–1850*, New York, 3 parts, 1927, 1937, 1948.

French, H. *List of early American silversmiths and their marks, with a silver collectors' glossary*, New York, 1917, ix, 164 pp., illustrated.

French, H. *Jacob Hurd and his sons Nathaniel and Benjamin, silversmiths, 1702–81*, Cambridge, Mass., 1939, xvi, 147 pp., 22 plates.

Graham, J. *Early American silver marks*, New York, 1936, 81 pp., illustrated.

Hiatt, N. W., and L. F. *The silversmiths of Kentucky, together with some watchmakers and jewelers, 1785–1850*, Louisville, Ky., 1954, xxi, 135 pp., illustrated.

Jones, E. A. *The old silver of American churches*, Letchworth, p.p., 1913, lxxxvii, 556 pp., 145 plates.

Phillips, J. M. *American silver*, New York, 1949, 128 pp., 32 plates.

Pleasants, J. H., and Sill, H. *Maryland silversmiths, 1715–1830, with illustrations of their silver and their marks*, Baltimore, Md., 1930, xiv, 324 pp., 67 plates.

Rosenbaum, J. W. *Myer Myers, Goldsmith, 1723–95*, Philadelphia, 1954, 141 pp., 30 plates.

B. Catalogues of Collections and Exhibitions

BOSTON, MUSEUM OF FINE ARTS

Buck, J. H., ed. *American silver, the work of seventeenth and eighteenth century silversmiths*, Boston, Mass, 1906, 100 pp., 29 plates.

Curtis, G. M. *American church silver of the seventeenth and eighteenth centuries*, Boston, 1911, xxv, 163 pp., 38 plates.

NEW YORK, METROPOLITAN MUSEUM

The collection of spoons made by S. P. Avery, New York, 1899, 23 pp., 9 plates.

Halsey, R. T. H. *Catalogue of an exhibition of silver used in New York, New Jersey, and the South*, New York, 1911, xxxvi, 85 pp., illustrated.

Avery, C. L. *An exhibition of early New York silver*, New York, 1931, 20 pp., illustrated.

PHILADELPHIA, PENNSYLVANIA MUSEUM OF ART

S., S. Y. *Exhibition of old American and English silver*, Philadelphia, 1917, 71 pp., illustrated.

YALE UNIVERSITY, GALLERY OF FINE ARTS

Art in New England: masterpieces of New England silver, New Haven, 1939, 97 pp., 15 plates.

C. List of Principal Public Collections

Albany, N.Y. — *Albany Institute of History and Art.*
Andover, Mass. — *Addison Gallery of American Art. Phillips Academy.*

Baltimore, Maryland — *Baltimore Museum of Art.*
Boston, Mass. — *Museum of Fine Arts.*
Cambridge, Mass. — *Fogg Art Museum (Harvard University)*
Chicago, Ill. — *Art Institute of Chicago.*
Cincinnatti, Ohio — *Cincinnatti Art Museum.*
Cleveland, Ohio — *Cleveland Museum of Art.*
Detroit, Mich. — *Detroit Institute of Arts.*
Minneapolis, Min. — *Minneapolis Institute of Arts.*
New Haven, Conn. — *Yale University Art Gallery.*
Philadelphia, Pa. — *Philadelphia Museum of Art. Historical Society of Pennsylvania.*

Providence, Rhode Island — *Rhode Island School of Design.*
St Louis, Mo. — *City Art Museum.*
Wilmington, Del. — *Winterthur Museum.*
Worcester, Mass. — *Worcester Art Museum.*

SELECT BIBLIOGRAPHY

III. PLATE OF CANADA

Jones, E. A. *Old church silver in Canada*, Transactions of the Royal Society of Canada, 3rd series, xii (1918), pp. 135–50.

Piers, H., and MacKay, D. C. *Master goldsmiths and silversmiths of Nova Scotia and their marks*, Halifax, N.S., 1948, 184 pp., 60 figs.

Traquair, R. *The old silver of Quebec*, Toronto, 1940, xi, 169 pp., 16 plates.

(Public collection: *Montreal, Museum of Fine Arts.*)

IV. PLATE OF THE UNION OF SOUTH AFRICA

Heller, D. *A history of Cape silver, 1700–1870*, Cape Town, 1949, 276 pp., [105] plates.

Morrison, M. N. *The silversmiths and goldsmiths of the Cape of Good Hope*, Johannesburg, 1936, 84 pp., 16 plates.

297

Index